LAW IN A MARKET CONTEXT
An Introduction to Market Concep

In *Law in a Market Context*, Robin Paul Malloy examines the way in which people, as social beings, *experience* the intersection of law, markets, and culture. His work recognizes that experience varies by such characteristics as culture, race, gender, age, and class, among others. Thus, market analysis must account for these variations. Through case examples, illustrative fact patterns, and problems based on hypothetical situations he demonstrates the implications and the ambiguities of law in a market society. In his analysis he provides a complete and accessible introduction to a vast array of economic terms, concepts, and ideas – making this book a valuable primer for anyone interested in understanding the use of market concepts in legal reasoning.

ROBIN PAUL MALLOY is Professor of Law, and Economics of Law, as well as Director of the Program in Law and Market Economy, at the College of Law, and a Professor of Economics (by courtesy appointment) in the Maxwell School of Citizenship and Public Affairs of Syracuse University. He has published seven other books including *Law and Market Economy: Reinterpreting the Values of Law and Economics* (Cambridge, 2000).

Advance Praise for *Law in a Market Context*
As someone who writes in the areas of critical race and feminist theory, I find Malloy's approach to be particularly useful because it provides critical scholars who are concerned with issues of social justice and equality with a new and theoretically sophisticated way to understand and reckon with the market. *Law in a Market Context* should find its way on to every critical scholar reading list.
Professor Emily Houh, University of Cincinnati, U.S.A.

Malloy builds a strong and long-needed bridge between humanistic and economic approaches to the study of law. I recommend this book to lawyers, judges, policymakers, and academics who want to sharpen their critiques of market thinking, as well as those who want to be better armed in the defense of markets.
Professor Shubha Ghosh, University at Buffalo, S.U.N.Y., U.S.A.

LAW IN A MARKET CONTEXT

An Introduction to Market Concepts in Legal Reasoning

ROBIN PAUL MALLOY

CAMBRIDGE
UNIVERSITY PRESS

PUBLISHED BY THE PRESS SYNDICATE OF THE UNIVERSITY OF CAMBRIDGE
The Pitt Building, Trumpington Street, Cambridge, United Kingdom

CAMBRIDGE UNIVERSITY PRESS
The Edinburgh Building, Cambridge, CB2 2RU, UK
40 West 20th Street, New York, NY 10011–4211, USA
477 Williamstown Road, Port Melbourne, VIC 3207, Australia
Ruiz de Alarcón 13, 28014 Madrid, Spain
Dock House, The Waterfront, Cape Town 8001, South Africa

http://www.cambridge.org

First published 2004

Printed in the United Kingdom at the University Press, Cambridge

Typeface Minion 10.5/13.5 pt.   *System* LATEX 2_ε [TB]

A catalogue record for this book is available from the British Library

Library of Congress Cataloguing in Publication data
Malloy, Robin Paul, 1956–
Law in a market context : an introduction to market concepts in legal reasoning /
by Robin Paul Malloy.
p.   cm.
ISBN 0 521 81624 6 (hardback) – ISBN 0 521 01655 X (pbk.)
1. Law and economics.   2. Sociological jurisprudence.   3. Markets – Social aspects.   I. Title.
K487.E3M355   2004   340′.11–dc21   2003055398

ISBN 0 521 81624 6 hardback
ISBN 0 521 01655 X paperback

For
Gina and Giovanni
and
in celebration of the first twenty-five years of marriage to
Margaret Ann
June 1978–June 2003

CONTENTS

Preface   *page* xi
Note for teachers   xvi
Acknowledgments   xviii
Note on citations   xix

1   **Introduction to law in a market context**   1
    An overview   1
    Conclusion   21
    Problems   22

2   **Understanding the contested meaning of markets**   26
    Self-interest and the public interest   27
    Framing the market in contemporary film   30
    Framing the market in case opinions   41
    Framing contested measures of market performance   50
    Conclusion   52
    Problems   52

3   **The law and market economy framework**   56
    Foundation for law and market economy   57
    A relationship among law, markets, and culture   62
    Mapping exchange relationships: a triadic approach   69
    The form of legal argument   80
    Some basic examples of mapping exchange
    relationships   85
    Clarifying the cultural-interpretive approach   93
    An outline of basic tools   104
    Conclusion   110
    Problems   110

4   **Market concepts of exchange**   114
    Single party or individual choice   114

Two-party transactions 115
Externalities and spillover effects 117
Multi-party coordination transactions 118
Public goods and commons problems 122
Cooperative exchange problems 130
Discrimination in exchange 132
Conclusion 135
Problems 136

5 **Additional economic concepts for law in a market context** **142**
Scarcity 143
Rationality 144
Rational ignorance 146
Opportunity cost 148
Accounting profits and economic profits 149
Production possibility curve 151
Substitute goods 152
Constructing the simple economic model: supply and demand 153
The basic model 156
Competition 161
Preferences 163
Valuation 165
Risk and return 169
Transactional misbehavior 174
Rent seeking and opportunistic behavior 175
Coase's Theorem 177
Pareto and Kaldor–Hicks efficiency 189
Public choice and Arrow's Impossibility Theorem 194
Efficient breach 199
Conclusion 203
Problems 204

6 **The not-for-profit exchange context** **212**
The non-profit organization 213
The three-sector economy 215
Demands on public services 222
Cross-over activities 222

Non-government organizations (NGOs)   223
Conclusion   224
Problems   224

7 **Parting thoughts**   **227**
Understanding law in a market context   227
Conclusion   232
Problems   232

Sources   235
Index   247

PREFACE

In this book, I offer a new way of thinking about the relationship between law and market theory. The approach is *not* the same as one would find in books on Law and Economics or an Economic Analysis of Law. In contrast to those types of books, I undertake to think more broadly about the way in which law is understood in a market context. I am *not* driven by concerns for particular conceptions of economic efficiency, but instead hope to explain how law and legal institutions work with markets and market institutions in shaping the contours of public policy and social organization.

I do not employ a traditional neoclassical economic methodology, and my audience is not made up of people in the law and economics movement. While a few progressive scholars of law and economics will find this work of interest, the book is primarily designed to assist non-law and economic scholars. It provides an introduction to using economic concepts in legal reasoning from a perspective of Law and Society, and Law, Culture, and the Humanities.

This book positions economics as an important and influential tool when used in legal reasoning and public policy making. It does not, however, treat economics as a "hard" science, nor does it present economics as independent of politics and ideology. Economics, because of its scientific appearance, has gained influence with lawyers and judges. This is because it gives the judge and the law an appearance of objectivity and neutrality in dealing with complex social problems. Appearance is not, however, reality. This book lifts the veil of economic objectivity and shows the subjectivity and malleability of economic reasoning in law. It explains that economic outcomes depend upon the way in which facts and issues are framed. Consequently, there is often more than one economically sound way of approaching a particular problem.

This book is also concerned with cultural differences in the relationship between law and market theory. With this in mind, it explores the way in which people, as social beings, *experience* the relationship between law, markets, and culture. This is a very different point of inquiry than that of traditional law and economics, which is concerned with an empirical or social science approach to understanding law within a particularized discourse of economics *as* science. This inquiry examines the relationship among law, markets, and culture with respect to a variety of characteristics such as race, gender, age, education level, class, income, and geographic location, among others. Thus, I see the primary audience as people who are interested in law, and its relationship to the social, political, and cultural structure of the marketplace. These are people who understand the significance of market forces in everyday life, appreciate the sense in which we are all embedded within markets, and yet question, doubt, or even reject some, or all, of the constraints of traditional approaches to an economic analysis of law.

There is, in this regard, a gap between the current works in law and economics, and the experiences of many people. This divergence carries over to the process of legal reasoning employed by many lawyers, judges, and public policy makers. This book is offered to bridge this gap. To achieve this goal I focus on building a basic conceptual vocabulary in economics rather than on promoting any particular conception of efficiency. I believe that there is a need for a book that simply and clearly explains the relationship between law and market economy with a concern for showing how certain market assumptions relate to legal reasoning, particular legal outcomes, and the formulation of public policy. I want the reader to become skilled at using and understanding various economic concepts and assumptions. I want the reader to appreciate the way in which these concepts and assumptions can be used to advance particular socio-legal values in legal reasoning, public policy, and the advancement of social justice and prosperity.

I also want readers to understand that the ideas and concepts discussed in this book are already part of our legal discourse. Courts, legislatures, and regulatory agencies already use many of these concepts. Consequently, it is important to understand these ideas and how they work. One needs to understand that knowledge of these ideas is fundamental to the modern-day practice of law. Just as lawyers must know property law, contract law, and tort law, they must also know basic economics and the market context in which law operates.

The book provides materials on all of the basic elements and concepts needed for understanding law in a market context. It discusses the relationship between law, markets, and culture. It also explains, in a non-quantitative way, all of the basic terms and concepts of economics that are used in the law and economics literature, and that are used in legal reasoning. In each chapter there are a number of examples and illustrations, and at the end of each chapter there are problems for thought and discussion. I designed these problems to assist the reader in thinking about the issues raised in the material. I also developed these problems to serve as the basis of group discussion or as essay questions that can be assigned when the book is used in conjunction with a course or seminar. The idea behind the problems is to use them to develop an ability to manipulate different frames, references, and representations for advancing a variety of logical and persuasive legal arguments.

In writing this book I realize that some people will suggest that more attention should have been paid to political theory, and others may suggest that there should be more material on cultural studies. I also realize that there are different approaches to interpretation theory and to semiotics. As with any book of this type, compromises have been made in an effort to make concepts accessible and understandable. I have made my own adjustments to Peirce's work so as to develop an approach with applicability to legal and economic reasoning. I do not purport to say that Peirce would say what I do, only that my approach has a clear Peircean influence. In particular, this influence is a product of my many years of work with Roberta Kevelson, who during her lifetime published numerous works on Peirce, and who served, for approximately fifteen years, as Director of the Center for the Study of Law and Semiotics at Penn State University.

As with any book of this kind, each individual reader is likely to have his or her own personal way of addressing the various issues covered. This is good because it can enrich the discussion of the material and lead to making further progress on the overall project of broadening our understanding of the relationship among law, markets, and culture. I hope that each reader understands that my effort is to offer an introduction to a new way of understanding law and market relationships. I do not purport to offer a new or definitive set of answers. Instead, I offer an invitation to anyone interested in taking this book as a starting point for rethinking the use of economic ideas in law. I am hopeful that my invitation will be taken up not only by people who think in a way similar to me, but also by people that merely find new ways of addressing the issues of law in a market society as a result of reading this book.

As an introductory book, this work is designed for people interested in jurisprudence; law and society; legal theory; law, culture, and the humanities; and law and markets. The book can be used to structure a course on the topic of "Law in a Market Context," "Law and Market Economy," or

"Law, Markets, and Culture." It can also be used to supplement materials in a variety of courses related to jurisprudence, and contemporary legal theory, including courses on law and society, law and humanities, law and culture, and feminist and other types of critical theory. Likewise, the book can be used as a supplement to law school courses such as property, contracts, torts, real estate transactions, and land use. This is particularly true when the course is taught with a casebook making reference to a variety of economic concepts applied to law. In such a course my book can be a useful supplement for the person seeking to integrate market concepts while wanting an approach that differs from that of traditional economic analysis of law. (See the notes on p. xvi for a few suggested ways to pair this book up with other readings when used in different types of courses.)

I can report that I developed and used these materials in a course with law students and graduate students. The course, titled "Law and Market Economy," is a cross-listed course that typically enrolls about thirty students. These students are primarily based in the College of Law but always include about a half dozen graduate students from other departments on campus. Many of these students would identify themselves as being interested in feminism, critical race theory, social justice, and public interest law. All of the students would identify themselves as interested in the problems of law, legal institutions, and public policy as related to the pressures and constraints of markets. In using the materials over several years I benefited greatly from student feedback. I also found that students completed the course with a clear ability to recognize, construct, and deconstruct a variety of economic arguments in law. This was even true for students with no prior study in economics or interpretation theory, and true for my graduate students with no prior work in law. The outline of "tools" included near the end of chapter 3 proved to be an important and valuable organizing kit for all of my students. It gave them an easy and useful way to go back and organize their notes and provided a structured guide for building the skills necessary to go on to advanced work.

I also used some of the materials in this book in teaching a first-year course on property and in teaching upper-level courses on real estate transactions and land use planning. The materials worked well to explain a number of concepts including, among others, risk, externalities, the commons problem, Coase, valuation, and cost and benefit analysis.

Many of the ideas in the book can be extended or expanded upon, but the goal is not to write the definitive word on the subject matter. The goal is to provide an accessible and reasonable-length primer. For a more detailed examination of some of the ideas and concepts addressed in this book I suggest that you refer to the list of sources, and in particular to Robin Paul Malloy, *Law and Market Economy: Reinterpreting the Values of Law and Economics* (Cambridge, 2000); and Robin Paul Malloy, *Framing the Market: Representations of Meaning and Value in Law, Markets, and Culture*, 51 Buffalo Law Review 1 (2003). Many of the ideas expressed and developed in chapters 1–3 are extensively footnoted in the article I wrote for the Buffalo Law Review.

In completing this book I benefited from the input and assistance of a number of people, and from the supplemental research support of the Syracuse University College of Law. Therefore, I wish to express my gratitude to those who supported me in this project. In particular, I thank Chris Ramsdell for her administrative assistance, and the following people who provided helpful comments and suggestions in reviewing various parts or drafts of this manuscript, including: Brian Bix, David Brennen, Alan Childress, Wythe Holt, and Martha McCluskey. I also benefited from ongoing discussion with my colleague, David Driesen. I thank Shawn Sauro, Nazakhtar Nikakhtar, and Meghan Honea for research assistance at various times over the time period involved in writing this book. I also thank the people who reviewed and commented upon the manuscript for Cambridge University Press. Mistakes and errors are of course my own. Finally, I wish to thank Finola O'Sullivan, Nikki Burton, Jackie Warren, Barbara Docherty, and others at Cambridge University Press for their support and assistance throughout the long and difficult process of publication.

NOTE FOR TEACHERS

I now offer a few suggestions on ways of pairing this book with other readings to be used in various types of courses. These are only suggestions, offered with the hope of giving the reader a more specific idea on how to integrate this book into different types of courses.

Courses on "Law and Market Economy," "Law in a Market Context," or "Law, Markets, and Culture"

The book can be used on its own with time devoted to discussion of the Problems. It can also be used with supplemental law review articles or with full text versions of the cases discussed in the text. Some books that can be paired with *Law in a Market Context* to build a one-semester course or seminar include the following books: David Throsby, *Economics and Culture* (Cambridge, 2001); Cass R. Sunstein, *Behavioral Law & Economics* (Cambridge, 2000); Robin Paul Malloy, *Law and Market Economy: Reinterpreting the Values of Law and Economics* (Cambridge, 2000); Nicholas Mercuro and Steven G. Medema, *Economics and the Law: From Posner to Post-Modernism* (Princeton, 1997); Regenia Gagnier, *The Insatiability of Human Wants: Economics and Aesthetics in Market Society* (Chicago, 2000); Deirdre N. McCloskey, *The Rhetoric of Economics* (2nd ed., Wisconsin, 1998); Hernando DeSoto, *The Mystery of Capital: Why Capitalism Triumphs in the West and Fails Everywhere Else* (Basic Books, 2000); *Beyond Economic Man: Feminist Theory and Economics* (Marianne A. Ferber and Julie A. Nelson, eds., Chicago, 1993); and Richard A. Epstein, *Simple Rules for A Complex World* (Harvard, 1995), David Driesen, *Economic Dynamics of Environmental Law* (MIT, 2003).

Courses on jurisprudence and contemporary legal theory

For these types of courses one might pair *Law in a Market Context* with one or two of the following: Robert Hayman, Nancy Levit, and Richard

Delgado, *Jurisprudence – Classical and Contemporary: From Natural Law to Postmodernism* (West, 2nd ed., 2002); Dennis Patterson, *Law and Truth* (Oxford, 1996); Martha Chapallas, *Introduction to Feminist Legal Theory* (Aspen, 1998); Peter Goodrich, *Reading the Law: A Critical Introduction to Legal Method and Techniques* (Blackwell, 1986); Brian Bix, *Law, Language, and Legal Determinacy* (Clarendon, 1996); Brian Bix, *Jurisprudence: Theory and Context* (Carolina Academic Press, 2000); Gary Minda, *Postmodern Legal Movements: Law and Jurisprudence at Century's End* (New York University, 1995); Randy E. Barnett, *The Structure of Liberty: Justice and the Rule of Law* (Oxford, 1998); and Samual J.M. Donally, *A Personalist Jurisprudence, The Next Step: A Person-Centered Philosophy of Law for the Twenty-first Century* (Carolina Academic Press, 2003).

Courses using *Law in a Market Context* as a supplemental reader

Most subject areas of law now have leading casebooks and textbooks that reference various economic terms and concepts. This is the result of the widespread acceptance by legal institutions of market theory as relevant to legal reasoning. This observation seems to be most true with respect to property law. Consequently, *Law in a Market Context* is especially helpful in addressing the many economic terms and concepts that are frequently expressed or implied in course books for the following subjects: Basic and advanced courses on Modern Property Law; Land Use, Zoning, and Development Law; and Environmental, and Natural Resources Law. Other courses such as Contracts, Torts, Corporate Law, Real Estate Transactions, and Intellectual Property depend upon the particular course book that is chosen.

Other courses

Law in a Market Context is also designed to be a primary or supplemental book for graduate and undergraduate courses on Legal Studies; Law and Policy; Law and Society; Sociology of Law; and other classes related to the subject areas identified above.

ACKNOWLEDGMENTS

In writing this book I benefited from the use of materials that I published in several previous works. I wish to thank the following publishers for granting permission for this use.

(1) Buffalo Law Review, for permission to include in chapters 1–3 and 7, substantial material published in Robin Paul Malloy, *Framing the Market: Representing Meanings and Values in Law, Markets, and Culture*, 51 Buffalo Law Review 1 (2003). There are material changes and differences between the chapters and the article.

(2) Aspen Law Publishers and James Charles Smith, for permission to include materials on valuation and risk in chapter 5, taken from Robin Paul Malloy and James C. Smith, *Real Estate Transactions: Problems, Cases, and Materials*, pp. 8–32 (2nd ed., 2002).

(3) West Publishing, for permission to intermittently include materials in chapter 5, taken from Robin Paul Malloy, *Law and Economics: A Comparative Approach to Theory and Practice*, pp. 14–45 (1990).

(4) Cambridge University Press, for permission to use materials from Robin Paul Malloy, *Law and Market Economy: Reinterpreting the Values of Law and Economics* (2000).

NOTE ON CITATIONS

All footnotes in the book are prepared as short-form citations of the identified sources listed in the Sources section (p. 235). All footnote citations have been prepared with reference to *The Bluebook: A Uniform System of Citation* (17th ed., 2000).

1

Introduction to law in a market context

An overview

This book examines the way in which people, as social beings, *experience* the relationship among law, markets, and culture. It does this with the recognition that people understand their experiences through the mediation of institutions of language, communication, and interpretation (interpretive institutions). Furthermore, it acknowledges that experience varies by a number of characteristics including race, gender, age, class, education, income, and geographic location, among others. Thus, law and market analysis must account for these variations.

With this in mind, the book advances two primary objectives. The first objective involves providing a framework for understanding the relationship among law, markets, and culture. This includes a framework for understanding the interpretive process and the ways in which interpretive institutions facilitate wealth formation and (re)distribution. In particular, attention is focused on understanding the way in which law functions to mediate the tension between culture (as an expression of a public and community interest) and the market (as an expression of private and self-interest). This involves an examination of the way in which legal actors and advocates understand and create legal arguments. This is important because it establishes a framework for understanding the way in which market ideas are borrowed and incorporated into law.

The second objective of the book involves providing an accessible introduction to a number of important economic terms and concepts that are frequently used in legal analysis. This involves an examination of economic terms and concepts as strategic "tools" for shaping legal reasoning. This is important because it provides a working vocabulary for understanding economic ideas that are already at work in the law, and it facilitates the use of these ideas in new situations. Attention is focused on understanding the way in which these tools create market advantages for

1

particular individuals and groups, and on learning to use these tools to one's own advantage.

The connection between these two objectives is in understanding how to use market concepts to influence the mediating process of law and legal institutions. This includes learning about the numerous ways of selecting, substituting, and re-characterizing the many economic terms and concepts available for advancing alternative lines of legal argument. This is important to effective legal reasoning – and to exercising favorable influence in the wealth formation and (re)distribution process.

As will be explained, understanding law in a market context is not the same as doing an economic analysis of law. This is because law in a market context focuses on the meanings and implications of using market concepts in law – not on doing an economic analysis of law. Before we begin our examination of this difference, however, it is appropriate to acknowledge the pioneering work of a few of the people that have greatly influenced the integration of legal and economic reasoning. This group includes such people as Gary Becker,[1] Guido Calabresi,[2] Ronald Coase,[3] and Richard Posner,[4] all of whom advanced new and thoughtful ways of understanding law and legal institutions. They, and others, made important contributions in many areas of law, and this should be recognized even though there may be disagreement with the subjective and political framing of their legal reasoning. Collectively, they helped develop

---

[1] *See generally* Becker, *Crime and Punishment* 169, 191–93; BECKER, ECONOMICS OF DISCRIMINATION; Becker, *A Theory of Competition*; BECKER, ECONOMIC APPROACH TO HUMAN BEHAVIOR; BECKER, HUMAN CAPITAL; BECKER & MURPHY, SOCIAL ECONOMICS; BECKER, ECONOMIC THEORY; GHEZ & BECKER, ALLOCATION OF TIME AND GOODS; BECKER, ACCOUNTING FOR TASTES; BECKER, ECONOMICS OF LIFE (a collection of essays on everyday topics).

[2] *See generally* CALABRESI, COST OF ACCIDENTS; Calabresi & Melamed, *Property Rules, Liability Rules, and Inalienability*; Calabresi, *The Pointlessness of Pareto*; CALABRESI, COMMON LAW FOR THE AGE OF STATUTES; CALABRESI, IDEALS, BELIEFS, ATTITUDES.

[3] *See generally* Coase, *The Problem of Social Cost*; COASE, THE FIRM, THE MARKET, AND THE LAW; Swygert & Yanes, *A Primer on the Coase Theorem*.

[4] *See generally* POSNER, ECONOMIC ANALYSIS OF LAW; Posner, *Utilitarianism, Economics, and Legal Theory*; Posner, *Rational Choice, Behavioral Economics*; POSNER, PROBLEMATICS OF MORAL AND LEGAL THEORY; POSNER, LAW AND ECONOMICS: THE INTERNATIONAL LIBRARY OF CRITICAL WRITINGS IN ECONOMICS (Posner & Parisi, eds.); POSNER, ECONOMIC STRUCTURE OF THE LAW (Parisi, ed.); POSNER, ECONOMICS OF JUSTICE; POSNER, FRONTIERS OF LEGAL THEORY; POSNER, LAW AND ECONOMICS (Posner & Parisi, eds.); POSNER, SEX AND REASON; POSNER, PROBLEMS OF JURISPRUDENCE; POSNER, ECONOMICS OF PRIVATE LAW (Parisi, ed.). *See also Debate: Is Law and Economics Moral?* (publication based on a live debate between Robin Paul Malloy and Richard A. Posner).

new frames of reference, and new patterns of legal thinking. As a result, we now have new rhetorical tools for discussing matters of liability, risk allocation, criminality, and property, among others. Our legal vocabulary has embraced new terms such as transaction costs, externalities, efficiency, wealth-maximization, preference shaping, reasonable investment-backed expectations, and cost-benefit analysis. We have also absorbed conceptual frameworks such as those referenced by such names as the Coase Theorem, the prisoner's dilemma, the tragedy of the commons, the anti-commons, the theory of path dependency, efficient breach, public choice, and game theory. Thus, for better or for worse, and without regard to one's politics, the borrowing of market concepts has *transformed* legal reasoning and captured an authoritative position in the legal imagination.

This book is concerned with the meanings and values created and promoted in law by the use of various market concepts. It seeks to examine and explain how these references to economics shape socio-legal meanings and values, and how they influence the allocation of scarce resources and the opportunities for capturing, creating, and distributing wealth.

The book also brings a humanities-based approach to recent trends in law and market scholarship. Thus, it contributes to an impressive expansion of law and market thinking brought on by a variety of approaches that might collectively be called the "new law and economics." Examples of "new" approaches include ventures into behavioral law and economics (referencing work in behavioral psychology and sociology),[5] the law and economics of norms (referencing theories of norm-building and of informal relationships and organizations),[6] institutional law and economics (referencing institutional economics rather than the more traditional appeal to neoclassical economics),[7] feminist law and economics

[5] See BEHAVIORAL LAW & ECONOMICS (Sunstein, ed.); Rostain, *Educating Homo Economicus.*

[6] See, e.g., *Symposium: Law, Economics and Norms*; LANDA, TRUST, ETHNICITY AND IDENTITY. See MALLOY, LAW AND MARKET ECONOMY at 136–37; McAdams, *Signaling Discount Rates*; Blair & Stout, *Trust, Trustworthiness, and the Behavioral Foundations of Corporate Law*; ELSTER, THE CEMENT OF SOCIETY.

[7] See generally MERCURO & MEDEMA, ECONOMICS AND THE LAW at 101–29, 130–56 (discussing Institutional law and economics, then discussing Neoinstitutional law and economics); NORTH, INSTITUTIONS, INSTITUTIONAL CHANGE AND ECONOMIC PERFORMANCE; NORTH, *Transaction Costs*; ADAMS, RELATION OF THE STATE TO INDUSTRIAL ACTION (Dorfman, ed.); COMMONS, INSTITUTIONAL ECONOMICS; Commons, *Law and Economics*; VEBLEN, THEORY OF THE LEISURE CLASS; SAMUELS, LAW AND ECONOMICS; SOLO, ECONOMIC ORGANIZATIONS AND SOCIAL SYSTEMS; AYRES, THEORY OF ECONOMIC PROGRESS.

(referencing feminist theory),[8] and interpretive and representational law and economics (referencing the humanities, various forms of interpretation and rhetoric theory, and law and society).[9]

In this book attention is focused on the emergent interest in interpretive and representational approaches to law and market theory, and on the experiential process by which legal and market reasoning is transformed. Therefore, in exploring an interpretive or representational approach, the book embraces the humanities, including references to esthetics, ethics, and logic. It explores the subjective nature of markets, the lack of universality in a number of economic concepts, and the role of interpretive institutions in generating value and redistributing resources. Moreover, it advances an understanding of the relationship among law, markets, and culture, indicating a need to democratize and enhance access to the meaning and value formation process.

At the outset, however, it must be noted that there are numerous approaches to interpretation theory, and to the cognitive processes that ground interpretation. The focus in this book is, therefore, limited. This book makes reference to the interpretation theory of one of America's greatest philosophers who was also a founder of the philosophical school identified as American Pragmatism, Charles Sanders Peirce.[10]

Peirce's work on interpretation and representation theory is categorized under the term or subject of semiotics, which means the study of "signs."

---

[8] *See generally* Hadfield, *Expressive Theory of Contract*; Hadfield, *Price of Law*; O'Connor, *Promoting Economic Justice in Plant Closings*; FERBER & NELSON, BEYOND ECONOMIC MAN; White, *Feminist Foundations for the Law of Business*; Meighan, *In a Similar Choice*; SUNSTEIN, FEMINISM & POLITICAL THEORY; Dennis, *The Lessons of Comparable Worth*; O'Neil, *Self-Interest and Concern for Others in the Owner-Managed Firm*; McCluskey, *Insurer Moral Hazard in the Workers' Compensation Crisis.*

[9] *See, e.g.,* Kevelson, *Transfer, Transaction, Asymmetry*; Malloy, *Toward A New Discourse of Law and Economics*; Brion, *Rhetoric and the Law of Enterprise*; McAdams, *A Focal Point Theory of Expressive Law*; McAdams, *An Attitudinal Theory of Expressive Law*; Lessig, *The Regulation of Social Meaning*; Malloy, *Law and Market Economy*; Brion, *The Ethics of Property*. The starting place for much of this work are two books by McCloskey, THE RHETORIC OF ECONOMICS and IF YOU'RE SO SMART. More recent books include: DESOTO, THE MYSTERY OF CAPITAL; GAGNIER, THE INSATIABILITY OF HUMAN WANTS; KIRZNER, MEANING OF MARKET PROCESS; MALLOY, LAW AND MARKET ECONOMY; NOOTEBOOM, LEARNING AND INNOVATION. While each of these books takes on a particular aspect of the representational relationship between law and economics, each demonstrates the significance of interpretation theory to an understanding of law, markets, and culture.

[10] *See* THE ESSENTIAL PEIRCE VOL. 1; THE ESSENTIAL PEIRCE VOL. 2. *See generally,* KEVELSON, PEIRCE, SCIENCE, SIGNS; KEVELSON, CHARLES S. PEIRCE'S METHOD OF METHODS; KEVELSON, THE LAW AS A SYSTEM OF SIGNS; KEVELSON, PEIRCE'S ESTHETICS OF FREEDOM; NOTH, HANDBOOK ON SEMIOTICS 39–47; SHERIFF, CHARLES PEIRCE'S GUESS AT THE RIDDLE; LISZKA, GENERAL

By this term Peirce simply meant to reaffirm the idea that humans are sign making and sign interpreting beings. Signs, as such, include language as spoken and written, visual images, colors, symbols, art, architecture, music, and a variety of other ways in which ideas are communicated. In this book I refer to semiotics as a *cultural-interpretive* approach, because this term expresses the semiotic ideas that the individual interpretive actor is situated within a cultural context and that a culture, in essence, is an implicit interpretive system. This is how one experiences the intersection of law and market economy – not as an isolated and atomistic individual but as an individualized participant in an interpretive community.

In popular culture perhaps the best known semiotician is Umberto Eco, who has numerous successes in both the popular and the academic communities.[11] It is, however, Peirce's work that is of particular value in exploring the relationship between law and market theory because it shares an affinity with a number of core ideas expressed in the works of Adam Smith,[12] and with work in Austrian economics.[13] The

INTRODUCTION TO THE SEMEIOTIC OF CHARLES SANDERS PEIRCE; COLAPIETRO, PEIRCE'S APPROACH TO THE SELF; APEL, CHARLES S. PEIRCE: PHILOSOPHICAL WRITINGS OF PEIRCE (Buchler, ed.); HOOKWAY, PEIRCE; REASONING AND THE LOGIC OF THINGS (Ketner, ed.); MERRELL, PEIRCE, SIGNS, AND MEANING; MERRELL, SEMIOSIS IN THE POSTMODERN AGE; SCOLES, SEMIOTICS AND INTERPRETATION; HAUSMAN, CHARLES S. PEIRCE'S EVOLUTIONARY PHILOSOPHY; POTTER, PEIRCE ON NORMS & IDEALS; MENAND, THE METAPHYSICAL CLUB; MILOVANOVIC, INTRODUCTION TO THE SOCIOLOGY OF LAW (discussing semiotics including Peirce).

[11] See ECO, SEARCH FOR THE PERFECT LANGUAGE; ECO, LIMITS OF INTERPRETATION 51; ECO, OPEN WORK; ECO, SEMIOTICS AND THE PHILOSOPHY OF LANGUAGE; THE SIGN OF THREE (Eco & Sebeok, eds); ECO, THEORY OF SEMIOTICS. His popular works include: ECO, MISREADINGS; ECO, FOUCAULT'S PENDULUM; ECO, THE NAME OF THE ROSE (made into a popular hit movie, THE NAME OF THE ROSE, starring Sean Connery, 1986, Fox Films).

[12] See, e.g., MALLOY, LAW AND MARKET ECONOMY 41–42, citing SMITH, THEORY OF MORAL SENTIMENTS 168; SMITH, ESSAYS ON PHILOSOPHICAL SUBJECTS 33–105; Smith argued that we exist in a social context and not as isolated beings; *id.* at 64–69, 106–24, 161–62, citing SMITH, THEORY OF MORAL SENTIMENTS, 71, 200–60, 352, 422 (discussing the impartial spectator), 264 (discussing the way in which general rules emerge from experience); SMITH, LECTURES ON JURISPRUDENCE 207, 311–30, 401–07 (discussing the idea of social organization based on many factors and not the idea of social contract), 14–37, 200–90, 311–30, 401–07 (addressing the dynamic stages of economic and legal evolution); SMITH, AN INQUIRY INTO THE NATURE AND CAUSES OF THE WEALTH OF NATIONS VOL. I 420–45, VOL. II 1, 231–44 (discussing the dynamic stages of economic development); SMITH, LECTURES ON RHETORIC AND BELLES LETTRES (provides a similar analysis with respect to the dynamic development of language).

[13] See, e.g., SHAND, THE CAPITALIST ALTERNATIVE; KUKATHAS, HAYEK AND MODERN LIBERALISM; HAYEK, CONSTITUTION OF LIBERTY; HAYEK, LAW, LEGISLATION, AND LIBERTY (VOL. 1, RULES AND ORDER) (VOL. 2, THE MIRAGE OF

compatibility with Austrian economics is most apparent with respect to the idea of "market process theory," as expressed in the work of such well-known economists as Friedrich Hayek and Israel Kirzner.[14] Peirce's work also shares a conceptual grounding that is similar to economist Joseph Schumpeter's theory of "creative destruction," which is central to an understanding of creativity in economics.[15] In addition, because Peirce was interested in developing a theory of the sciences, his approach lends itself to the deconstruction and interpretation of empirical and social science work, such as that done within the framework of an economic analysis of law. Peirce's concern for understanding the way in which we experience the sciences makes his approach readily applicable to the study of law and market theory.[16]

Peirce's work and the idea of understanding law in a market context should also be of interest to critical theory scholars.[17] Critical theorists have contributed a great deal to our understanding of the experiential nature of law, and these insights are valuable to the cultural-interpretive process. Critical theorists, and other non-law and economics scholars, have also reminded us of the fact that law is not a natural science. And, even though references to the natural and social sciences can be helpful, law involves human practices and experiences that are not fully explainable or understandable in scientific terms.

This book, therefore, examines the way in which the "institutions" of language, communication, and interpretation function to redistribute and create wealth. It also explores ways in which an interpretive approach can make us better and more effective lawyers by facilitating an understanding of law in its market context. This can be done in at least three ways. First, Peirce's approach enhances our ability to use *framing* devices to identify value-enhancing opportunities in the exchange process. Framing

---

SOCIAL JUSTICE, 1976) (VOL. 3, THE POLITICAL ORDER OF A FREE PEOPLE, 1979); KIRZNER, MEANING OF MARKET PROCESS; KIRZNER, DISCOVERY AND THE CAPITALIST PROCESS.

[14] *Id.*   [15] *See* SCHUMPETER, CAPITALISM, SOCIALISM, AND DEMOCRACY 81–106.

[16] Thus, it is not surprising that Peirce's work has been cited and favorably discussed by Richard Posner in two of his books (PROBLEMS OF JURISPRUDENCE 462–64; PROBLEMATICS OF MORAL AND LEGAL THEORY 99, 104, 264; and MERCURO & MEDEMA, ECONOMICS AND THE LAW).

[17] *See, e.g.,* Houh, *Critical Interventions.* In this excellent article the author reconsiders the good faith rule in contract law. With specific reference to race and employment matters, she uses critical theory and law and market economy theory (with reference to Peirce) to rethink and restructure the established approach in the area. In integrating her approach she reforms our thinking about the good faith rule in contract law and develops a new cultural-interpretive pattern of legal argument.

involves identifying a category or general viewpoint from which a fact pattern or problem will be addressed. Second, it facilitates the use of *referencing* devices that enhance our ability to mediate between contested matters within a given interpretive framework. Referencing involves the identification and selection of particular criteria, from among several, for use in analyzing issues *within* a given frame. And, third, it explains how semiotic devices can be used to create value by transforming legal convention – by creating new *representations* that extend the networks and patterns of exchange. Representation involves the way in which abstract ideas and concepts are made comprehensible and able to be exchanged, as in using a written deed to represent an estate interest in land so that it can be sold or mortgaged. Each of these points can be initially illustrated with some simple examples.

As to the idea of framing, consider a typical real estate financing transaction.[18] Imagine that a developer has formed a corporate entity to deal in real estate transactions. In an effort to raise needed cash for a new venture, the developer seeks to borrow against $10 million in equity that it has in an office building. At the outset one needs to consider the way in which this financing transaction might be framed. It might be framed as a loan secured by a mortgage on the office building. In this setup the developer retains full ownership of the building and gives a mortgage lien as collateral for the promise of repayment. On the other hand, the transaction could be set up as a sale and lease back of the property. Here the developer sells the building to a buyer to raise cash and then leases it back to use the space. The proceeds of sale provide funding as a substitute for the mortgage loan, and the lease payments to the buyer mimic the repayment of a mortgage. Now the transaction involves a sales contract, coordinated leasing terms, and no mortgage. A third way of doing this transaction might involve the sale or pledge of the stock in the corporate entity holding legal title to the property. In this framing of the transaction the exchange is shifted out of real property law and into the law governing corporate stock transfers. Each of these three transactional frames is common practice and collectively they illustrate several different ways of approaching the problem. Each framing of the transaction triggers different aspects of law, and different cash flow, tax, and other economic consequences.

Once a specific frame and transactional view have been decided upon, there are still many points to be considered and evaluated. Within the

---

[18] *See* MALLOY & SMITH, REAL ESTATE TRANSACTIONS 3–43.

chosen frame there are multiple ways of structuring the details of the transaction. Interpretive references may be made to internal rates of return,
out-of-pocket costs, sunk costs, opportunity costs, market penetration,
and net and gross cash flows, among others. Different references used
to evaluate the desirability of a given transactional frame will provide
different conclusions about the consequences of the proposed project.

In a similar way, particular drafting points may be referenced against
different interpretive criteria to evaluate the status of the terms as
covenants, warranties, or one of three types of conditions (simultaneous conditions, conditions precedent, and conditions subsequent). The
point is, that these different interpretive references may result in different
risk allocations and in different legal and economic opportunities. This
is true even when operating within the given transactional frame. Moreover, understanding the meanings that each side attaches to particular
words, terms, or conditions used in documenting a transaction is essential to advancing a client's transactional expectation. Being an effective
advocate for *either* side, therefore, involves an ability to understand the
framing and referencing of the transaction from *each* side.[19]

We can appreciate another aspect of framing and referencing when we
consider a transaction in a cross-cultural context.[20] Consider, for example, a real estate transaction involving an American developer negotiating
for a project in a transitional economy such as China. Here, the developer must contend with additional framing and referencing issues. Here,
she must appreciate the interpretive implications of *different* worldviews
as value frames – different conceptions of property, capitalism, profit,
individual autonomy, and different formulations of the proper balance
between private and public interest in market exchange. Consequently,
understanding the deal requires an ability to effectively use the tools of
interpretation theory to successfully navigate the cross-cultural waters of

[19] There are a number of classic examples of this type of interpretive problem in structuring
exchange. In the area of contract law, consider two cases that appear in most first-year
casebooks. *See* Frigaliment Importing Co. v. B.N.S. Int'l. Sales Corp., 190 F. supp. 116
(S.D.N.Y. 1960) (Litigating the meaning of the word "chicken" as used in a contract:
did "chicken" include more expensive "fryers" or simply make reference to lower value
"stewing chickens"?); Raffles v. Wichelhaus, 2H.&C. 906, 159 Eng. Rep. 375 (EX. 1864)
(Litigating confusion as to which of two ships by the name of *Peerless* was the one that was
the subject of the contract between the parties.)

[20] *See* MALLOY, LAW AND MARKET ECONOMY 12–15, 66–70; Hom & Malloy, *China's
Market Economy. See generally,* CHINESE WOMEN TRAVERSING DIASPORA (Hom,
ed.) (exploring meaning in alternative cultural-interpretive frames).

commerce, and this ability is of even more importance as we consider the process of globalization.

We can also examine these framing and referencing conflicts between interpretive communities within one country. Consider, for example, the case of *American Nurses' Ass'n* v. *Illinois*.[21] This case involved a class action suit that challenged the appropriate frame of reference for determining wages for certain classifications of workers.[22] The plaintiffs in the case, brought on behalf of nurses and typists employed by the state of Illinois, alleged that the state pay scales were unfair and discriminatory.[23] The claim was that jobs associated with women paid less than jobs traditionally done by men.[24] On the surface of the text, the dispute seemed to be one of *contested facts* concerning the determination of wages when a comparison was made between the "work of women" and the "work of men."[25] The underlying tension in the case, however, really involved deeply *contested values* regarding market operations.[26] The State of Illinois, for instance, defended its wage structure by showing that it was implemented with reference to the wage rates established by the supply and demand for particular types of employees in the general labor market.[27] The plaintiffs, however, rejected the fairness of the marketplace and interpreted the market frame as inappropriate.[28] To them, markets were inherently biased in favor of men, and a market frame simply served to perpetuate the unfairness of the labor market to women.

Understanding the underlying debate in a case such as *American Nurses' Ass'n*, and working to effectively mediate the tension between the two conflicting interpretive frames, requires an understanding of the conflicting meanings and values dividing the two sides of the case. The dispute is not simply about *facts* (differences in wages between jobs); it's about *values* and the interpretation of market relationships. Both sides can recognize that getting the court to understand the dispute from their own particular frame and reference will affect the outcome, and ultimately the allocation of economic resources.[29] Thus, interpretation theory facilitates a

---

[21] American Nurses' Ass'n v. State of Illinois, 783 F.2d 716 (1986). This case is also discussed in MALLOY, LAW AND ECONOMICS 134–45.

[22] *Id.*   [23] *Id.*, at 718–19.   [24] *Id.*   [25] *Id.*

[26] American Nurses' Ass'n, 783 F.2d 716, at 719–20. *See* CHAMALLAS, INTRODUCTION TO FEMINIST LEGAL THEORY 184–96; PAUL, EQUITY AND GENDER.

[27] American Nurses' Ass'n, 783 F.2d 716, at 719–20.   [28] *Id.*

[29] Once the court selects a particular interpretive frame and reference concerning the nature of the dispute and its resolution, the outcome and implications must be justified within

deeper understanding of conflicts such as the one illustrated by the case of *American Nurses' Ass'n*, while directing attention to the use of law in positioning social and gender relations.[30]

In addition to explaining the significance of framing and referencing, this book addresses the way in which Peirce's semiotic interpretation theory facilitates exchange.[31] In general, semiotics deals with the way in which abstract ideas are *represented*.[32] This simply means that it deals with the devices, concepts, and tools that we use to communicate and interact with each other. The ability, for instance, to represent different forms of property ownership in terms of deeds, leases, and mortgages, permits exchange in ways that would not be possible without such representational or interpretive devices.[33] A deed representing fee ownership of real property, for example, permits a homeowner to control a property as a physical object and at the same time use it as collateral for a secured loan, or lease it for rental income.[34] Law, through legal convention, permits the property to serve multiple market functions. Not only does it provide a home and shelter, it can provide access to credit and to cash flow. In a similar manner, the ability to use a credit card as a recognized symbol or representation of financial ability enhances market exchange by eliminating the need for individuals to carry large sums of gold when they shop or travel.[35] In so doing, it raises the possibility of extending exchange beyond the boundaries of small or informal communities, and thus expands the potential for meaningful and profitable market interaction. In this way, the transformation of the interpretive frames and references of legal representation enhances our ability to create value.[36]

In the hope of further advancing an understanding of framing, referencing, and representing, I wish to briefly discuss several more cases that

---

that frame and reference. In a sense one might think of selecting the appropriate frame and reference as generally related to the idea of the judge acting on a cultural-interpretive hunch; and once the judge makes a framing and referencing choice the logic of that choice constrains the decision. *See generally*, Dewey, *Logical Method and Law*; Hutchenson; *The Function of the "Hunch" in Judicial Decisions*; Frank, *What Courts Do In Fact*; Brion, *The Pragmatic Genesis of Constitutional Meaning*; Yablon, *Justifying the Judge's Hunch*; Modak-Truan, *Pragmatic Justification of the Judicial Hunch*.

[30] When this case is analyzed in a cultural-interpretive manner, one better understands the conflict, while also appreciating the way in which dominant frames and references are used to inform gender politics. *See generally*, BEYOND ECONOMIC MAN (Ferber & Nelson, eds.).

[31] MALLOY, LAW AND MARKET ECONOMY 23–56,148–53.

[32] *Id.*   [33] *See* DESOTO, MYSTERY OF CAPITAL 4–10, 39–67.

[34] *Id.*   [35] *Id.*   [36] *Id.*

illustrate these ideas in law. These additional case examples should help in setting a foundation for further discussion. These cases include *Pennsylvania Coal* v. *Mahon*,[37] *Keystone Bituminous Coal Ass'n.* v. *DeBenedictis*,[38] *Dolan* v. *City of Tigard*,[39] and *Moore* v. *Regents of the Univ. of California*.[40]

The two cases of *Pennsylvania Coal* and *Keystone Bituminous Coal Ass'n* work together to illustrate the idea of framing. Each case involved a state statutory scheme designed to regulate underground mining operations in Pennsylvania. In each case the regulations were designed to preserve support for the surface estate property interest at the expense of the subsurface estate interest owned by mining companies. The regulations required the subsurface owners to leave a percentage of their coal in the ground in order to ensure adequate support for the surface estate owners. The concern was that extensive subsurface coal extraction would result in the collapse of the surface estate and the destruction of homes, roads and other land improvements. The problem was that the mining companies held property entitlements to the subsurface estate, and they alleged that a restriction on their ability to extract all of their coal amounted to an unlawful taking of their property without just compensation in violation of the Fifth Amendment to the United States Constitution.[41]

In addressing the conflict between surface and subsurface owners, the United States Supreme Court reached completely different outcomes in each case, despite the virtually identical statutory schemes. The key to understanding the different outcomes is in appreciating the different frames used to position each case. In *Pennsylvania Coal* the dispute was framed as a two-party exchange. A willing buyer purchased a surface estate knowing that it was subject to the rights of the subsurface estate owner. The Court found no reason to interfere in a voluntary and consensual market exchange between two competent parties. Moreover, it held that the State could not restrict the extraction of subsurface coal without violating the takings clause of the Fifth Amendment.[42]

In *Keystone Bituminous Coal Ass'n* the Court rejected the two party transactional framing of *Pennsylvania Coal*, and reached the opposite result by framing the dispute as a transaction with multi-party

---

[37] Pennsylvania Coal v. Mahon, 260 U.S. 393 (1922).
[38] Keystone Bituminous Coal Ass'n. v. DeBenedictis, 480 U.S. 470 (1987).
[39] Dolan v. City of Tigard, 512 U.S. 374 (1994).
[40] Moore v. Regents of the Univ. of California, 793 P.2d. 479 (Cal. 1990). *See generally* Resnik, *DNA Patents and Human Dignity*; Harris & Alcorn, *To Solve A Deadly Shortage*; Rao, *Property, Privacy and the Human Body*.
[41] Pennsylvania Coal, at 412.   [42] *Id.*, at 414.

implications.[43] The Court focused on the implications for multiple surface owners, including the public in terms of protecting such improvements as schools, roads, and parks. It also looked at the safety needs of mine workers. If a mining shaft collapsed workers could be hurt or killed. Thinking in terms of a broadly framed legal problem, the Court was able to logically reason that the matter was not one capable of being fully addressed in a private market exchange because two private parties to a contract would not take into account the many third-party interests involved. Consequently, the legislature, empowered to protect the public, was capable of restricting the amount of coal that could be extracted, and as long as the coal companies retained substantial value in their holdings there would be no violation of the takings clause.[44]

Thus, we see an important example of the power to frame a legal and market dispute. Where the frame is focused on two well-informed individuals with the capacity to freely contract and with few barriers to overcome, the courts are more likely to follow the logic of avoiding interference with the exchange relationship. On the other hand, the more extensive and complex the exchange network, the more likely it is that a logical argument can be made for interference. This is because of the difficulty individuals have in assessing the necessary information and interests to be accounted for in the transaction. As the number of parties with an interest in the transaction increases, there are also numerous problems of coordination and cooperation. Consequently, a great deal of power resides in one's ability to influence the frame and definition of the exchange relationship.

In the case of *Dolan* v. *City of Tigard* we have a nice example of what I would call a referencing problem.[45] *Dolan* involved a situation in which a property owner argued that the city engaged in an unlawful taking of private property without just compensation. Dolan owned some property near a river. She operated a hardware store on the property and sought to expand her commercial operations. The city passed regulations restricting use and development on the property in order to provide open space within the river floodplain. It also required a bike path to be placed across part of the property.[46] In this case, both the majority and minority opinions of the United States Supreme Court framed the dispute in terms of takings law. They both agreed on the fundamental nature of the exchange and on the nature of the competing interests. They even agreed

[43] Keystone, 480 U.S. 470 (1987).   [44] *Id.*, at 472.   [45] Dolan, 512 U.S. 374 (1994).
[46] *Id.*, at 380.

on the basic idea of the need for the regulations to have an essential nexus and rough proportionality to the stated purpose to be accomplished by the regulation.

One important difference in the opinions, however, involved a reference to the rule governing the burden of proof in this situation. The majority opinion held that the regulation was enacted as a quasi-judicial function of the zoning and land use board. Thus, the appropriate reference was to the rule that required the city of Tigard to carry the burden, by substantial competent evidence, of demonstrating compliance with the essential nexus and rough proportionality requirements. The majority determined that the City did not meet its burden even if it could be argued that there was a nexus.[47] The minority, in contrast with the majority, argued that the regulations were typical legislative acts rather than quasi-judicial acts. The applicable rule of reference in such a case is one that presumes the validity of the regulation and places a burden on the property owner to show that it is not even fairly debatable that the appropriate nexus and rough proportionality tests have been met. The minority opinion concluded, therefore, that the burden had been met and that there was no unlawful taking.[48]

Thus, in *Dolan* we see that a particular rule referenced within the frame of the case helps to explain a key difference in the outcome.

I identify the choice of interpretive rule in *Dolan* as a reference primarily because a reference is a narrower and more specific concept than a frame. It is true, for instance, that one could say that the majority framed the dispute in terms of a quasi-adjudicative process whereas the minority framed it as a legislative process. The line between framing and referencing is generally one of degree and of emphasis. The idea of framing and referencing (and of representing) is that they are to function as flexible and dynamic tools for thinking about and organizing analysis. They are simply meant to be organizing concepts. In organizing the analysis of any given fact pattern, for example, the frame is generally a broader and more primary concept than a reference. The idea of referencing is one that recognizes that there are still many interpretive moves and devices to select and employ, even after the primary interpretive frame is set. These narrower and more specific choices within any given frame are usefully thought of in terms of referencing devices.

Finally, in *Moore* v. *Regents of the Univ. of California* we have a useful example of a representation problem.[49] In *Moore* a dispute arose over

---

[47] *Id.*, at 388.   [48] *Id.*, at 411.   [49] Moore, 793 P. 2d 479 (Cal. 1990).

claims of ownership with respect to body fluids and genetic information. The case involved John Moore who was a patient at UCLA medical
hospital. Moore was receiving treatment related to his spleen and this
involved repeated visits to and treatment by doctors over an extended
number of years. While performing their work, doctors discovered that
Moore had some unique genetic qualities. They extracted genetic materials from him and used it in their research. The research led to the
eventual development of some very valuable drugs. The potential market
value of the pharmaceutical products derived from Moore's cell line was
estimated to be worth 3 billion dollars in 1990. Upon learning of this,
Moore sued for damages asserting that his privacy and property rights
had been violated. He sought adequate compensation for the value of his
cell line.[50]

There are many interesting aspects of the case including framing and
referencing issues.[51] In terms of representation the case raises the problem
of how the human body is to be represented in law. Should the body be
treated as property subject to the usual rights of use and possession,
exclusion, ability to transfer, and the right to the profits of ownership?
Should the law commodify the body and make it an ordinary article of
commerce, of barter and trade? Or should the human body be represented
as sacred, as the creation of God? If the body is to be property then what
type of property should it be – personal property or intangible property,
for instance?

The case raises questions with respect to our ability to assert an ownership interest or property right in our bodies, and if we have such a right,
what does it mean for purposes of market exchange? Should people such
as Moore be able to use a property right to block, hinder, or raise the
expense of scientific research that can benefit the greater public? Is the
value of any product related to a given cell line really the outcome of
the research or does it remain attributed forever to the fortuitous identity
of the person from which it originally came? Can these differences be
reconciled or coordinated by private contract?

---

[50] *Id.*, at 482.
[51] For example, is this to be framed as a two-party transaction between Moore and his
doctor or as a multi-party transaction involving additional parties such as the hospital,
the university, and the public? Should the dispute be framed in terms of property law, in
terms of the patient and doctor relationship, or otherwise? Within any given frame, how
are we to value or measure the costs and benefits of the medical service provided to Moore,
the research, and the pharmaceutical products? These valuations all involve referencing
problems that we will explore later in the book when we learn about alternative valuation
methods in chapter 5.

Another problem in *Moore* involves consent and the matter of a voluntary exchange. The facts of the case indicate that Moore consented to treatment but he asserted that this consent did not extend to the research and commercial use of his cell line.[52] Even if Moore had been asked to consent to research and potential commercial use of products derived from his cell line, how would the parties arrive at a suitable contract price? An *ex ante* agreement might look very low if *ex post* the research led to a multi-billion-dollar line of products. The representation problems in *Moore* are several. Should the relationship between Moore and his doctor be represented as professional (the doctor-patient relationship), as one of contract, or as one of agency? Each raises different socio-legal issues. And what is to be made of the relationship between the hospital and Moore, and as between the hospital and the doctor? Furthermore, what of the difficulty of factoring in the community value of such research that might lead to important improvements in public health.

By failing to represent the body in property terms, the court in *Moore* removed the controversy from standard market analysis. It did this by refusing to commodify the body as an object of market exchange. Refusing to represent the body as property, of course, is not the same as saying that the Court made a decision of no economic consequence. The decision had major economic consequences that were much less favorable to Moore than they might have been had the Court been willing to represent the body as property.

At this point there should be a sufficient basis for appreciating the general idea of framing, referencing, and representing in law. These concepts will be further developed in this book. In chapter 3, for instance, these ideas will be discussed in terms of the structure of legal reasoning and legal argument.

Before concluding this introductory chapter, however, I wish to discuss one further example of the framing process and the implication it raises when considering law in a market context. This example is designed to show the connection between a particular frame for justifying private property in the legal system and the use of alternative allocation rules in distributing initial rights over particular resources. The discussion is not meant to fully elaborate on the various property rules and allocation rules described. It is meant to provide a brief sketch of a relationship between concepts that illustrate an important part of understanding law in a market context.

[52] *Id.*, at 485.

In a market economy there are four general justifications that are typically offered as a basis for private property rights over valuable resources. These justifications can be identified as approaches based on natural rights, distributive justice, economics, and identity.[53] There are also three major ways of structuring a simple resource allocation model. These three ways include allocation based on a first in time rule, allocation based on the highest bidder rule, and an allocation based on a lottery. The allocation rules are self-explanatory, but a brief description of each of the justifications is provided.

Natural rights[54]

The natural rights model centers on the idea of people having a natural right to the "fruits of their labor." In this sense it relates to a labor theory of value. This approach is generally associated with the first appropriation rule. A property interest is created in favor of the person that first appropriates the resource. In the context of real property it is also usually associated with the need to change the natural environment and to build permanent improvements on the land.

Distributive justice[55]

This model involves political and social organization. It is concerned with fairness and with an equitable distribution of resources. In this model, rules related to private property are justified against a background organizing principle developed under a "veil of ignorance." The idea is that equitable distribution rules are ones that we would select if we were unable to know our natural endowments at the time of the vote. In other words, we are asked to think hypothetically about our own self-interest in a context where we do not know if we will be black or white, strong or weak, rich or poor, or enabled or disabled in any particular way. Only after the organizing rules are adopted would we know our own circumstances.

---

[53] *See generally,* SINGER, INTRODUCTION TO PROPERTY 2–19; SPRANKLING, UNDERSTANDING PROPERTY LAW 11–44; ALLEN, RIGHT TO PROPERTY 119–61; DWYER & MENELL, PROPERTY LAW AND POLICY 2–17; EPSTEIN, SIMPLE RULES 57–70.

[54] This approach relates to the ideas of John Locke as expressed in his SECOND TREATISE ON GOVERNMENT.

[55] This approach makes reference to RAWLS, THEORY OF JUSTICE. Rawls developed the idea of a background organizing principle based on a "veil of ignorance."

The idea is that most people are risk averse and will opt for a fair rule that protects the interests of the weakest individuals since they may themselves be in such a position when the veil of ignorance is removed.

Economics[56]

The economic justification of private property is pragmatic. The basic idea is that a private property system promotes productivity and efficient use of scarce resources. This approach seeks to put resources into the hands of the people that value them most. That is the people that are willing and able to pay the most for a particular resource. This system seeks to reward people for their productivity and gives primacy to the ordering rules of self directed individuals pursuing their own self-interest. The underlying assumption of this approach being that the pursuit of self-interest promotes the public interest.

Identity[57]

This approach to private property focuses on the way in which identity is related to property. One contemporary way of understanding this approach is with the idea that "we are what we own." In this approach we think of a person acquiring rights in resources that are essential to individual or group identity. Resources that extend beyond this narrowly defined conception would not be private property. Another way of thinking about this idea is in terms of aboriginal identity. Aboriginal people often times link identity to place, and believe that they imprint the land on which they live just as the land imprints them.[58] In this understanding some resources are so closely linked to identity that they cease to be understandable as property, in the sense in which we typically think of commodifying resources for exchange in the marketplace.

Given these four brief and basic definitions, let us consider the way in which these legal approaches relate to our three market allocation rules. Assume we have identified a small lake with rich deposits of valuable

---

[56] This approach has its modern expression in such works as POSNER, ECONOMIC ANALYSIS OF LAW.

[57] This approach makes reference to Hegel. *See* Radin, *Property and Personhood* (she makes reference to Hegel's book on the PHILOSOPHY OF RIGHT).

[58] *See generally,* Malloy, *Letters from the Longhouse* at 1576; CHATWIN, SONGLINES; Mosley, *Laying Down the Law.*

minerals beneath its bed. At the time of our discovery the lake is in a natural and undeveloped state. No one is using the lake other than members of a small aboriginal tribe, and they only visit it for a three-week time period once each spring and fall. During these time periods they conduct some of their most sacred ceremonies.

As a result of the discovery of the valuable minerals many people now want to move to the lake and claim ownership over the resource. In an effort to prevent overcrowding and a wasteful depletion of the resources an attempt is to be made to use property rules to achieve a proper allocation of the resource. Given our four basic approaches to private property and our three simple allocation rules, consider the ways in which this matter might be framed.

Assume that we frame the property justification in terms of a natural rights approach. From this point of view the most appropriate allocation rule would seem to be the first in time rule. This means that we might have a legal rule that recognizes ownership in the person that first possesses the resource by successfully getting equipment in place and extracting it from the lake bed.

If instead we were to frame the property justification in terms of a distributive justice approach we might allocate the resource on the basis of a lottery. In this situation people would enter the lottery and one lucky person would win. This allocation treats everyone equally since it does not rely on an ability to get to the lake or exploit the resource before others, and it does not require one to have a great deal of wealth to make an original purchase of the lake.

If we were to frame the property justification in terms of an economic approach we would probably favor allocating the resource to the highest bidder. This method would put the resource in the hands of the person willing and able to pay the most for the resource. This should be the person that expects to get the most value out of the resource, and assuming that the pursuit of self-interest equates to the promotion of the public interest everyone will gain from this approach.

A problem with the first in time and highest bidder rules is that poor people will be disadvantaged. If one lacks the technology and wealth to get there first or to bid the most, these rules seem unfair. This is often the claim in the global community when developing countries object to such allocation rules when addressing difficult to reach resources such as minerals below the ocean beds, resources in Antarctica, and the use of inner and outer space. Developing countries tend to favor a distributive justice approach whereas developed countries tend to advocate for either an economic or natural rights approach. This is understandable since the allocation rules favor different outcomes. Each of the rules appears neutral on its face but the power to shape a particular frame of analysis favors a particular outcome. Therefore, understanding the relationship between one's particular point of view and the power to influence the framing of legal reasoning is important and of economic consequence.

In our simple lake example the aboriginal people are likely to be in the position of a developing or underdeveloped country. Thus, they might prefer the lottery as an allocation system. Preferable to a lottery, however, would be a system based on the identity approach, assuming they can convince the legal system to respect their claim to the lake as an essential part of their personhood. If the lake can be protected as a sacred place intimately associated with the cultural identity and existence of the aboriginal people it might be possible to allocate the resource to them, particularly if they are prohibited from transferring the lake and required to continue to use it as they have for generations. The problem here is that the lake is then removed from the marketplace. Its economic value is not exploited and there is likely to be great pressure to resist this outcome.

In this example we see the important implications of framing. Framing a particular legal justification for law favors a particular allocation rule. Note, however, that this is not a one-way relationship. If we were to approach this legal problem with a predisposition for framing the matter in terms of a given allocation rule we would get similar results. For example, if we favor a first in time rule we will likely adopt a natural rights justification, if we favor a highest bidder allocation rule we will likely prefer an economic justification, and if we are inclined to use a lottery allocation rule we will find justification for that rule in a distributive justice approach. Consequently, we need to recognize and use our understanding of these relationships in legal reasoning and public policy making. Understanding these relationships and learning to use them to the advantage of one's client and constituents is an important part of doing law in a market context.

At this point it should be understood that examining law in a market context is not the same thing as doing an economic analysis of law. The difference is both exciting and challenging.

In concluding this introduction it should be noted that the initial points raised in this chapter are just examples of the way in which an interpretive approach advances our understanding of the relationship between law and market theory. These and other points will be further elaborated upon in this book. In addition to discussion of numerous market concepts and ideas, the book assumes and implicitly supports the following conclusions.

Knowledge and information are fragmented and constrained by differences in individual and group experience and culture. Legal and market institutions also vary with reference to the cultural-interpretive framework in which they operate. The market system is seldom completely established in any particular society. Thus, opportunities exist for capturing or creating value in mediating between different groups.

Cultural-interpretive frameworks can vary by such factors as historical context, race, gender, age, class, income, education, and geographical location, among others. The variance in these frameworks creates asymmetrical positionings that can be used to shape markets, to segment markets, and to discriminate within and between markets.

Understanding law in its market context, and making sound market judgments do not require adherence to an efficiency or wealth-maximization criterion. Efficiency and wealth maximization are both ambiguous and highly contested ideas. Addressing these ambiguities and mediating these contested ideas requires an implicit, if not express, reference to esthetics, ethics, and logic. Moreover, understanding law in a market context means understanding the various economic consequences associated with legal action, and simultaneously appreciating the market constraints upon law and legal institutions. This awareness and understanding is important even when efficiency and wealth maximization are not the primary economic criteria under consideration.

In an interpretive approach, successful market economies can be understood as being facilitated by legal institutions that promote a concern for others – for third parties and for a public interest that is not always advanced by the fragmented pursuit of self-interest. Markets involve exchange and exchange, like interpretation, occurs between publicly situated human actors. In this regard, it is important to explore exchange in ways that go beyond assumptions of methodological individualism.

Finally, it is important to say something about the term "culture." As used in this book the term culture is given a broad meaning that can be usefully defined with reference to two quotes. The first is from a book edited by Stuart Hall and the second from a book by David Throsby.

> Culture . . . is not so much a set of things – novels and paintings or T.V. programs and comics – as a process, a set of practices. Primarily, culture is concerned with the production and the exchange of meanings – the "giving and taking of meaning" – between members of a society or group. To say that two people belong

to the same culture is to say that they interpret the world in roughly the same ways and can express themselves, their thoughts and feelings about the world, in ways which will be understood by each other.[59]

> "culture" is . . . a set of attitudes, beliefs, mores, customs, values and practices which are common to or shared by any group. The group may be defined in terms of politics, geography, religion, ethnicity or some other characteristic . . . The characteristics which define the group may be substantiated in the form of signs, symbols, texts, language, artifacts, oral and written tradition and by other means.[60]

Thus, this book explores the connection between culture, law, and markets. It does this in several steps. Chapter 2 explores the contested meanings of markets related to the differences in experience among people. Chapter 3 develops an interpretive framework for understanding and examining the connection between cultural-interpretation theory and an explanation of the way in which these ideas relate to the process of creating and capturing wealth in the marketplace. Chapters 4 and 5 explore particular market concepts and terms. This includes discussion of a wide range of terms such as, but not limited to, externalities, adverse selection, asymmetrical information, scarcity, risk, rent seeking, opportunistic behavior, moral hazard, Pareto and Kaldor–Hicks efficiency, preferences, wealth effects, path dependency, and hedonic and contingent valuation. The discussion also covers important concepts such as the tragedy of the commons, the prisoner's dilemma, cost and benefit analysis, the Coase Theorem, public choice, and the theory of efficient breach. Chapter 6 addresses some special considerations relevant to the non-profit sector of the economy. This is an important part of the marketplace, and is of particular interest when considered in the context of a society such as the United States that is so publicly committed to the pursuit of profits. Finally, chapter 7 offers some parting thoughts while raising some questions about the economic assumption of methodological individualism as applied to law and legal reasoning.

Conclusion

Understanding law in a market context is different from doing an economic analysis of law. Law in a market context involves an examination of the way in which people *experience* the relationship among law, markets,

---

[59] REPRESENTATION 1–2 (Hall, ed.).   [60] THROSBY, ECONOMICS AND CULTURE 3–4.

and culture. And it recognizes that this experience varies by a number of characteristics including race, gender, age, class, education, income, and geographic location. Furthermore, a primary way in which people experience these relationships is through the "institutions" of language, communication, and interpretation. Thus, law in a market context explores the cultural-interpretive process and its implications for wealth formation and (re)distribution.

Problems

Consider the problems that follow in terms of the way in which different people experience the marketplace. If you change the age, race, income level, education level, gender, or other characteristics of the parties involved how might that change our understanding of the problem and its resolution?

(1) In the aftermath of a big storm (a hurricane, for example), a major violent incident or act of war (the attack on the World Trade Center for instance), or a prolonged drought people are dislocated and public services are disrupted. Housing and basic shelter are in short supply, and safe drinking water is scarce. In these emergency situations difficult distributional questions arise. In the face of a great need and a very limited supply, how should these resources be distributed?

Assume that such an emergency arises in a major population center. While homes have been damaged and destroyed in a given neighborhood, and city water supplies have been cut off in that area, nearby hotels have rooms, electricity, and clean potable water. The hotels could be used to provide shelter, water, and comfortable accommodation to people who would otherwise be left on the streets. With a very high demand for hotel rooms, to serve as temporary accommodations, devise a fair and just way to distribute the limited supply of space. Should the hotels be able to distribute space on the basis of the highest bidder? Must they conduct a lottery? Should they give space to the first people on line using a first come first served rule? Should there be a redistribution each day or every couple of days so that more people get at least some chance to recover and use the accommodation? How many people should be limited to each room, and must they be married or immediate family members to share a room? What potential problems may arise in terms of the incentive to get around any given rule that is adopted? In other words, does any given rule create an opportunity for someone to earn a fee or bribe by admitting people in circumvention of the rule, and can this be policed? Discuss the trade off in selecting any given rule rather than another, and explain the reason for believing that one distribution rule is more fair than another.

(2) A law enacted in Hupeh Province, China, in the late 1990s to regulate premarital sexual relations required a premarital physical examination of the woman as a condition for a couple to obtain a marriage license. The purpose of the examination is to determine whether she had lost her virginity. If the doctor concluded that she had lost her virginity a monetary fine would be imposed against the woman in an amount equal to a month to four months' wages. In addition, the women would have to write a self-criticism essay. If an examination revealed that the woman was pregnant she would be fined additional amounts for each month into the pregnancy. These fines were designed to raise the cost of immoral practices. The policy behind the law is to crack down on the "immoral influences" of western values. The justification for the law is based on the interest of the People (represented by the Party and the government) in preventing premarital sexual relations.

Consider the rule in this situation, its objective and the way it was enforced. Provide both a justification for and a criticism of the law. How is this law experienced by different people? How might such a law work in a different country or in a different cultural context? What are the market implications of laws such as this one with respect to gender differences?

(3) Utopia is a newly independent country with an emerging economy. It has been in the process of writing and implementing a variety of new laws. Utopia is a country with several distinct regions. Each region has a dominant ethnic, racial, and religious population, and there are a number of tensions between the different regions. Utopia has not passed any positive law on the subject of equal rights or on the prohibition of discrimination based on characteristics such as race, gender, and religion.

Utopia has passed a law that forbids action by private parties that would hinder or interfere with interregional commerce. In passing the new "Commerce Law," Utopia stated that the public purpose of the law involved the promotion of interregional trade, travel, and commerce. The hope of the law is that it will facilitate the growth of a more integrated and dynamic national economy free of local restrictions and interference.

Citing the New Commerce Law, Ahmed, an individual, brought a legal action against The Friendly East Motel. According to Ahmed, he was traveling in his car from his home in the Southwest Region of Utopia, a predominantly Moslem area, to a small town in the Northeast Region. There he planned to meet with a businessman to discuss production and distribution of inexpensive "last-generation" computers. Last-generation computers are ones that use chips and processors that are about eighteen months behind the technology being used in basic home computers in the United Kingdom, the United States, Canada, and Australia.

Ahmed was driving to his destination on the newly completed National Highway. It was getting late and Ahmed was tired so he pulled into a motel that was located in a city just a few miles before the town where he was to have his meeting on the next day. The motel was named the Friendly East Motel and there was a sign on the front entrance stating that there were vacancies. When Ahmed approached the desk clerk at the motel he was told that there were no rooms available. As he stood in the lobby thinking about his next move, a young couple entered and asked for a room. They were told that several types of rooms were available. They made a selection and were given a key to a room. On witnessing this activity Ahmed went back to the desk clerk and again asked for a room. The clerk responded by informing Ahmed that there were no rooms available for him. The clerk stated, "The Friendly East Motel does not provide rooms for people from the Southwest. In the East we are all good Christians and we do not want any Muslims in our motel. Go now before trouble happens!"

Ahmed spent several hours driving around looking for a motel that had a vacancy for him. He found none so he had to sleep in his car. He was thus forced to go to his business meeting the next day wearing the clothes that he had slept in. He was not able to groom himself before the meeting and he was very tired from lack of sleep. The meeting did not go well.

Under the procedural law of Utopia the case was brought for trial in the National Trial Court for the Eastern Region. The following is a brief summary of the trial court opinion. The trial court did not find any violation in either the letter or spirit of the new Commerce Law. It explained that individuals are free to enter into contracts in the open marketplace. It described the situation as one between two individuals, Ahmed and the Friendly East Motel. In this case, the Friendly East Motel decided that it did not want to enter into a contractual relationship with Ahmed. Ahmed was free to go to one of the fifty other motels in the area. (Ahmed provided evidence of three other motels that refused him a room.) In the alternative, Ahmed could have gone about half way back to his hometown and found accommodation "suitable" for a person of his position. The trial court explained that in a free market people are free to exchange and to buy and sell with whomever they please. Thinking in terms of mutuality of remedies, the court reasoned that it could no more force the Motel to let Ahmed a room, than it could force Ahmed to pull off the road and give his custom to that particular establishment. The court said that the entire situation was a private matter between two individual parties and that the government had no business intruding upon private relationships. Furthermore, the court referenced natural rights as a basis for private property and declared that the Friendly East Motel enjoyed the ability to exclude others from their property, and this included Ahmed.

The matter is now set for an appeal to the National Appeals Court located in the Central District of Utopia. The Central District is the Capital City Region and has a diverse population containing significant representation of people from each of the various regions of the country. Ahmed is hiring you to take his case on appeal. He also has the "silent" support of a number of businesses located throughout the various regions of Utopia. Develop a plan for reframing this exchange on appeal so that it might better fit a favorable analysis under the new Commercial Law. (The lower court framed the situation in terms of a two-party market transaction.) Also provide an alternative or refocused approach to property rights that might help Ahmed and other business people in similar situations. It is your job to develop a persuasive argument in support of Ahmed. Your argument should enable the appellate court to justify ruling in favor of Ahmed.

2

Understanding the contested meaning of markets

We engage in market action through a process of interpretation, and we interpret the information that the market communicates to us in order to ascribe meaning to it. Even the process of economic calculation requires interpretation as we must perceive and interpret the valuation of various costs and benefits. Similarly, market choice requires an interpretive process to identify, evaluate, and act upon market options. These interpretive processes can be examined from a variety of perspectives including those of cognitive theory, behavioral theory, and assorted approaches to interpretation theory. This chapter explores only one of these approaches. It focuses on cultural-interpretation theory as related to an applied semiotics influenced by the work of Charles S. Peirce.

This chapter explores contested understandings of the market. It is designed to set the groundwork for analysis of the way in which shifting frames and references alter the meanings and values of exchange. In illustrating several key areas of contested interpretations of the market, this chapter advances the idea that substantive economic consequences, in terms of resource allocation and distribution, flow from influence over the process of framing, referencing, and representing in law. It also points to the ambiguity of much work in law and economics in as much as different cultural-interpretive frames, references, and representations allow for ranges of plausibly good economic results. In other words, economics can not help us identify an optimal course of action. Economics can, however, be helpful in directing our attention to a finite set of alternative choices, all of which may be desirable or socially plausible within one or another particular frame.

While there are many aspects of the social and market exchange relationship that can be explored, this chapter highlights the cultural-interpretive tension between the pursuit of *self-interest* and the promotion of the *public interest*. Reference is made to examples in contemporary film, case opinions, and comparative measures of economic performance. The point of each example is to illustrate contested understandings of the market. This is important because it highlights the cultural-interpretive conflict that must be mediated by law and legal institutions.

Self-interest and the public interest

The traditional approach to market analysis starts from a presumption that there is a relative or close equivalence between the pursuit of self-interest and the promotion of the public interest. This idea is implicit in the standard economic assumption that in competitive markets, marginal private benefits equal marginal social benefits, and marginal private costs equal marginal social costs.[1] This means that self-interest equals the public interest, and that there are no negative or positive externalities from market exchange. The private side of the equation equals the public side. The same idea dates all the way back to Adam Smith and his notion of the invisible hand.[2] Smith argued, for instance, that when individuals pursue their own self-interest, they end up promoting the public interest even though it is not part of their original intention. He suggested that an "invisible hand" guides us to benefit the public even as we think first and foremost of ourselves. His basic point is that we must offer goods and services that the public values if we are to attract the attention, resources, and praise that benefit us. Thus, if I want to get wealthy as a computer manufacturer and my only concern is for my own self-interest, I will have to provide the products and services the public demands or I will not make money. In this way, the pursuit of my private or self-interest corresponds to the promotion of the public interest.

This "equivalence theory" of markets can make sense under traditional assumptions of perfect competition. Such markets assume that all actors (1) act rationally, (2) in their own self-interest, (3) with good and full information, (4) all goods and resources are freely transferable, (5) in which all markets permit free and easy entry and exit, and (6) in which

[1] MERCURO & MEDEMA, ECONOMICS AND THE LAW 14–15. (Discussing assumptions of the market such as: marginal public benefit equals marginal social benefit (MPB = MSB), meaning that private interest equals public interest; and marginal private benefit equals the product price (MPB = PP), meaning that there are no positive externalities or public goods effects; and marginal private costs equals marginal social costs (MPC = MSC), meaning that there are no negative externalities.)

[2] See MALLOY, LAW AND MARKET ECONOMY 89–90. For an interesting history of the idea of self-interest see, SELF-INTEREST: AN ANTHOLOGY OF PHILOSOPHICAL PERSPECTIVES (Rogers, ed.).

prior distributions of wealth and resources do not unfairly impact on competition. In this ideal world we are all buyers and sellers of something. For instance, I sell my labor for a wage and I use my income to purchase food and shelter. At the same time, we observe that sellers have no power, since perfect competition means that sellers must respond to consumer demands and preferences or lose market share to others who will gladly step in to meet the demand. This system means that countless individual consumers drive the allocation of resources by pursuing their own self-interest in the marketplace.

In the real world we know that the above assumptions of perfect competition do not always hold true. Sometimes people do not act rationally, and sometimes we act altruistically rather than with self-interest. We do not have perfect information and access to information is not evenly distributed. We also know that transferring goods and services is not always easy, just as it is not always easy to pack up and move to a distant location in pursuit of a job. It is difficult to leave family, friends, and one's roots. Similarly, markets are not always open to free entry and exit. Some markets have huge economies of scale or require licenses, or have other formal and informal restrictions in place. Likewise, we know that prior distribution does make a difference to competition. People who come into the market with more training, prior experience, and greater resources have better odds of being successful. This is true even though it is also true that the market does not guarantee success; some very rich people have gone broke because they were unable to stay competitive against new upstarts.

One possible conclusion that might be drawn from this analysis is simple. The more a transactional relationship appears to resemble key elements of our hypothetical model of perfect competition, the more it validates letting individuals arrange the relationship on their own. Their pursuit of self-interest will come close to approximating the public interest. On the other hand, the less resemblance between a given market context and the hypothetical state of perfect competition the closer we must look at ways to facilitate the coordination of private and public interest. In this regard we must consider the ways in which law might be used to enhance the process of exchange so as to make it come closer to the ideal.

There are several factors that can prevent market action from conforming private (self-) interest with the public interest. These factors include high transaction or coordination costs when multiple parties are involved; lack of good information; irrational discrimination directed at certain market participants; extensive externalities; path dependencies; public goods or commons problems; and poorly defined legal rights.[3]

There is, of course, another perhaps more fundamental problem with equating the pursuit of self-interest with the promotion of the public interest. In traditional approaches to law and economics this assumption works to focus attention on the actions of detached and atomistic individuals. It also operates to frame the vast majority of socio-legal disputes as ones of contested facts, within the given economic framework, rather than of contested values between claimants in differently situated interpretive communities. This assumption is highly contestable because it is based on the concept of methodological individualism[4] – that market actors are detached and purely rational individuals. Individuals, however, as interpretive beings, are not isolated, detached, and atomistic; they are embedded within communities. And successful market economies may succeed, in part, precisely because they construct legal institutions capable of representing a public interest that is not expressed by the fragmented pursuit of individual self-interest.

Even Adam Smith understood, for instance, that individuals exchange and act within a social fabric.[5] Economic calculus does not occur in isolation nor is it detached from a conception of meaning and value informed by a process of social interaction. Consequently, to the extent that markets involve the actions of individuals embedded within a social fabric, we need to know something about how these individuals understand and communicate. We need to understand human action in terms of

---

[3] *See* Ayres & Talley, *Solomonic Bargaining* (regarding transaction costs when multiple parties are involved); Akerlof, *The Market for Lemons* 239 (Katz, ed.) (regarding information availability in the market); BECKER, ECONOMICS OF DISCRIMINATION 14–15 (regarding irrational discrimination in the marketplace); BARNES & STOUT, LAW & ECONOMICS at 40–42 (regarding externalities); MALLOY, LAW AND MARKET ECONOMY 101–02 (regarding path dependency and citing ARROW, SOCIAL CHOICE AND INDIVIDUAL VALUES); Hardin, *Tragedy of the Commons*; COOTER & ULEN, LAW AND ECONOMICS 94–95 (demonstrating delineation of legal rights).

[4] "Methodological individualism" refers to the traditional economic focus on individuals as rational and self-interested calculators of efficiency. *See* BLAUG, METHODOLOGY OF ECONOMICS 46, 49, 50, 227–28; MERCURO & MEDEMA, ECONOMICS AND THE LAW 114–15 (institutional economics focuses on "mutual interdependence rather than atomistic independence," *id.* at 114); MALLOY, LAW AND MARKET ECONOMY 57–70 (an interpretive critique of the concept).

[5] *See* MALLOY, LAW AND MARKET ECONOMY 64–69, 106–15, 118; SMITH, THEORY OF MORAL SENTIMENTS 71, 200–60, 352, 422 (discussing the impartial spectator). Smith also discusses the need to humble the pursuit of self-interest and to realize that we all operate within a social context, *id.* at 161–62.

the meaning and value formation process. We need to understand market choice not as a form of mathematical calculus but as a process of experiential interpretation involving individuals embedded within and between different communities. Market choice and market action are therefore socially situated, and we need to think in terms of the legal institutions that can enable us to exchange beyond our own community boundaries.

Consequently, market transactions are constrained and influenced by an individual's experience, position, and frame of reference within a community. The idea of promoting the pursuit of self-interest as a means of advancing the public interest is, therefore, contingent upon one's interpretive conception of self and public – of self and other – of autonomy (freedom) and coercion (necessity).[6] From a cultural-interpretive point of view, this means that market analysis is contested not only in terms of *facts* but also in terms of *values*. And, from the perspective of legal decision making, it is important to develop a pragmatic understanding of the contested frames and references at issue in a given dispute.

We can begin to understand the contested nature of the relationship between law and markets by examining a few illustrations from contemporary film, case opinions, and comparative measures of economic performance.

Framing the market in contemporary film

Contemporary films include numerous examples of contested interpretations of market values and meanings. These films explore underlying tensions in legal, cultural, and economic relationships. The point of these examples is that they illustrate conflicting cultural-interpretive understandings of the marketplace. These conflicts, as presented on film, project images of the tension present in real life. Thus, a first step in exploring law in its market context is to appreciate the idea of different people, and different communities having very different experiences of market exchange. These differences in experience foster differences in understanding, and raise important concerns for law and legal institutions. For law to mediate these tensions and command respect across diverse peoples and communities, it can not presume a singular and universal interpretation of the marketplace. In this part of the chapter discussion focuses

---

[6] *See* KEVELSON, PIERCE'S ESTHETICS OF FREEDOM 1–47. Freedom is the opposite of necessity, *id.* at 16. *See also*, HAYEK, CONSTITUTION OF LIBERTY 20–21 (discussing the conflict between coercion and individual liberty).

on five films: *Wall Street,*[7] *Other People's Money,*[8] *Do The Right Thing,*[9] *Class Action,*[10] and *Disney's Pocahontas.*[11] While having viewed these films may be helpful it is not necessary as the relevant facts are presented in the text.

The first two films, *Wall Street* and *Other People's Money,*[12] contain significant scenes involving corporate stockholder meetings and raise interesting issues about the nature of market values and the purpose of exchange. They also raise questions about the nature of the firm, the characteristics of ownership, and the community obligations of business. Both films involve a takeover bid by an investor seeking to break up a company as a way of enhancing stockholder value. The lead characters in each film make appeals to the stockholders urging the stockholders to vote in favor of the takeover, and for liquidation of the firm in an effort to maximize stockholder value.

In *Wall Street* the character of Gordon Gekko, played by Michael Douglas, takes center stage at a stockholder meeting held in the surroundings of a well-appointed convention center. In the room are plenty of well-dressed stockholders who are seated at floor level looking up to a platform stage. Sitting on the stage are the president of the company and his thirty-three corporate vice presidents. After the corporate president warns stockholders that Gekko is a destroyer of companies and that they should reject any takeover offer from him, Gekko takes up the microphone, from the floor, and declares, "I am not a destroyer of companies, I am a liberator of them." Gekko goes on to tell stockholders to vote in favor of his takeover bid because he will make them rich. He tells them "greed is good, greed simplifies, greed clarifies, greed in all of its forms makes the marketplace work." He tells them to ignore the concerns of the inefficient management of the company, and to pursue their own self-interest – to follow their greed in the pursuit of wealth. The clarity of the self-interested pursuit of greed will bring to them a freedom that only Gekko can deliver.

---

[7] WALL STREET, Twentieth Century Fox (1987) (discussed in MALLOY, LAW AND MARKET ECONOMY 168–70).

[8] OTHER PEOPLE'S MONEY, Warner Bros. (1991) (discussed in MALLOY, LAW AND MARKET ECONOMY 168–70).

[9] DO THE RIGHT THING, MCA Universal (1989).

[10] CLASS ACTION, Twentieth Century Fox (1990).

[11] POCAHONTAS, Walt Disney (1995).

[12] *See* MALLOY, LAW AND MARKET ECONOMY 168–70 (discussion here expands on an example used in my earlier book).

Similarly, in *Other People's Money* Danny DeVito, playing Larry the Liquidator, makes an appeal to stockholders to vote in favor of his takeover bid because he will make them money. He tells them that the company, while profitable, is worth more dead (liquidated) than alive. He tells stockholders to vote for making the best return on their money and that they have no obligation to the employees of the company or to the community where its factory is located. Their only obligation is to make the best profit for themselves.

In contrast to these views Gregory Peck, playing the role of the eighty-one-year-old founder and president of the New England Wire and Cable Company in *Other People's Money*, argues that a company is worth more than the value of its stock. He says that a business is about people. It's about people who work together pursuing a common purpose and who share the same friendships and live in the same community. He cautions the stockholders to avoid selfish and greedy actions and asks them to vote instead with their feelings. He asks them to vote for the continuation of a profitable business. He asserts that a business is more than a collection of capital goods. He tells them that a business is a community.

In contrast to the scene from *Wall Street*, the stockholder meeting in *Other People's Money* occurs at the factory and the film's director presents us with images of the "blue-collar" town and workers who are present both inside and outside of the meeting. The meeting is not set in some sterile convention hall, as in *Wall Street*, but is held in the very town that will be affected by closing the plant. The dispute is not about an inefficient management team it is about a company that is no longer as productive as other investments because new technologies are cutting into its market. The common theme between these films is the same, however. Each involves the takeover of a company by a rational but "heartless" Wall Street "money-man" declaring that the only obligation people owe one another is to maximize wealth in the pursuit of self-interest.

In *Wall Street* and in *Other People's Money* the takeover advocates address the legal owners of the company, the stockholders, and tell them to maximize their wealth by voting to liquidate the companies while they are still valuable. In contrast, Peck's character frames the appeal differently. He basically asserts that a company has obligations to its "stakeholders" and not just to its legal owners. He positions the proper market analysis as including the community, the schools, residents, workers, and others that have contributed to the company over the years. The company is not simply a detached and impersonal capital good . . . it is more than a physical object; it is a web of interconnected interests and values. He argues that resource determinations should account for a broader set of interests than those reflected by *legal owners* simply pursuing self-interest. In part, therefore, Peck's character questions the frame and the interpretive reference set by the wealth-maximizing character, Larry the Liquidator. By changing the frame and the interpretive reference, Peck's character can logically promote a different economic calculus.

In viewing these scenes one gets a close-up look at the real tension between two different visions of the market. It becomes clear that the disagreements are as much, or more, about *values* as they are about *facts*. It is not just a debate about the profitability of the various companies in question, for instance, but about the values to be promoted and endorsed by a market economy.

These two films also deal with other tensions: tensions regarding the nature of capitalism and the meaning of property. Therefore, another way to frame the dispute is in terms of the nature of the form of economic and social organization. For example, capitalism involves the private ownership of the means of production. In *Other People's Money*, the company president seems to be saying that the enterprise, and certain of its constituent parts, ought not be subject to private ownership and traded in the market. The company is, in a sense, not a commodity or freely transferable resource. Thus, the company president has a different vision from that of Larry the Liquidator about whether certain resources should be treated as freely exchangeable commodities in the marketplace. In this frame the debate is about the values to be embodied within capitalist society.

Many of these same issues are addressed in *Dynamics Corporation of America* v. *CTS Corp.*[13] In this case Dynamics made a tender offer to acquire stock in CTS. If successful in its bid Dynamics would have stock holdings of 27.5 percent of CTS and the power of control. The Board of Directors and management of CTS resisted the takeover bid. CTS management acted to frustrate the takeover by following a protected strategy (involving a "poison pill" for the takeover entity) permitted by the state law of Indiana, the state of its incorporation. The state law was designed to protect entities incorporated under Indiana law. This made Indiana a favorable state for incorporation from the point of view of management because it made it more difficult for the company to be taken over, and consequently more difficult to replace management.

One key issue in the case involved the question of ownership of CTS. As a corporation with publicly held stock, the stockholders and not management are the owners. The management acts as an agent and fiduciary for the stockholders. Thus, management should act to enhance shareholder

---

[13] Dynamics Corp. of Am. v. CTS Corp., 794 F.2d 250 (7th Cir., 1986).

value rather than to protect management. The court felt that the failure to do this should be considered a breach of the duty owed by management to the owners.

The CTS case explores the same type of tension as depicted in each of the above movies. The court was concerned with owners rather than stakeholders and framed the case in efficient market terms. In this context the court considered two polar positions in the debate over hostile takeovers.[14] On the one hand it understood the argument that takeovers were bad because they forced managers to take actions that made short-term profits look good in an effort to avoid a takeover, and they understood that a takeover often resulted in moving a corporate headquarters and creating an element of absentee control.

On the other hand, the court, favoring an efficient market frame, addressed the market for corporate control and discussed the value of having corporate assets and control move to the highest bidder. In an efficient market resources move to the person that values them the most and who will presumably put the resources to their best use. Assuming that the pursuit of self-interest equates to the promotion of the public interest this means that society gains by permitting such a market in corporate control. The market for corporate control helps to police management because it provides a way of eliminating bad managers. And managers who spend their time erecting barriers to a takeover fail in their fiduciary duty to the shareholder owners. This view puts primacy on the immediate shareholders as owners and discounts the interests of other stakeholders. It also assumes the equivalence of self-interest and the public interest.

Extending its efficient market frame to other matters, the court also addressed the market for incorporations.[15] It envisioned the fifty states as competing for the revenue of attracting incorporations under their own state laws in competition with each other. In this market the various states should not be competing to attract the self-interested actions of managers seeking to protect their jobs. States that offered extensive protection from takeovers frustrate the broader marketplace for interstate commerce and for the moving of corporate control to the highest-value users. Thus, we should discourage laws of the type in place in Indiana.

The CTS case is interesting because of the way in which it addresses a number of the same issues identified in the two movies just discussed, and because of the clear way in which a particular market frame shapes the analysis and outcome of the Court's decision.

[14] *Id.* at 253.   [15] *Id.* at 263–64.

Thus, both of the above films and the CTS case involve a corporate takeover and in a similar way each raises fundamental questions about ownership and the corporate form. Each asks us to consider who owns a company – the stockholders, the management, the workers, the community? How does ownership relate to having a "stakeholder" interest? Are claims by the community in this type of situation any different from the ones made by fans when their favorite major league football or baseball team threatens to pull out and move to a new city? Do corporations exist simply to maximize profit for the stockholders? Is there such a thing as good corporate citizenship? What is the basic nature and role of the firm in law and society, and how do alternative conceptions of the firm, and of the market, relate to matters of information costs, risk assessment and management, production costs, market price, firm valuation, and labor relations? These considerations set up an examination of the exchange relationships within the firm, and between the firm, its constituent parts, and the community. Understanding these relationships helps us to establish a map or plan for a more detailed investigation of factors to address in legal reasoning and public policy making.

Another insightful contemporary film that contests the meanings and values of the marketplace is Spike Lee's *Do the Right Thing*.[16] There are two important scenes to consider in this film. The first involves a discussion between Sal, the owner of Sal's World Famous Pizzeria, and his oldest son, Pino, who works at the Pizzeria. Sal operates his Pizza shop in a neighborhood that has been transformed. Once it was an Italian-American community with which Sal identified. Over the twenty-five-year period in which Sal has been there, the neighborhood has become home to a Latino and African-American community. Sal is very Italian and his shop celebrates this by having a "wall of fame" with pictures of great Italian-Americans. The problem is that Sal's customers are African-American and Latino, and they do not identify with these heroes.

At several points in the film some of his teenage customers complain that they want to see "some Black heroes on the wall of fame." This causes a lot of heated debate and tension. It is interesting that Sal's response is positioned in the classic framework of neoclassical economics. Sal argues that "it is his shop, he built it, he worked it, he owns it, and he will put whomever he wants on his wall of fame." Sal's response is understandable and justifiable in the individualist framework of traditional law and economics. On the other hand, Sal fails to appreciate the nature of the

---

[16] Do the Right Thing, MCA Universal (1989).

claim being raised. While the teenagers are talking about specific pictures on a wall, they are also "representing" a broader question about the
community responsibility of a business. The teenagers reject Sal's individualist model and take a more critical stance. Here the dispute seems
to be about the claim that a community has on the people and activities within its boundaries. Sal is a part of the neighborhood, but like the
detached and atomistic figure of "homo-economicus," he is not a part of
their community. He claims his pizza shop as an island, but the community questions his ability to be there without being a part of the people he
serves.

The conflict in this scene raises the issue of the community responsibility of a business. Is this an economic responsibility or a legal responsibility?
If this responsibility is economic in nature, won't the market constrain
Sal and require him to meet the demands of his customers? Otherwise,
Sal goes out of business for lack of customers. If the responsibility is legal
in nature, to whom is it owed – the community in a public sense or the
potential customers in a private sense? More importantly, how will this
tension be resolved? In the film, law seems to break down and community members trash and burn Sal's pizza shop while declaring him an
unwanted outsider.

The hope should be for law to provide a mediating mechanism to avoid
the kind of violence that takes place in the film. To do this, however, law
(and a theory of law and market economy) must account for alternative
market experiences, and embrace flexible interpretive frames. Law can not
simply presuppose a singular or universal market frame if it is to provide
a credible and meaningful resolution to tensions of this type.

In another scene from the same film, Sal is talking with Pino inside
the pizza shop. The son looks through the window and outside to the
neighborhood to complain that he hates working in this place. He hates
all the black people, it drives him crazy, and his friends laugh at him for
working in that community. Sal tells his son that these people who laugh
at him for working in this neighborhood are not his friends. He asks,
"who puts the food on your table, who pays for your clothes, and who
puts a roof over your head? These people, and I am proud that they have
grown up on my food." In this scene Sal is once again representing the
traditional economic concept of the market. He is not really connected
to his customers as people, as friends, as part of his community; instead,
he sees them, through a glass enclosure, as a means to serving his own
self-interest. They are the source of his income, and in pursuing his own
self-interest he has promoted the public interest by providing these people
with food. In the end, Sal seems to be telling his son that his son's friends

are not really friends because they do not understand how the market works. They do not understand how Pino gets an economic advantage from selling pizza to the people in this neighborhood. These so-called friends should not make fun of Pino for serving African-American and Hispanic people; instead, they should applaud Pino for so cleverly serving his own self-interest.

This scene, once again, raises important issues about the patterns of exchange and the nature of social meanings in market society. It opens the door to a discussion of self-interest and the degree to which people understand their relationships in terms of being partners in trade or in terms of being a means to one's own economic ends.

Two other contemporary films to consider include *Class Action*,[17] and *Disney's Pocahontas*.[18]

One scene from the film *Class Action* involves a discussion of cost and benefit analysis related to the question of repairing a defect in an automobile that a company has on the market. This scene is reminiscent of the *Ford Pinto* litigation (*Grimshaw* v. *Ford Motor Co.*) and reflective of the more recent rash of law suits involving allegedly defective Firestone tires.[19] In the film, the automobile in question has a defective turn signal switch that causes sparks to ignite the vehicle in certain types of collisions. The sparks cause the vehicle to explode and a number of plaintiffs are suing the company for burns, and for deaths. In this particular scene the company president explains to the corporate lawyers that statistical studies were done by the company indicating that it would be cheaper to deal with potential law suits than to recall and fix all of the cars. The potential cost associated with paying victims was substantially less than the cost of recalling and retrofitting the cars. "It's a simple cost and benefit analysis." Thus, the company knowingly chose to leave the defective cars on the market and allow people to be injured and killed.

The scene provides a glimpse into a purely "rational choice" discussion that leaves the viewer wondering about the nature of justice, and the decision making process of the corporate enterprise. The scene clearly depicts the nature of discussion within a given cultural-interpretive frame and viewers are challenged to understand the implications. Viewers are confronted with the consequential meaning of promoting a system of

---

[17] CLASS ACTION, Twentieth Century Fox (1990).

[18] POCAHONTAS, Walt Disney (1995).

[19] *See* Grimshaw v. Ford Motor Co., 174 Cal. Rptr. 348 (Ct. App. 1981); Ciscusi, *Corporate Risk Analysis* 547, 568–70; STROBEL, RECKLESS HOMICIDE? Voris & Fleischer, *Feeding Frenzy over Firestone*; Fick, *Calif. Jury Rules Ford Explorer "Defective"* at B.1. *See generally* Beveridge, *Does the Corporate Director Have a Duty to Obey the Law?*

social organization grounded in simple cost and benefit analysis, and driven by a desire for wealth maximization. They are also challenged to formulate alternative strategies based on competing values, and different interpretive frameworks.

The question that remains is, if the company does not use cost and benefit analysis, what should it use as a guide to decision making? A reasonable response might involve reframing the question. One might ask, what considerations and information beyond a cost and benefit analysis should be used to guide us in decision making? In this respect the challenge is to see that multiple frames and references can be used together, at the same time. There is no need to accept a simple dualistic frame that positions the choice as between using only cost and benefit analysis, or suggesting a complete rejection of cost and benefit analysis. Life in a modern market economy is too complex for simple dualistic responses. Moreover, social and market choices are too complex to be simplified into mere factual disputes. As this example illustrates, the underlying dispute is more profound than a contest between two different teams of experts and their calculation of the proper costs and benefits for announcing a recall on the defective automobile. The deeper issue concerns the proper frame to be used in identifying and evaluating the appropriate facts to be considered in making a decision with major individual and community implications.

We can even find images of deep-seated social tension about the meanings and values of the marketplace in films for children. Disney's *Pocahontas* presents the contrast between two competing cultural-interpretive frames for market analysis. One view, put forward by the character of Captain John Smith, is based on a belief in science, technology, and the separation of man from the natural world.[20] The other view, represented in the character of Pocahontas, is grounded in a connection to nature, based on an emotive sense of belonging, and a non-monetary sense of value.[21] The scene, therefore positions tension between two competing value frames and different sets of interpretive references.

In one particular scene Captain Smith is alone with Pocahontas in the woods. He is telling her about his home in London and explaining the way in which the English will show Pocahontas and her people how

---

[20] *See* BEYOND ECONOMIC MAN (Ferber & Nelson, eds.) at 1–93. (Discussing the "objective" male perspective in economics and the bias that this has relative to the differences indicated by a feminist view of the market.)

[21] *Id.*

"to make the most of their land." He explains how England has civilized "savages" all over the world and showed them how to industrialize and make progress. Smith sees the land and its resources in terms of the ability to commodify them for purposes of economic gain and wealth maximization. Pocahontas responds that her people already know how to make good use of the land, and that they are not savages just because they understand the world in a way that is different from that of the English. She explains the connection between nature and her people and wonders if Smith can ever understand the value of the land without calculating its monetary worth.

In a sense, *Pocahontas* reiterates the theme of each of the other films. Each reflects a deeply contested public discourse regarding the nature of market life. Each contests assertions of ownership, and of the pursuit of self-interest as a sustainable and worthy criterion for social organization. Each raises questions of valuation, and of participation in the decision making process. Each offers competing frames and references, and challenges us to develop supportable and persuasive justifications for invoking one frame rather than another. Similarly, each provides us with an understanding of the way in which alternative cultural-interpretive frames promote different potential distributions, as well as competing meanings and values.

Pursuing useful information about the nature of these exchange relationships and contested interpretations is important to developing a responsive and pragmatic approach to law. Before we can make useful legal arguments for policy change, however, we must understand the problem. And an important part of understanding many socio-legal problems involves an appreciation of the different ways in which people experience the intersection of law and market economy.

The idea of different people experiencing and understanding the relationship between law and markets in alternative ways is important. An interesting case exploring this idea is *Suntrust Bank* v. *Houghton-Mifflin Co.*[22] This case involved a question of copyright infringement with respect to a book by Alice Randall titled *The Wind Done Gone*,[23] and an earlier work by Margaret Mitchell titled *Gone With the Wind*.[24] Mitchell's book

---

[22] Suntrust Bank v. Houghton Mifflin Co., 268 F.3d 1257 (11th Cir., 2001).

[23] Randall's book was withheld from release to the public when a trial court granted a temporary restraining order. Suntrust Bank v. Houghton Mifflin Co., 136 F. Supp.2d 1357 (N.D. GA. 2001).

[24] Since its publication in 1936 it has become one of the best-selling books in the world second only to the Bible. Suntrust Bank, 268 F.3d 1257, 1259.

and the film by the same title have become legendary classics. In *Gone With The Wind* a romantic depiction of life in the antebellum American South is presented from the point of view of Scarlett, a southern beauty and daughter of a wealthy plantation owner. Alice Randall in *The Wind Done Gone* sets out to tell that same story but this time from the point of view of Cynara, a beautiful slave on the plantation who is the daughter of the white plantation owner (Scarlett's father) and a house slave. In *The Wind Done Gone* most of the same characters from Mitchell's book appear, the character of Scarlett, for example, appears as a southern belle addressed as "the other."

The interesting part of this case, as relates to our discussion, is that Randall admits that she uses characters, events, and depictions from the original work by Mitchell. At the same time she insists that she is telling a different story. She complains that for many Americans, and for many non-Americans alike, the understanding of life in the "Old South" is miscomprehended because of the popularity of its depiction in Mitchell's work and the portrayal of that work in the classic film. She argues that Mitchell presents a narrow and one-sided view of life in the Civil War era and that the presentation of African-Americans is one-dimensional, wrong, and inappropriate. In her work she undertakes to retell the classic story from the point of view of the various black characters in the story. She expresses their concerns, their complexity, and their humanity.

The heart of the case concerns the ability to comprehend that there are at least two different stories that can be told about the same facts, characters, and events without one infringing upon the other. This is at the core of our discussion of the above-mentioned films and of central importance in understanding the application of interpretation theory to an understanding of law in a market context. In the *Suntrust* case, the court largely accepts the idea of Randall's perspective as being another story, or at least as being a protected fair use of Mitchell's story to make a very different point.[25] In understanding law in a market context we have to be able to comprehend the idea of different people having different experiences and thus different interpretations of both the law and the market. We have to understand that this results in a contested and ambiguous meaning for markets in our society. Our goal, therefore, is to take this understanding and use it to improve our legal reasoning skills.

---

[25] The Circuit Court lifted the temporary restraining order and remanded the case for further proceedings, indicating that the work should be able to be released even if some infringement damages might be appropriate.

The *Suntrust* case and the various scenes from contemporary films discussed in this part of the book illustrate, at a popular culture level, the highly contested meanings of modern legal and economic discourse. Debates concerning these same issues fill law reviews, law school curriculums, courthouses, and legislative hearings. We need to understand that an economic analysis of law will not supply us with a ready calculus for mediating the type of tensions illustrated by the fact patterns in these films and played out in real life. While market concepts can help us improve our understanding of these issues we are ultimately required to make normative judgments: judgments informed by market information but not controlled by an economic calculus.

Framing the market in case opinions

There are numerous case opinions that contain illustrations of contested visions of market relationships. This section of the chapter discusses several cases with the hope that they will serve as an adequate introduction to cultural–interpretive framing issues at play in using market analysis to address pressing socio-legal problems.

In *Merritt* v. *Faulkner*, a prisoner in the Indiana State Prison, Billy Merritt, challenged the denial of appointment of counsel in a civil action.[26] While in prison Merritt experienced medical problems with his eye related to sickle cell disease.[27] As a result of incomplete and allegedly incompetent medical treatment, and as a product of the alleged deliberate indifference of prison officials, Merritt suffered the loss of his eyesight.[28] In reviewing the denial of appointed counsel for Merritt, the majority of a three-judge panel of the Seventh Circuit Court of Appeals held that it was improper to deny appointed counsel to Merritt who, as an indigent prisoner, was seeking to advance a claim against prison officials based on the denial of his civil rights.[29]

The majority opinion delivered by Judge Swygert recognized that indigent civil litigants have no constitutional or statutory right to be represented by a lawyer.[30] Yet he found that "when rights of a constitutional dimension are at stake, a poor person's access to the federal courts must not be turned into an exercise in futility."[31] Furthermore, he stated that

---

[26] Merritt v. Faulkner, 697 F.2d 761 (7th Cir. 1983). This case is also discussed in MALLOY, LAW AND ECONOMICS 126–32.

[27] *Id*. at 762.   [28] *Id*.   [29] *Id*. at 766–66.

[30] *Id*. at 763.   [31] Merritt, 697 F.2d 761, 763.

"[i]n some civil cases meaningful access requires representation by a lawyer."[32] The Court then went on to set out five non-exclusive factors to be considered and balanced in determining an indigent individual's right to appointed counsel in such a case. These factors included:

> (1) whether the merits of the indigent's claim are colorable; (2) the ability of the indigent plaintiff to investigate the crucial facts; (3) whether the nature of the evidence indicates that the truth will more likely be exposed where both sides are represented by counsel; (4) the capability of the indigent litigant to present the case; and, (5) the complexity of the legal issues raised by the complaint.[33]

Using these factors the court held that the trial court had abused its discretion in not providing Merritt with appointed counsel.[34]

Judge Posner, concurring in part and dissenting in part, offered a separate opinion.[35] Posner framed his analysis of the case in market terms. He argued for a presumption against appointed counsel in such a civil action.[36] His general reasoning was that any individual with a good case for tort liability would be able to get a lawyer because of the economic incentive of recovering a contingency fee.[37] Thus, it was unnecessary to do an after-the-fact balancing test because the market could more readily and efficiently pass upon the merits of the case. If it was a strong case with substantial prospects of prevailing against the state the indigent would show up with an attorney. In other words, the market would respond to the need and the potential for economic gain. The fact that Merritt showed up without an attorney resolved the matter against the indigent claimant.

Posner's position is altogether consistent with framing this issue within an individualist, and self-interested market model. He suggests that prisoners have ample access to information about lawyers and that lawyers have ample access to information about potential civil claims within the prison system.[38] He imagines a competitive market for providing civil legal services to indigent prisoners, and he rejects the statement in the majority opinion that "[a]n underlying assumption of the adversarial system is that both parties will have roughly equal legal resources."[39] To the contrary, Posner asserts that this has never been an assumption of the adversarial system.[40]

Such a view is consistent with Posner's assumptions about a perfectly competitive market. In the perfectly competitive market there is

---

[32] *Id.*   [33] *Id.* at 764.   [34] *Id.*   [35] *Id.* at 769.   [36] *Merritt*, 697 F.2d 761, 769.
[37] *Id.*   [38] *Id.* at 770.   [39] *Id.* at 771.   [40] *Id.*

no assumption about equality of resource allocation, and inequalities in prior distributions are dismissed as unproblematic. Posner frames his investigation in terms of the organizing principles of self-interest. In this frame, the lawyer and the indigent prisoner will both be led by an invisible hand to achieve justice without the need for government intervention into the marketplace. But Posner's framing misses an important element in the framing of the majority opinion with which he disagrees.

A problem with Posner's opinion, even if one were to accept the idea of a well-functioning and competitive market in this context, is that it leaves the indigent claimant with no legal representation unless there is a significant contingency fee available. This means that slight injuries, or injuries that are important but difficult to quantify in economic terms may well go unaddressed. This is because the market responds to the *willingness and ability to pay*. And when an injury is slight, the potential fee to a lawyer will be negligible. Thus, there will be little, if any, incentive for a lawyer to aid the indigent claimant. A similar problem arises with slight or technical violations of the Constitution. The violation may impose only a minor cost or burden on the individual but the redress of the violation may be costly to society. Thus, a simple cost and benefit analysis may lead one to overlook the technical or minor violation. It would make rational economic sense to do so. The problem with this conclusion, however, is that it ignores the positive externalities that flow to the benefit of others from requiring the State to uphold the Constitution and to respect the human dignity of all of its citizens.

In other words, litigation that addresses constitutional considerations about the relationship between individuals and the state has implications for people beyond those that are the immediate parties to the suit. Where Posner uses a "zoom lens" to focus in on a two-party transaction to calculate efficiency, the majority seemingly takes a "wide-angle" look at the public interest represented by the underlying issues at stake in the dispute. Where Posner imagines that the pursuit of self-interest leads to the promotion of the public interest, the majority identifies a problem with this rationale. The majority opinion expresses a concern that justice, even justice based on a desire for efficiency, might not prevail where extensive positive externalities are present.[41]

Consequently, the case can be interpreted in different ways. It can be understood in terms of a difference in the cultural-interpretive referencing

---

[41] Geuss, Public Goods, Private Goods; Cooter & Ulen, Law and Economics 42–43; Rosen, Public Finance 55–58.

of individual rights, and of the relevant market concepts to be considered. The case is not so much about disputed facts concerning Merritt's injury, or about the cost of an attorney to represent him. It is about the underlying values we seek to promote in our particular form of constitutional and representative government. We must, therefore, work to develop a logical and useful method of analysis that includes both fact-based and value-based components – one that balances the relationship between the humanities and the sciences.

From a cultural-interpretive perspective, most legal disputes involve contested understandings of both *facts* and *values*. This can be observed readily in cases dealing with issues of commodification and entitlement respecting the human body.[42] Consider, for example, *In the Matter of Baby M.*[43]

The *Baby M* case involved a private contractual attempt by three individuals to provide an alternative family formation process.[44] The exchange in question involved William Stern, Elizabeth Stern (his wife), and Mary Beth Whitehead (the surrogate mother).[45] Mr. and Mrs. Stern were unable to have a child but they desperately wanted to start a family. They were discouraged by the adoption process, and they wanted a child that would reflect some of their own genetic makeup. This prompted the Sterns to enter into a contract with Whitehead providing for Mr. Stern's sperm to be used to inseminate Whitehead artificially.[46] Mrs. Whitehead agreed to carry the resulting child to term and upon birth to deliver the baby to the Sterns.[47] Upon delivery of the baby Mrs. Stern would adopt the child and Mary Beth Whitehead would relinquish all maternal rights.[48] For her services, Whitehead was to be paid $10,000 and the Sterns agreed to cover the costs of fertilization and maternity.[49]

The case is interesting because it involves issues of representation, framing, and referencing. At the outset we need to consider the way in which the law represents Mrs. Whitehead's body and that of Baby M. Are they beings endowed by their creator with certain inalienable rights, or are they

---

[42] *See, e.g.,* In the Matter of Baby M, 109 N.J. 396 (1988); Moore v. Regents of the Univ. of California, 793 P. 2d 479 (Cal. 1990).

[43] In the Matter of Baby M, 109 N.J. 396 (1988).

[44] Baby M, 109 N.J. at 410. *See* Gostin, *Surrogacy From the Perspectives of Economic and Civil Liberties*; Carol Sanger, *(Baby) M is for the Many Things*; Garrison, *Law Making for Baby Making*; Carbone, *The Role of Contract Principles in Determining the Validity of Surrogacy Contracts.*

[45] Baby M, 109 N.J. at 411.   [46] *Id.* at 412.

[47] *Id.*   [48] *Id.*   [49] *Id.* at 410.

simply new examples of post-industrial commodities, available for sale or lease? Is this a case about the degradation of human life or a celebration of the legal commodification of children and of the woman's womb? The case also raises further questions concerning the legal representation of family formation, motherhood, and paternity.

Beyond these issues, we can describe the attempted transaction in three different ways. The transaction might be described as the sale of a baby, or as payment for incubation services, or as a lease of space in an otherwise empty or underutilized womb. The legal system, given the tragic experience with treating people as objects of sale in the United States, is generally not inclined to view these transactions favorably when they are cast as baby sales. On the other hand, as a contract for services, or perhaps even as a lease of space, the transaction may be sustainable.

First of all, the transaction seems to have been consensual among all of the parties. Consequently, under the rationality assumption, it was initially a Pareto efficient arrangement.[50] This means that at least one party to the exchange was made better off while no one was made worse off by the transaction. The Sterns wanted a child and had sufficient income to make the payments necessary to attract a willing person to participate in their plan. Mrs. Whitehead consented to all of the contract terms, presumably finding that this was a viable way to earn additional income by taking advantage of her fertility and her ability to carry a child to term.[51] Her payment would reflect the value of other income-producing opportunities that she would forgo in order to perform her part of the contract. In economic terms, she was paid enough to cover her opportunity costs.[52] In the end, however, after the baby was born, Mrs. Whitehead had a change of mind and did not want to give up the baby.[53] This resulted in litigation to enforce the contract.

While an initial review of the case can be framed as a consensual two-party transaction between Whitehead and the Sterns, a closer examination

---

[50] A Pareto efficient arrangement is one in which at least one party is made better off as a result of the exchange while no one is made worse off. This describes a typical voluntary market exchange. *See* chapter 5, *infra*. *See generally* MALLOY, LAW AND MARKET ECONOMY 108, 154 (discussing consent and basic definitional issues with respect to Pareto and Kaldor–Hicks efficiency).

[51] Baby M, 109 N.J. at 414.

[52] An opportunity cost involves the potential benefits one could get from taking an alternative course of action. For example, when a person leaves a full-time job to become a full-time student, she not only has the expense of her education but also the loss of her forgone salary. The income that she gives up is an opportunity cost.

[53] Baby M, 109 N.J. at 415.

indicates the possibility of an alternative framing. The exchange can also be understood as either embracing or affecting Baby M, relatives of the Sterns and of Mrs. Whitehead, and the public. First, Baby M is a person with constitutional rights. The Sterns and Whitehead acted in an agency capacity in contracting over the status and identity of this baby. Baby M, however, has rights independent of the contract to be accounted for in the transaction. This raises a question of how these rights would or could be properly represented and incorporated into such an agreement. Second, the Sterns and Whitehead made a contract that had implications not only for themselves but also for people who would be genetic or contractual relatives to Baby M. Other children of Mrs. Whitehead, for example, would be denied a relationship with their sibling as a result of this contract. The contract also had a public implication. Beyond the public policy question related to upholding such private contracts there is a public interest in family stability, and in factors related to the healthcare, schooling, and parenting implications of new children brought into a community. For example, if the baby had been born with severe genetic defects, would it have been permissible for the Sterns to reject delivery on the grounds that the baby was a non-conforming good? Would Mrs. Whitehead be able to refuse a return of the baby under such circumstances, and would the baby end up as a charge of the public?

When Mrs. Whitehead breached the contract by seeking to retain maternal rights, the question for traditional law and economics might be whether the initial contract or the subsequent breach was efficient. In addressing these questions within a frame of efficiency, references could be made to more than one measure. Pareto efficiency considers the contract and the breach with respect to no party being made worse off as a result of the exchange. On the other hand, a Kaldor–Hicks efficiency test measures efficiency in terms of the winners winning more than the losers lose as a result of the exchange.[54] Using a Pareto efficiency test, we know that the breach is inefficient because at least one party is made worse off as a result of the breach. With reference to Kaldor–Hicks efficiency we can generate alternative views of the case. As between the parties it might be

---

[54] Kaldor–Hicks efficiency is an alternative measure to that of Pareto efficiency. The Kaldor–Hicks test does not depend upon a voluntary exchange. A coercive exchange can be Kaldor–Hicks efficient as long as the value to the winning party exceeds the loss to the losing party. For example, it may be Kaldor–Hicks efficient to breach a contract if the breaching party has a new economic opportunity that will allow it to pay damages and still come out with a greater profit than would have been the case under the original agreement. *See* chapter 5, *infra*.

asked if Mrs. Whitehead wins more than the Sterns lose, or perhaps there is a need to expand the scope of this calculation to one of asking if Mrs. Whitehead and Baby M win more than the Sterns and Baby M lose. We also have to view this from a publicly positioned evaluation of Kaldor–Hicks efficiency and ask if the public gains more than these private parties lose by taking one position or another as to the validity of such transactions. In each situation one must consider the extremely difficult matter of valuation on all sides of the exchange. From the point of view of this book, we need to appreciate the ambiguity of the traditional efficiency analysis.

In the actual case, the court decided that the contract could not be enforced.[55] Public policy favored other channels, such as formal adoption, as an alternative way to establish a family. Stated differently, the court simply withdrew certain human resources – for example, the services of the womb – from the market.

Thus, the court denied private parties a right to fashion an alternative conception of the family and the family formation process, at least until such time as the legislature might expressly provide otherwise.

As important as recognizing the ambiguity of economic calculation in this situation is the understanding of how the authority to represent the meanings and values of this relationship inform the outcome. The case illustrates the flexible nature of an economic calculus, with different outcomes able to be declared efficient based on the use of particular framing and referencing devices. Framing the transaction as a simple two-party exchange to be analyzed under a Pareto efficiency standard, for instance, leads to a very different result from the result that would be obtained by framing it as a multi-party transaction with numerous public externalities, and with a reference to a Kaldor–Hicks efficiency standard. The authority, therefore, to set the cultural-interpretive frame and reference has implications for resource definition and allocation. More fundamentally, and perhaps more difficult to appreciate, is the matter of representation in this exchange. Who should have the authority to define the relationships between the parties, and who should control the representation of meaning and value in this complex human exchange? These are important questions because the authority to represent and to interpret relationships involves the power to create and redistribute wealth and resources.

---

[55] Baby M, 109 N.J. at 415.

We can observe contested understandings of the market in a variety of situations. Shifting from the commodification of the body, as represented in the *Baby M* case, we can consider another case, *Honorable v. Easy Life Real Estate Sys.*[56] This case addressed the issue of market power in housing markets in the context of a claim that Easy Life had engaged in racially discriminatory practices.[57] Easy Life was in the business of rehabbing houses and financing their acquisition by homebuyers.[58] The aggrieved homebuyers in the case were African-Americans.[59] They claimed that Easy Life exploited them in the market, and that Easy Life violated both the Civil Rights Act and the Fair Housing Act.[60]

In *Honorable,* the evidence indicated that Easy Life targeted a sales market in a neighborhood that was 95 percent African-American, and that the products sold in this market were priced at substantially higher rates than comparable ones sold to white customers in other neighborhoods.[61] The basis of the claim was, therefore, that Easy Life was following a dual market strategy and exploiting African-American consumers. Easy Life argued that it did not and could not exploit African-American homebuyers in this way, and that it could not be held liable for exploitation because it lacked the market power needed to successfully advance such a discriminatory strategy.[62] It cited a Federal Trade Commission (FTC) guideline for the proposition that a seller with less than a 35 percent market share was presumed not to have the market power necessary to split and exploit the market.[63]

The FTC guideline in question can be understood as embodying a traditional neoclassical economic assumption that a seller in a competitive market lacks the power to set terms and to exploit consumers. In the perfectly competitive market paradigm, sellers are without power. Power resides in consumers because they can easily shift to a new seller if one seller attempts to deal on undesirable terms. Easy Life presented economic information about the definition of the market and its relevant market share.[64] It argued that in the absence of market power it could not accomplish the ends alleged by the plaintiffs.[65] In essence, Easy Life asserted an inability to influence the meanings and values of the exchange because formal equality existed between the parties in the absence of market power.

The court rejected the arguments offered by Easy Life and refused to frame the matter in terms of the perfectly competitive market paradigm.

---

[56] Honorable v. Easy Life Real Estate System, 100 F. Supp. 2d 885 (N.D.Ill. 2000).
[57] *Id.* at 886–87.   [58] *Id.* at 886.   [59] *Id.*   [60] *Id.*
[61] Honorable, 100 F. Supp.2d at 887.   [62] *Id.* at 890.   [63] *Id.*   [64] *Id.*   [65] *Id.*

It reasoned instead that sellers can have power and market exploitation is possible in the absence of a 35 percent market share.[66] It held that markets could be segmented and fragmented into enclaves informed by certain behavioral and interpretive practices.[67] Here Easy Life controlled information and market access for the consumers in question.[68] Thus, Easy Life used its influence over information to segment the market, and it could, by such practices, exploit a particular set of consumers even if it otherwise lacked broad market power.

The analysis in *Honorable* worked to frame the market in terms of potential submarkets, and in terms of the inability of assumptions about perfectly competitive markets to inform the situation fully. The court was persuaded that behavioral practices and cultural experiences could undermine some assumptions of the perfectly competitive market paradigm. Asymmetrical positioning within the community, therefore, made it possible for Easy Life to segment and exploit an identifiable group within the community. This raised clear questions of discrimination that could not be understood or addressed by simplified concepts of efficiency, wealth-maximization, and perfect competition.

The opinion is important because it confirms the difference between an economic analysis and a concern for the authority to represent and interpret meanings and values in the relationship among law, markets, and culture. Where traditional economic analysis of law focuses on individuals stripped of their character, culture, history, and other human qualities, an interpretive approach recognizes these qualities. This means that it does not assume that people are fungible, detached, and atomistic. To the contrary, an interpretive approach understands the individual as embedded within particular social and market networks that can vary by such factors as history, race, gender, age, class, education, and geographic location, among others. Variances among individuals and groups create asymmetrical relationships with respect to the authority to influence the cultural-interpretive framework of an exchange. Consequently, there are real opportunities for market and social segmentation, and for exploitation that are independent of broad based and generalized conceptions of market power.

In *Merritt, Baby M*, and *Honorable*, we find illustrations of the way in which market framing can shape both the legal and the economic

---

[66] *Id.* at 890–91.
[67] Honorable, 100 F. Supp.2d at 889. The court references Hanson & Kysar, *Taking Behavioralism Seriously*.
[68] Honorable, 100 F. Supp.2d at 889.

approach to an exchange relationship. Referencing different assumptions about self-interest and the public interest, or viewing the exchange from a variety of different perspectives changes the way in which the legal argument develops. It also influences the ultimate outcome of the case.

Framing contested measures of market performance

There are a number of ways to measure the way in which individuals and groups experience market performance. At an individual firm level one might look at market share, stock price, or price to earnings (P/E) ratios, for instance. At a national level, one might look at statistics on gross national product (GNP), gross domestic product (GDP), inflation, or unemployment. Interpreting the importance or relevance of these measures is once again a matter of framing.

This part of the chapter briefly illustrates the problem of assessing market performance by making reference to two examples from Amartya Sen's book *Development as Freedom*.[69] Sen's book is concerned with a number of issues. Of particular interest is his analysis of the incompleteness of a wealth indicator and of an efficiency indicator as measures of how a given market arrangement is experienced by different people. The first example discussed concerns the incompleteness of a wealth indicator as a reference for well-being in a given community. The second concerns the use of an efficiency criterion when referencing unemployment rates relative to social welfare payments.

Sen argues that a variety of measures must be employed to map a reasonable understanding of well-being in a given market context.[70] One of the examples he gives involves the position of African-American men in the US economy.[71] He points out that by reference to a wealth indicator, African-American men are among the richest black people in the world.[72] As a group they have higher incomes than black men located almost anywhere else.[73] At the same time, when he compares the same population groups for life expectancy and mortality rates, he finds that African-American men are doing much worse than black men in some of the most impoverished countries in the world.[74] Consequently, it is difficult to say that the market system in the United States provides better outcomes. His point is that one needs to consider a variety of measures if

---

[69] SEN, DEVELOPMENT AS FREEDOM.
[70] *Id.* at 13–14.   [71] *Id.* at 21–24.   [72] *Id.* at 21.   [73] *Id.*   [74] *Id.* at 21–24.

one is to gain real insight into the condition of African-American men in the US economy.

At the same time, his work supports the observation that the power to frame the interpretive reference of analysis influences the understanding of the market relationship being investigated. When we frame our inquiry in terms of wealth and income we get a very different picture of the market experience than when we measure other important qualities of life, such as health and mortality rates. This observation is important because different public policy approaches will be triggered or justified based on the meanings and values presented in any particular frame.

A second illustration used by Sen references a difference in economic policy and social welfare between the United States and Europe. He points out that by American standards Europe has generous social welfare benefits.[75] The social safety net, as it were, is thicker in Europe than in America. This, as many Americans like to point out, can create incentives for staying on welfare and can increase market costs resulting in higher unemployment rates in Europe than in the United States. In general, generous social welfare benefits are thought to be less efficient. To better evaluate the difference between US and European social policy, however, one must look more closely at the US frame of reference. Sen points out that the United States, while providing less of a social safety net than Europe, focuses much more attention on employment rate policy.[76] He argues that the United States is able to spend less on social welfare primarily because it spends more time and focuses more attention than Europe on employment.[77] US policy tends to tinker with market mechanisms designed to keep unemployment rates very low by European standards. This permits it to pay less attention to social welfare as long as it can hold out the promise of available employment for those who seek it.[78] European policy, by way of contrast, is focused less on low employment numbers.[79]

The basic point to be gathered from the distinction is that both the United States and Europe need to be concerned with providing for the needs of their citizens; there are, however, different ways in which to frame the issues and the responses. In response to the effects of unemployment or economic dislocation European countries tend to redistribute resources through social welfare programs. The United States, on the other hand, redistributes resources under policies intended to create jobs

---

[75] *Id.* at 21.   [76] *Id.* at 95.   [77] *Id.*   [78] *Id.*   [79] *Id.* at 95.

and stimulate employment. Thus, both countries intervene in the market to advance social policy, and the way in which they frame their concern has different substantive impacts in terms of the distribution of wealth – there are different winners and losers under each approach. Understanding the interpretive frames and references for different situations permits one to gain a deeper insight into the broader socio-economic considerations at work in each community.

Conclusion

In the various examples discussed in this chapter we see that alternative frames and references highlight different facts, values, and policies. Interpretation theory helps us identify alternative understandings and approaches so that a broader set of facts and values can be investigated as relevant to mediating and resolving a particular dispute. To conclude simply that a particular course of action is or is not efficient, wealth-maximizing, or inevitable on a given set of facts, begs the question. The *facts and the values* behind those facts are often times contested and subject to interpretive ambiguity. Therefore, better-informed legal reasoning and policy making requires attention to a variety of contested market meanings.

Problems

Use the following problems to think about and discuss the contested nature of market assumptions in each situation.

(1) Juan and Martha have been married for ten years and are in their mid-forties. They have been trying to start a family for three years. They have recently decided to adopt a baby. As they look into the adoption process they learn that potential babies are a scarce and valuable resource. They also learn that access to a baby is essentially controlled by a vast network of social workers and adoption agencies. While there are many agencies to choose from and fees vary, all have a similar set up with similar fees for services. "Winning" approval for a placement is based on passing the screening interviews of the various social workers. The fact that Juan and Martha are both successful surgeons each earning in excess of $300,000 per year entitles them to no better or quicker process than the plumber and auto mechanic they met at a recent prospective parent meeting. They are told that a placement will take between eighteen and twenty-four months. Juan and Martha think that the system is inefficient,

causing undue delay and preventing some babies from getting into a good family. They recently read about two countries in the international adoption market that allow prospective parents to come to the country, visit an orphanage and place a bid for a child. Every Friday bids are tabulated and children are delivered to the highest bidders. A minimum bid is set to cover costs to the agency in caring for the child up until a market placement occurs. Juan and Martha think that the idea of "market placement" is a good one and they want to fly to one of these countries and obtain a child so that they can start their family. They are told by their lawyer, however, that such procedures may be risky under US law because they by-pass the social worker and agency system.

What are the pro and con arguments for the market placement system vs. the current adoption system? As an alternative, consider the situation of Martha being seriously ill and in need of an organ transplant. Martha's name is put on a list of people needing an organ transplant. There are 2,000 people ahead of her on the waiting list. Juan places an advertisment in the newspaper and on the Internet offering $750,000 for the needed organ donation. Should organ transplants be organized by the market? Is a market allocation to the highest bidder better or worse than a lottery, or a first-in-time approach?

(2) Bill is hired as an associate with the largest law firm in his mid-sized city. He is a new law school graduate. He is also the father of two young children, one aged four and one aged seven. He is a recently divorced single parent, having won custody of both children in a protracted legal custody battle that lasted over two years. Despite this stress he finished near the top of his class at law school and joins the firm along with four other new law school graduates. At the time he is hired Bill explains that he has full parenting obligations and will generally not be able to work on weekends, will not be able to do extensive travel and will have to leave the office by 5:00 on week days, although he will be able to take some work home with him. The firm says they understand and want to give him a chance at becoming a partner. All of the other new hires are single with no plans for marriage or family. Of the five hires, three are women and two are men.

After three years with the firm, a firm committee meets to assess the progress of the class of associates that Bill is in. At that meeting all five members of the class are told that it is time to evaluate the partnership potential of each of them and to start sorting out the best people for senior associate positions based on ability and potential to become a partner. The partner in charge says that all of them are bright and have done high-quality work. For the most part they have each been billing about 2,100 hours/year with the exception of Bill and Lisa. Bill has been billing about 1,800 hours and Lisa about 2,400 hours. All of them except Bill have done considerable travel in representing the interests of clients. All except Bill have been able to attend the annual four-day firm retreat where partners and associates participate in "corporate games" and social activities designed to enhance team-building and bonding among the lawyers. Likewise, all but Bill have participated in the weekly Friday night "social hour" where beer, wine, and food are served in the law firm lounge area on Fridays between 6:30 and 8:00. In the past three years all of the associates have earned the same base salary with differences in bonus structure payments. Now the base pay will change substantially along with bonus structure.

After the meeting, Bill is called aside by the managing partner. He is told that he is doing some excellent work, some very complex stuff, but he is not keeping up with the other associates or fitting in as well as he should be. The partner says, "you know Bill, here at Smith, Smith, and Smith, we like to think of all of our 127 lawyers as one big family . . . You know everyone is just one of the guys." He then offered Bill a chance to improve his standing by taking a four-month assignment with a corporate client 900 miles away which will involve weekends and lots of travel. Bill says, "you know I have family commitments and I can't do that kind of work." The partner than tells Bill, "I kind of thought we were your family too Bill." Then the partner explains that they would like to keep Bill on as a permanent junior associate in what they call the "mommy track . . . we call it that because it is usually where we end up placing women and you will be the first man to whom we offer this opportunity. This way you keep a good job and we keep a good associate. Everyone wins."

Bill objects and says that he should have the right to continue to pursue a senior associate position and a partnership, because the "mommy track" is dead-end work with little respect in the firm, inadequate staff support, and no hope of having a voting stake in the firm. Bill says he is being punished just because he has a family and has parenting obligations that the other male partners do not have since they all have stay-at-home wives or nannies, and the women associates are single with no life beyond that of the firm. The partner replies, "we pay people based on what they add to the bottom line not based on their family or personal needs."

Consider the perspective of Bill and of the firm. Also take into account the various subgroups within the firm. Identify and discuss the various ways in which the different individuals and groups might be experiencing the market process in this situation. How might the situation be similar or distinguishable from the relationships discussed in this chapter (for example, the relationships in the films *Wall Street, Other People's Money, Do The Right Thing*, and the cases of *Baby M*, and *Honorable*)? Outline some of the alternative positions that might be taken in support of Bill and, in the alternative, in support of the firm.

3

The law and market economy framework

A primary objective of Chapter 2 involved showing the various ways in which market interpretations are contested in our society.

In this chapter, attention turns to the development of a better understanding of the interpretive process in law and market economy, and to the outlining of some basic "tools" for an interpretive approach. This includes a discussion of the way in which interpretive institutions facilitate wealth formation and distribution. It also addresses the way in which law functions to mediate the tension between culture (as an expression of a public or community interest) and the market (as an expression of private or self-interest). The basic objective is to offer a broader and more inclusive way of thinking about the market, and about the way in which market ideas are borrowed and incorporated into law.

It is important to understand the way in which legal argument is organized and developed. Appreciating this process will make it easier to understand how, when, and why certain market concepts get used in law. Thus, this chapter undertakes to provide the background and framework needed for understanding the use of the many market concepts discussed in chapters 4–6. In reading this material, keep in mind that law and legal institutions operate within markets, and markets operate in relation to law and legal institutions. At the same time, broadly conceived notions of culture influence law, markets, and legal institutions. The relationship is triadic and multi-directional. Therefore, legal reasoning and legal argument should respond to a variety of interrelated concerns.

This book also undertakes to introduce cultural factors into the understanding of law and market economy. While economists generally discount the role of culture, this book actively integrates cultural considerations. Consequently, this chapter focuses on taking an *interpretive and representational turn* in understanding the relationship among law, markets, and culture.[1] It does this by using semiotic, or cultural–interpretation

[1] *See, e.g.*, HAUSMAN, CHARLES S. PEIRCE'S EVOLUTIONARY PHILOSOPHY 194–225 (discussing Peirce's work in terms of a "linguistic turn"); PATTERSON, LAW & TRUTH 71–127 (discussing the "interpretive turn" in contemporary theories of jurisprudence).

theory to investigate this relationship. I call this approach *law and market economy.*[2]

Naturally, there are multiple ways to approach interpretation theory and to integrate culture into an understanding of law and market economy. This chapter offers one useful way of accomplishing this objective. Moreover, the framework provided in this chapter is designed to be readily adaptable to a variety of theories such as those informed by feminist, critical, and alternative political theories.[3] This can be accomplished by changing the identification of the particular frames and references of the interpretive institutions to be discussed in connection with figure 3.1 (p. 63), and likewise by changing the theory used for the second step in Peirce's triadic approach to legal argument to be discussed in connection with figure 3.3 (p. 73).

In developing an interpretive approach to law and market economy, this chapter first introduces some of the basic ideas explored in law and market economy.[4] Second, it presents a simple interpretive framework for understanding the relationship among law, markets, and culture. Third, it develops a way of "mapping" exchange relationships (of thinking in terms of alternative diagrams of the exchange relationship). Fourth, this mapping process is explained in terms of the lawyer's role in formulating legal argument. Fifth, further clarification of the cultural-interpretive approach is provided. This material addresses the relationship between the subjective and objective in the interpretive process, and it explains the need for normative analysis in legal reasoning. And sixth, some basic "tools" are outlined to assist in organizing and understanding the process of framing, referencing, and representing in law and market economy.

Foundation for law and market economy

This part of the chapter starts by offering, as background, a few brief comments regarding some basic ideas concerning law and market economy and the understanding of law in a market context.

First, it is important to understand that the market operates as a *place of meaning and value formation.* Meanings and values arise from the process

---

[2] Malloy, Law and Market Economy.
[3] *See generally,* Hayman, Levitt, & Delgado, Jurisprudence; Minda, Post-modern Legal Movements; Chamallas, Introduction to Feminist Legal Theory.
[4] *Id.*

of people seeking to equate between different items of exchange – between work and pay, for example. In addition, choice in the marketplace involves a process of interpretation. Understanding the value and nature of the objects of exchange, and the purpose and terms of exchange, presupposes an interpretive process. This includes the idea that cost and benefit analysis, in traditional law and economics, is really about *an interpretation of costs and benefits* and not simply about a calculus of choice. This is important because the interpretive process is *grounded in experience*, and experience varies by such factors as culture, race, age, gender, education level, and rural or urban location, among others. This helps to explain the contested understandings of the market. It also helps to explain some of the differences in practice when legal and economic concepts are borrowed from one culture and translated into another culture. The market process in China is not the same as in the United States, for example, because the translation into practice is grounded in a different cultural-interpretive experience.[5]

We can also understand the role of culture in the borrowing process when we think of the Uniform Commercial Code (UCC). The UCC was adopted by the various states in the United States and was envisioned as an attempt to be a code in the French, German, or Italian civil law tradition. In practice, however, the UCC does not function in the same way as a civil law code.[6] Despite its code-like organization, it is used and interpreted by lawyers trained in a common law tradition. The legal culture of the American common law lawyer is different from that of the Continental civil law attorney. The difference in legal culture expresses itself in the different way in which each understands and deals with a "code."

The idea of interpretation being grounded in experience also helps to explain one aspect of the market information problem. Information and knowledge are fragmented, in part because experiences are different. These experiences function as key interpretive ingredients for exchange and are important for market coordination. An important function of the market involves maximizing the creative and value-enhancing potential of dispersed information and knowledge. Thus, the more extensive, accessible, and diverse the networks and patterns of exchange, the greater will be the potential for wealth formation.[7]

---

[5] *Id.* at 12–15. *See also* Hom & Malloy, *China's Market Economy* (this article takes the form of a unique exchange of letters and observations between the authors when they worked in China).

[6] *See generally,* MERRYMAN, CIVIL LAW TRADITION.

[7] MALLOY, LAW AND MARKET ECONOMY.

This idea is similar to the concept of a *positive network externality*.[8] For instance, having a telephone system with one phone on it is not very valuable but when you have two, four, 100, 10,000, 200 million or a billion users, you add a lot of value. Value arises from the potential to greatly multiply the exchange potential of the system. The more extensive, diverse, and accessible the exchange system the more information and knowledge that can be traded. And, the more trading and exchanging in the system, the more potential there is for promoting and discovering value-enhancing relationships. In this analysis, the "institutions" of language, communication, and interpretation function like the "telephone system," providing the interpretive network that facilitates exchange and the process of wealth formation.

Another important idea is that law and market economy explores the ambiguity of efficiency as a criterion for decision making.[9] As discussed in chapters 1 and 2, efficiency is an ambiguous concept apart from a given situational context. In addition, we know from the studies of *complex systems* that it is impossible to use a criterion such as efficiency to determine the optimal course of action to be taken in a market economy.[10] The best that can be achieved, through careful process analysis, is the formulation of sets of plausibly good courses of action.[11]

In this context "complexity" refers to the idea expressed in complex systems and chaos theory.[12] Research in these areas indicates that there is no optimal outcome that can be determined in a complex system.[13]

---

[8] *See* DE SOTO, MYSTERY OF CAPITAL 72 (citing "Metcalfes's Law" dealing with computer networks. While stand-alone computers are useful, value really takes off when they are linked in networks. This is my point as well – market values take off and are made sustainable by extensive networks and patterns of exchange, and these networks and patterns are facilitated by institutions of language, communication, and interpretation.)

[9] *Id.* at 78–105. *See generally*, KIRZNER, DISCOVERY AND THE CAPITALIST PROCESS; KIRZNER, MEANING OF MARKET PROCESS.

[10] *Id.* Complexity involves complex systems theory or chaos theory and research in this area holds that there is no optimal outcome that can be determined in a complex system. *Id.* at 139–40. *See also* KAUFFMAN, AT HOME IN THE UNIVERSE 248–62, 267–69 (it is impossible to determine an optimal course of action even in a system with only a few independent variables, much less one with as many variables and actors as a market economy); AUYANG, FOUNDATIONS OF COMPLEX-SYSTEMS 80–82 (in a complex system, the idea of optimization is limited and relative, and even then it is in the nature of a *set* of possibilities rather than any absolute optima); BRIGGS & PEAT, TURBULENT MIRROR; GLEICK, CHAOS; GREENE, ELEGANT UNIVERSE. *See* MALLOY, LAW AND MARKET ECONOMY 112–13.

[11] *See* MALLOY, LAW AND MARKET ECONOMY 139–40. *See also id.* at 78–135.

[12] *Id.* at 139–40. *See also* KAUFFMAN, AT HOME IN THE UNIVERSE 248–62, 267–69.

[13] AUYANG, FOUNDATIONS OF COMPLEX-SYSTEMS 80–82.

In a complex system the idea of optimization is limited and relative, and even then it is in the nature of generating a set of possibilities rather than any absolute optima.[14] The market, like nature, is a good example of a complex system because it has so many degrees of freedom and points of interaction. The market is complex because it has so many individual participants and thus innumerable degrees of freedom. It is precisely this complexity that gives the market exchange process its dynamic nature and its ability to produce wealth.[15] Legal systems function in a similar way. For example, rules that create complex market exchange possibilities create more value than simple rules. A property system that recognizes only a fee simple absolute interest in land is simple, and it produces far less wealth than a system with numerous property interests that can be broken down and targeted to increased numbers of potential investors. Similarly, the real estate markets in the United States produce tremendous amounts of wealth not because they are simple but because our conceptions of property and property interests are complex. Furthermore, government is not always bad in this regard as government regulation is responsible for creating much of the wealth-enhancing infrastructure of American real estate markets. Some examples include government-backed insurance and mortgage programs, and the development of the secondary mortgage market.[16] In many ways, these programs make law more complex yet they facilitate market exchange and involve trillions of dollars of economic activity.

In this complex market environment, economics can facilitate the filtering of information in a way that can assist in developing a finite set of decisional options (sets of plausibly good courses of action). Ultimately, however, we can not rely on an economic calculus to identify an optimal course of action and selecting a particular course of action from a number of plausibly good alternatives requires an appeal to values, meanings, and mechanisms that go beyond traditional economic tools. Selecting from among alternatives, just like the process of market framing, requires

[14] BRIGGS & PEAT, TURBULENT MIRROR; GLEICK, CHAOS; GREENE, ELEGANT UNIVERSE.

[15] Richard Epstein addresses the idea of complexity but his conception of complexity is very confusing if one actually has an understanding of complex systems theory, or the more formal meaning of complexity. See EPSTEIN, SIMPLE RULES FOR A COMPLEX WORLD. Epstein erroneously presumes that nature and the market are simple, and he seems to suggest that government regulations (even when simple) are complex, while private arrangements (even when complex) are simple. It seems to me that Epstein uses an unusual definition of complexity when compared to the literature on the subject.

[16] MALLOY & SMITH, REAL ESTATE TRANSACTIONS 505–61, 597–658.

reference to Peirce's idea of the normative sciences of esthetics, ethics, and logic (ideas to be further developed later in this chapter). After a given course of action is selected, on normative grounds, economics can then be helpful in identifying a more cost effective, or perhaps a least-cost method, for achieving a particular goal.

In law and market economy attention is also directed at the promotion of a process of *sustainable wealth formation* rather than at the idea of wealth-maximization.[17] This is a broader concept than wealth maximization as it focuses on a *market process approach* to wealth formation and long-term economic growth.[18] It also involves an understanding of the difference between seeking to improve one's position and seeking to maximize one's wealth advantage. In a complex exchange system, such as the market, it is not always clear that people act to maximize wealth even if they do seek to improve their position. It is reasonable to believe that people frequently seek to improve on their own circumstances within a community context – not acting merely to maximize their own self-interest but simply seeking to improve their condition while recognizing the needs of the greater community. Sustainability requires a broader and longer-term community reference than does self-interested wealth-maximization. Therefore, a process of sustainable wealth formation considers a variety of factors, along with efficiency and creativity, that work together to sustain market operations and social prosperity over the long run.

Finally, a primary assumption in law and market economy is that "institutions" of language, communication, and interpretation play an important role in the creation of wealth, and in the allocation and redistribution of wealth. These institutions are of central importance in understanding the question of market economy. For example, wealth formation, economic development, and creativity expand with the specialization and transformation of interpretation. Markets are enhanced by increases in grammatical forms, styles of legal discourse, and by advancing representations of ideas such as property. Interpretive processes, in other words, have substantive economic implications.

---

[17] *See* MALLOY, LAW AND MARKET ECONOMY 78–105. The idea of a process of sustainable wealth formation is similar to the concept of sustainable development. It means that we can have market growth, but that such growth should not simply follow a path of unconstrained self-interest in the pursuit of wealth maximization. Sustainable growth should be balanced and constrained by a concern for the public interest. In balancing self-interest and public interest we can promote the common interest.

[18] *Id.*

A relationship among law, markets, and culture

Law and market economy involves the study of the social and market exchange process by focusing on the relationship among law, culture, and markets. This relationship is triadic, dynamic and multi-directional. Moreover, in this relationship, one can understand the *market* sphere as expressing a concern for the individual,[19] with a market focus on the pursuit of self-interest. On the other hand, *culture* is more of a collective concept, and therefore the cultural sphere can be understood as expressing a community perspective or norm.[20] In a sense it also expresses a notion of the public interest. *Law*, in this relationship, functions as a mediator between the expression of private and public interest. Therefore, the primary idea behind this approach involves the recognition of the dynamic relationship among these three spheres.

In understanding law in a market context it is important to appreciate these connections and to avoid putting too much emphasis on isolated criteria such as wealth-maximization. Moreover, cultural context and cultural practices will vary across communities and, thus, the understanding of law in a market context will also vary. This means that differently situated people will understand the exchange process differently, and this is an important observation in understanding law in any particular market setting.

It is even more important when we think globally. In the global context this means, for example, that the neoclassical economic model and the economic practices of the United States do not have universal application. While economics may appear to be a universal "language" the market exchange process is understood and practiced differently in different cultures. Thus, while the United States may generally have the power to significantly influence interpretive conventions for discussing market issues in an international forum, these conventions do not have the same applicability and meaning in every country.

Figure 3.1 depicts the triadic relationship among law, markets, and culture. The sides of the triangle represent the semiotic or cultural–interpretive connectors that link each of the key spheres of the law and market economy relationship. These links represent the cognitive processes of understanding, communicating, and referencing. They include "institutions" of language, communication, and interpretation. Specific interpretive "tools" include the use of metaphor, rhetoric, linguistics, grammar, and narrative.

---

[19] *See generally*, THROSBY, ECONOMICS AND CULTURE 13.   [20] *Id.*

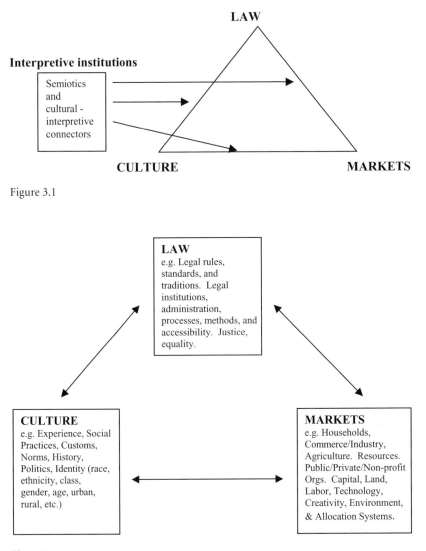

Figure 3.1

Figure 3.2

Figure 3.2 provides a further elaboration of the basic model. It indicates some of the traditional or typical categories and concepts to be included within each sphere of law, markets, and culture.

As these diagrams indicate, law and market economy theory is not the same as law and economics. Market theory goes beyond the interests and concerns of economics. This is evident to anyone who has ever been to business school or worked in a commercial enterprise. Markets involve sociology, organizational theory, marketing, behavioral psychology, and interpretation theory, among others. Thus, while market actors can benefit from an understanding of economics, something more is needed to understand the relationship between law and market economy. In other words, there is a need for a clear recognition of approaches that study market activities as relationships and exchanges that go beyond the traditional boundaries of economics. We need to understand law and markets in terms of the cultural context and practices that give them meaning. And, we need to bring a variety of information, gathered from multiple disciplines, to bear upon our understanding of law in its market context.

Law and market economy has, as two of its primary concerns, a desire to understand (a) the way in which we, as social beings, *experience* the relationship between law and markets, and (b) the way in which this experience, as a ground in Peircean semiotics, translates and transforms human relations through an on-going process of meaning and value formation (and re-formation). In this regard, the intersection of law and market economy is *experienced* in a variety of ways. It is experienced in terms of the networks and patterns of exchange in which people participate, and in terms of the way in which these networks and patterns relate to such characteristics as race, gender, age, education level, income, and geographic location, among others. It is also experienced in terms of the way in which the institutions of language, communication, and interpretation facilitate our understanding of choice while bringing coherence and comprehensibility to the process of wealth formation and resource allocation or distribution. Furthermore, law in its market context is experienced culturally and collectively, with reference to contested interpretations of market functions, outcomes, consequences, and assumptions. It is experienced in ways that can be personal and individualized, and thus not fully universal.

Law and market economy is also about the human practice of exchange and the strategies for directing exchange toward worthy esthetic and ethical values. To this end, law and market economy uses semiotics, or cultural-interpretation theory, to address the meanings and values of market relationships. It does this by identifying and "mapping" the networks and patterns of social/market exchange.

In doing this, law and market economy proceeds from the proposition that law, as a semiotic system, is the product of human agency, and a primary motivation for human action is the pursuit of authoritative influence over the process of cultural-interpretive framing, referencing, and representation. This process of framing, referencing, and representing translates and transforms meanings and values, and the ability to influence these cultural-interpretive connectors is a primary concern of self-interest. This influence is important because authority in this regard informs the process of interpretive choice and produces substantive outcomes in terms of the generation and allocation of resources.

This aspect of self-interest can be understood in simple terms. Self-interest includes a desire to influence or control the spaces and forms of socio-legal discourse. We seek this control for a variety of reasons, some of which can not be easily quantified. All of us recognize a motivation, at some level, to influence people's opinions and viewpoints: to have people agree with us on how to improve the economy, fight terrorism, promote racial equality, and what have you. We can even observe this in very young children. At an early age children seek to define and claim space in the world around them by telling others, "that's *my* toy, *my* book, *my* mommy, *my* daddy." In this way, they lay claim to specific resources and power sources. We observe a continuation of this practice as children get older. As teens, people seek to define a sphere or space of authority apart from their parents and use clothing, music, and other accessories in this process. They also seek to define who is "cool" and who is not. As adults, people try to convince others to read certain books or articles and to understand them in a particular way; they want other people to agree in judgments as to the best sports teams, the best computer, and the hottest car. They want to influence each other on political issues and on voting. These are all examples of the basic idea of self-interest related to the desire to shape and influence the process of interpretive framing and referencing.

Importantly, the motivation for action is the gaining of power over the definition of one's world, and of the forms and patterns of discourse that are considered authoritative in the decision making process. While not mutually exclusive, this motivation differs from ones based on a desire to maximize wealth and efficiency. In a sense it is like following a market-share strategy in business where one pursues a strategy of maximizing market share rather than profit margin.[21] Such a strategy might be compared to the behavior of an animal "marking" and defining its

---

[21] *See generally* GORDON, COMPETITOR TARGETING; ROSENBAUM, MARKET DOMINANCE (the strategy can include efficiency but does not require efficiency); TYNAN, MULTI-CHANNEL MARKETING. A market share strategy might also be compared to an animal "marking" and defining its territory. Humans use language and other semiotic devices to "mark" their "territory" or authority over particular cultural-interpretive space. This authority gives rise to value-enhancing opportunities.

territory. Humans use language and other semiotic devices to "mark" their "territory" and authority over particular discursive places and spaces. This authority expresses itself in the power to influence the process of framing, referencing, and representing. The idea being that it is sometimes more valuable and satisfying to control the decision making process than to simply maximize profit in an environment controlled by others.

The point is that success in this process of framing, referencing, and representing generates opportunities for capturing and creating value. Various legal forms facilitate this process and give us influence over extended spaces. We can operate through the corporate form, for instance, to develop and shape a particular corporate culture, and to promote the values of commodification and wealth-maximization. We can also work within a non-profit organization to shape a *private* definition of the public interest,[22] or work within the public sector to direct community resources at our own conception of the public welfare.[23] All of these institutional and organizational forms, in which we can operate, are products of legal convention. They create mechanisms and manageable frameworks for exerting influence over interpretive hierarchies and worldviews, that shape the generation and allocation of resources.

More specifically, the ability to establish or influence a frame, reference, or interpretive hierarchy conventionalizes decision making authority in favor of a particular interpretive community. This then influences and constrains the people, groups, and institutions having responsibility for generating, responding to, or otherwise participating in future decisions or exchanges.[24] In this way we use particular legal forms and conventions to exercise a self-interested authority over the meanings and values of the world around us.

For example, if the interpretive hierarchy (conventionalized interpretive norm), expressed in the corporate form or in a judicial or legislative convention, requires that cost and benefit analysis be used in all decision making, values that are difficult to price will be highly discounted or ignored. Correspondingly, the pursuit of profit will be elevated and extended at the expense of other normative values such as those related to the environment, public health, or family services.

With influence over the institutions of interpretation, language, and communication, one can shape the understanding of socio-legal problems, and facilitate particular outcomes. Thus, the ability to

---

[22] *See* chapter 6, *infra* for discussion of non-profit organizations.   [23] *Id.*
[24] *See* KAY, PATTERNS IN CORPORATE EVOLUTION 50–58, 91–93, 234–44.

conventionalize choice-selecting and decisional rules and norms provides individuals and groups with an ability to influence the distribution and allocation of wealth and resources.

In this way, interpretive hierarchies provide continuity and guidance for future decision making while framing the boundaries and alternative paths of market exchange. In the language of semiotics, interpretive hierarchies (conventionalized interpretive norms) operate as *indexical referents* that mediate and inform the process of interpretive choice. In this context, the pursuit of self-interested behavior is directed at two primary objectives. First, it is directed at the pursuit of strategic opportunities for interpretive influence within the given hierarchy (within a particular worldview or market frame), and second, either at the pursuit of reinforcing or replacing the given interpretive hierarchy. This means that we either try to act strategically within the rules that we are confronted with, or we try to change the rules. Thus, contested understandings of the market reflect struggles over the conventionalized decision making process, with the understanding that authoritative influence in this process can result in a greater share of the distribution of wealth.

This idea of a *cultural-interpretive hierarchy* can be understood by comparison to an operating system in a computer.[25] The operating system conventionalizes the computing environment and only compatible software will work in the system. Any software that is incompatible with the conventionalized operating system is rendered inoperative. This control over the meanings and values that are expressed within the system is very valuable as is evidenced by the market position of Microsoft Corporation. Microsoft dominates the market with its operating system and this makes it very difficult for software companies that do not have compatible software. By dominating the market for operating systems, Microsoft controls the interpretive hierarchy of computer software and this enhances both its market power and its economic position. In a similar way, control over the cultural-interpretive environment of law and market economy gives primacy and power to discourses, meanings, and values, which are compatible with the dominant interpretive hierarchy. In other words, if I have the power of a high court judge and I require all legal cases to be approached from an economic point of view, I make legal argument difficult for those people who want to discuss problems in terms of feminist or critical race theory. Dissenting and contested points of view must struggle

---

[25] MALLOY, LAW AND MARKET ECONOMY 170–71.

for recognition. In order to challenge the conventionalized discourse they must generate doubt in the current mode of thinking, and they must suggest "better" alternative framings, references, and representations.

Economic concepts are important in all of this analysis because economics provides a formal representational sign system, or "language," for "mapping" the process of exchange to which semiotics refers.[26] It provides a mechanism for conventionalizing decision making because it offers a way to understand the process of exchange, and this is useful even as we appreciate the fact that "the map is not the territory" – as we acknowledge that our models are partial and incomplete representations.[27] To the extent, however, that we seek to understand exchange we must deal with economics. Economics is the formally accepted discourse of market analysis, and we must be able to understand and use economics if we are to address law in a market context.

We can use economic terms and concepts in law even though we understand that they offer a partial and incomplete picture for legal reasoning. Economic concepts and models are used to represent the exchange process, but they are not the exchange process itself. This can be better understood if one thinks in terms of the way in which a legal description "represents" a particular piece of property even though it is not itself the property to which it refers.[28] The legal description simplifies the process

---

[26] *See generally* KEVELSON, LAW AS A SYSTEM OF SIGNS 167–201; KEVELSON, PEIRCE'S ESTHETICS OF FREEDOM 199–218. Kevelson explains:

> the triadic linking of law, economics, and semiotics makes its most recent debut in the work of Robin Paul Malloy . . .
>
> Malloy shows how signification of cultural values evolve and are transformed through use and exchange in living community. He suggests that it is by using the instrument of semiotic inquiry, in the sense that all theories have instrumental purpose, that we can begin to perceive and explain previously undisclosed processes of value development, i.e., aspects of emerging value which appear only as a result of a certain way of being observed.
>
> Every use and mention of a term and every attempt to redefine and sharpen the meaning of a term creates an asymmetrical relationship between the known and the new, just as every marketplace transaction changes the value of the objects exchanged and increases the meaning of each, so that the value of each becomes off-balanced from its previous marketplace value and acquires, as if repricing were redefinition, an increase in meaning. (*Id.* at 205–06.)

[27] *See also* HAYAKAWA & HAYAKAWA, LANGUAGE IN THOUGHT AND ACTION 13–21 (the map is not the territory and the symbol is not the thing symbolized). Likewise, our market models and theories are symbols and sign systems of the exchange process. MALLOY, LAW AND MARKET ECONOMY 39–44 (discussing the idea of "the map is not the territory" as related to law and to market theory); GLEICK, CHAOS 92–121 (mapping and measuring depend upon scale and point of reference – fractals in complex system theory).

[28] I am talking about the formal metes and bounds, government survey or a plat-based legal description that appears in the deed and mortgage for example. *See* MALLOY &

of identifying and transferring the property, but it is not the property and it does not represent all of the characteristics of the property. It is a partial and incomplete representation. In a similar sense, economic concepts function as signs that define, simplify, and facilitate exchange but like the legal description mentioned above, these concepts are merely partial and incomplete representations of underlying exchange processes which are complex and dynamic.

Thus, economic concepts function as partial and incomplete representations even though they may be useful for understanding the constraints and the dynamics of a particular situation. In this way, economics is like a map. A road map, for example, is useful for assisting in the task of driving around town but it tells one little or nothing about the quality of schools or home prices, and gives no indication of crime rates, climate or other important characteristics that collectively give meaning to a particular property located along a particular street in a given community. In this respect, the map is not the territory, and the market model is not the market exchange process. Nonetheless, economics, as a cultural- interpretive device, facilitates the mapping process and can help us identify a finite set of plausibly useful courses of socio-legal action. Furthermore, once a normative decision is made about the particular map or path that we want to take, economics can assist in advancing our objective in a more cost effective or least-cost manner.

In a semiotic sense, therefore, markets are important because they function as primary cultural-interpretive systems for the process of meaning and value formation. Furthermore, law, markets, and culture interact to continuously transmit, and to encode and decode, social meanings and values. In this transmission process, opportunities arise for generating and capturing value.

Mapping exchange relationships: a triadic approach

Understanding law in a market context differs from other approaches to understanding the relationship between law and economics. A primary

SMITH, REAL ESTATE TRANSACTIONS, at 317–60. Note that representation occurs in a variety of areas and not just with respect to real estate. For example, the corporate form of organization operates as a representation that extends the authority and action of an individual or group. It permits action and exchange with a different and legally distinct identity, and permits the legal entity to act beyond the identity of the real people whose interests it represents. This extended representation can itself be limited, however, with such concepts as acting *ultra-vires* (beyond the authority of the entity), or by the process of "piercing the corporate veil."

difference is that it does not seek so much to ask questions about efficiency as it does seek to explore the nature, scope, and consequence of various exchange relationships. It attempts to develop a method that will help us formulate better legal reasoning and public policy by addressing the process of exchange in terms of alternative cultural-interpretive frames and references. It seeks, therefore, to understand the market process as a meaningful human experience, and not merely as an exercise in "scientific" calculation.

In developing the method of law and market economy, reference is made to the semiotic method of Charles Sanders Peirce. Peirce developed a theory of semiotics based on a triadic theory of signs involving three modes of logic. We can use Peirce's idea of a triadic theory of signs to improve our understanding of law in a market context. The triadic approach is consistent with thinking in terms of the dynamic relationship among law, markets, and culture. It also helps us think about legal argument in terms of first, identifying and working with facts; second, using interpretive tools to make the facts understandable; and third, drawing persuasive conclusions from the relationship between steps one and two.

Peirce identified the three modes of his triadic theory as firstness (icon), secondness (index), and thirdness (symbol).[29] These three modes, when taken together, function as the semiotic sign or idea. The relationship between these modes is dynamic, and the process of semiosis is continuous, with every third re-informing a first.

Peirce's theory describes an understanding of the cognitive process. It offers a way of visualizing the mind at work. Our mind responds to stimuli such as facts and information, and these are processed and translated into meanings, values, feelings, and actions, including the triggering of further thought. Peirce's contribution to our understanding of this process is his idea of the triadic relationship between firstness, secondness, and thirdness. This understanding differs in an important way from the

---

[29] *See generally*, LISZKA, GENERAL INTRODUCTION TO THE SEMEIOTIC OF CHARLES SANDERS PEIRCE. These three categories are further broken down and discussed in Liszka's book. They are: *Speculative Grammar, Pure Grammar,* and *Universal Grammar* involving deduction, induction, and objective (hypothetical) reasoning; and *Speculative Rhetoric, Formal Rhetoric,* and *Universal Rhetoric, id.* at 10. In general, Peirce's classifications for this approach to signs involve *grammar* as the "study of formal features of the sign and its modes of expression," *id.* at 9–10, 18–52; *Logic* as "concerned with the manner in which signs can be used to discern truth," *id.* at 9–10, 53–77; and *Rhetorics* as "the investigation; the manner in which signs are used to communicate and express claims within a community," *id.* at 9–10, 78–108. Each of these areas is explained with good illustrations throughout the book.

more traditional idea of a bilateral model of interpretation. For example, consider the relationship between the word "table" and the object that we identify as a table. One way to view the relationship between the word and the object is to see them in a bilateral relationship. In a bilateral model the word is a representation of the table to which it refers. There is the table, and the representation of the table in the word. Peirce's insight involves the recognition of an intermediary step in the interpretive process that he called "secondness." This additional step expands the model into one that is triadic rather than bilateral. In this approach, secondness involves a reference/referent and comparison. In simple terms, Peirce's logic suggests that between the word "table" and the object, our mind searches, as a computer might, for something in its memory that can be used to process the connection between the word and the object. Upon seeing the table (firstness), for example, the mind searches its memory for other objects of similar look, design, purpose, and quality (secondness). This referencing triggers the conclusion, "table" (thirdness). Likewise, when we encounter the word "table" we search our memory banks for things that we have previously associated with that word, and we draw a conclusion about the image of the thing being represented by the word "table."

In a like manner we might view a trademark such as the Nike "swoosh" and understand it as the signifier of the Nike brand. When we see this trademark on clothing or running shoes we identify it with the Nike company, and associate it with feelings and experiences related to the promotional campaign in support of the brand. Nike spends valuable resources creating images to associate with their name and with their swoosh. They understand the power and value of being able to create meaning through the process of association in an indexical sense. A primary contribution of Peirce is in recognizing that when we observe the word "table" or the Nike swoosh, we reference this to other images or signs already stored in our memory. After making an indexical reference, we then draw a conclusion. In this way Peirce gave express recognition to the importance of the indexical reference in the interpretive process. This is important because it provides a foundation for understanding the power associated with being able to influence the process of framing, referencing, and representing in law.

We can appreciate, for instance, the power of a judge and of a legislator in posing the questions to be asked and in setting the criteria for resolving a certain dispute or tension. They can set the frame of inquiry (as secondness) and establish the requisite legal and market "memories" required to be referenced in a given matter. If they frame the matter in terms of feminist theory, for example, this will force the discourse to take a very different shape than if the frame were one of cost and benefit analysis from a conservative neoclassical economic perspective. By changing the nature of the discourse and the relevance of particular frames and references these legal actors also influence the range of plausibly good outcome choices that are available. Consequently, their power to influence the interpretive process facilitates their power over resource allocation and distribution.

This triadic approach is important to an understanding of law and market economy because it permits us to explore the process of framing, referencing, and representing in the structure of legal argument. It is this process, and in particular the function of secondness, that assists us in understanding economic concepts and tools as important devices for framing, referencing, and representing exchange relationships in law. Secondness also helps us understand the idea of culture and experience in this model of law and market economy. Culture and experience play a significant role in shaping the frames, references, and comparisons that are metaphorically stored in our cognitive memory banks. Consequently, they influence our understanding and the meaning of law and of exchange. Furthermore, this idea of secondness also helps us to visualize the power involved in controlling or influencing the frames, references, and representations used in the interpretive institutions of the law. It does this by showing us that meaning is filtered through the idea of secondness, and thus conclusions are influenced by and differ with reference to such things as culture and experience, and these are further varied by reference to such characteristics as race, gender, age, education, class, income, geographic location, and history, among others.

Using Peirce's method of analysis, law and market economy positions the market as a complex and dynamic web of representational networks and patterns of exchange wherein the nature, scope, and content of these exchange relationships inform social meaning and value.[30] Law and market economy undertakes an examination of these relationships by using a multi-valued approach.

---

[30] Law and market economy examines exchange systems, and the scientific method of inquiry used in semiotics to understand exchange systems reveals that they are like a "web" with indefinite boundaries. *See* PHILOSOPHICAL WRITINGS OF PEIRCE (Buchler, ed.), at xii. This is also a point raised in general chaos or complex systems theory. *See* KAUFFMAN, AT HOME IN THE UNIVERSE 270–87 (discussing co-evolving webs in complex systems). In studying these webs of exchange it is important to investigate and understand discourse across a number of conventionalized boundaries. *See*, KEVELSON, PEIRCE, SCIENCE, SIGNS 11, 63, 78, 109, 131; KEVELSON, PEIRCE'S ESTHETICS OF FREEDOM 27–28, 62–64.

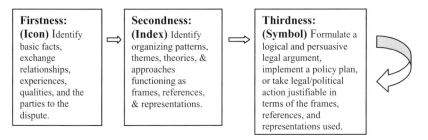

| Firstness:
(Icon) Identify basic facts, exchange relationships, experiences, qualities, and the parties to the dispute. | ⇒ | Secondness:
(Index) Identify organizing patterns, themes, theories, & approaches functioning as frames, references, & representations. | ⇒ | Thirdness:
(Symbol) Formulate a logical and persuasive legal argument, implement a policy plan, or take legal/political action justifiable in terms of the frames, references, and representations used. |

Figure 3.3

Figure 3.3 depicts the semiotic process in the form of legal argument for law and market economy using Peirce's triadic theory of signs (icon, index, and symbol).[31] In this diagram the *icon* is of firstness, and of quality. It is the exchange itself, standing for itself and for all exchange in general. It arises in an experiential context of social or interpretive conflict or tension. It involves the generation or identification of information fragments or "facts." It requires an initial identification of relevant facts and qualities regarding the dispute and the immediate parties to the exchange.

The *index* is of secondness, and of comparative reference. It functions as an interpretive screen. It frames, filters, and influences the encoding and decoding of socio-legal meanings and values. It "maps" the relationship between a particular quality or exchange and other such exchanges or qualities. Alternative mappings (alternative ways of diagramming and situating the exchange relationship) are possible with different cultural-interpretive referents. This involves the process of understanding the relationship between particular information fragments or facts, and a varying set of organizing principles, comparative measures, and referents. In practice this involves organizing the facts in relation to particular patterns of legal argument, and connecting the facts to legal themes and approaches that serve as potentially good frames, references, and representations for resolving the matter in a favorable manner.

The *symbol* is of thirdness, and of argument, action, or contingent "truth." It involves the development of a logical and persuasive argument in support of the frames, references, and representations used in reaching a given conclusion. It also supports the identification of "significant" facts relative to facts that are argued to be of less or no significance to the given exchange. Thirdness is what gets constituted as law, or what gets justified

[31] *See* MALLOY, LAW AND MARKET ECONOMY 23–50.

and represented as a legal rule, holding, or conclusion. It provides a basis for further investigation of quality and of exchange. That is, we move from thirdness back to firstness to refine and re-evaluate the facts in light of our initial conclusions. Perhaps new or different facts emerge as significant after we finish our first review of the situation. For example, on further review we may focus on third-party effects and externalities that cause us to expand the consideration of relevant parties beyond that of the most immediate parties to the transaction. We might also experiment with the organizing principles available for considering the problem, and thus further fine-tune our analysis, causing us to revise our initial and tentative conclusions. Theoretically this process of moving from firstness to thirdness and back can go on indefinitely, but the demands of everyday life will cut it short. This process is referred to as *semiosis*,[32] and as we move through this process we construct alternative mappings of the exchange relationship.

In simple terms this three-step model provides an organized way of thinking about legal reasoning and legal argument. First, it indicates the need to identify the basic nature of the exchange and dispute. Second, it tells us to look for ways of understanding the exchange or dispute in relationship to patterns of legal argument. Thus, we think in terms of classifying and categorizing the basic facts with reference to particular areas of law and various approaches to contemporary legal theory, history, culture, and other interpretive frames, references, and representations. Third, it indicates the need to formulate a legal argument and a plan of action that can be supported in terms of the pattern of argument (the frames, references, and representations) ultimately selected from step two.[33]

This triadic approach to legal reasoning and legal argument helps us to reframe market analysis in a way that differs from the approach of an economic analysis of law. The triadic relationship introduced above and depicted in figure 3.3, indicates the way in which law and market

---

[32] *Id.* at 21, 33–35, 87.

[33] The idea of *patterns* of legal argument is important because of the evidence that we understand meaning with reference to activity patterns in the brain. Interpretation is pattern based. *See* Freeman, *A Neurobiological Interpretation of Semiotics.* It may also be helpful to go back and review the example in chapter 1 concerning the allocation of rights to minerals beneath the lakebed of an isolated lake. Recall the basic facts of the exchange and the connections between the approach to justifying private property and the selection of an allocation rule. These are the type of relationships to look for in moving between the basic qualities and facts of firstness, the alternative organizing principles used in secondness, and the conclusions to be drawn in thirdness.

economy approaches the analysis of legal problems. Law and market economy undertakes the identification and formulation of legal argument or action based on the use of particular cultural-interpretive frames and references. The process is not one of calculating efficiency, but of *mapping* and representing alternative cultural-interpretive understandings of the market as a human exchange process capable of continuously generating and transforming meanings and values. The goal is not to assume an ability to calculate an economically optimal course of action, but to improve legal reasoning and public policy making by exploring alternative ways of logically and ethically advancing worthy esthetic values.

Peirce's approach is also helpful because it enhances our ability to appreciate a primary focus of tension in law and public policy. Using Peirce's triadic model it is easy to grasp the idea that the index, or secondness, is a focal point for competition between alternative interpretive communities and socio-legal theories. The greater the ability of an individual or a group to influence or control the index (cultural-interpretive frames, references, and representations) the more power she or they will have over the conventionalizing of an interpretive hierarchy. This provides influence over future decision making by constraining the people, groups, and institutions having responsibility for making and responding to future decisions and policies. Consequently, an important part of law and market economy involves understanding the competition for influence over the cultural-interpretive frames and references of exchange. It also involves a need to explore institutional arrangements capable of mediating between and beyond the boundaries of individuals and the particular cultural-interpretive communities in which they are situated.

The development of law and market economy, and the mapping of exchange using the process depicted in figure 3.3, is also important because it involves matters of resource allocation and distribution, as well as matters of law and legal institutions. In this context, law and legal institutions provide the infrastructure for social and market exchange. Law operates to define the terms of permissible exchange and provides the social and public definition of the various objects of trade. Law also maps the consequences of certain types of trade, and facilitates the coordination of exchange with particular importance for multi-party trades, trade between impersonal or distant market actors, and non-simultaneous exchanges that take place over extended periods of time, place, and space. In all of these exchange relationships, cultural-interpretive or semiotic theory is at work because market actors must make choices based on meanings and values derived from the application of interpretive frames references, and representations to factual experiences and information fragments.[34] Moreover, the more distant, extended, and diverse the networks of exchange the more they need to be formalized and conventionalized through interpretive mechanisms facilitated by law.

In using Peirce's approach, economics helps us to understand and filter information through a cultural-interpretive "language" of market exchange. Economic concepts can be used initially to help filter a potentially endless number of viewpoints down to a finite set of plausibly good outcome choices, or decision paths. And, once normative analysis directs us to the selection of a given choice option, economics can direct our attention to more cost effective mechanisms for achieving our given objective.

Peirce's three-step process also advances a lawyer's ability to understand and to generate useful legal arguments. The lawyer's stock-in-trade involves the ability to draw on an inventory of familiar *patterns* of legal argument. By working through the process of seeking and manipulating alternative frames, references, and representations the lawyer continually revises and adds to her inventory of legal argument patterns. And, in seeking to remain attentive to the way in which law is *experienced* by people situated in various and competing cultural-interpretive communities, the lawyer expands her mapping and argument tools while facilitating her creativity.

Expanding her ability to understand law and market relationships from an increasing number of perspectives enhances her creativity. This creates tension between the dynamic aspects of exchange as experienced in a dynamic world and the tendency of legal argument to become conventionalized. This tension fosters a constant re-evaluation of law and creates the potential for developing entirely new frames, references, and representations.

In this process, we can understand that the primary professional skill of lawyers and legal actors relates to language, communication, and

---

[34] *See* KEVELSON, PEIRCE'S ESTHETICS OF FREEDOM 59–69. When we reason we bring experience, subjective bias, and various values to the process. The things that shape our experiences and values will thus affect the meanings we derive from present and later exchanges. KEVELSON, LAW AS A SYSTEM OF SIGNS 81–87. It is possible to influence interpretation and meaning by shifting the referential baseline of inquiry. We can "contribute to the reformulation and transformation of official, ideal Law Language and Law Discourse as authoritative symbol," KEVELSON, PEIRCE'S ESTHETICS OF FREEDOM 115. Rules of interpretation constrain and mediate the privilege of the reader and this would be similar to the way in which conventionalized theories of the market exchange process constrain and mediate the market as a text. *See generally*, ECO, LIMITS OF INTERPRETATION 51.

interpretation. Legal actors read cases, legislation, contracts, court proceedings, and a variety of other texts. They write memoranda, pleadings, briefs, position papers, contracts, wills, and legislation. They make oral arguments, take depositions, conduct interviews, address the jury, appear before boards, negotiate with one another, and make a variety of persuasive appeals in formal and informal settings. In order to do their work they must be able to interpret the meanings of the texts and arguments they encounter, and they must make sure that their own writings and arguments embody the intended meanings that they hope to express. To be persuasive, they must understand their audience, and work effectively within and around legal conventions. They must appreciate the way in which the intended and unintended interpreter will read and hear their words, their mannerisms, and their entire delivery. All of this involves cultural-interpretation theory and an indirect, if not direct, knowledge of semiotic connectors such as linguistics, metaphor, rhetoric, narrative, and logic.[35] It also involves working through Peirce's three-step process to identify and organize basic facts, to filter those facts through a variety of frames, references, and representations, and to construct logical and persuasive justifications for the selection of given frames, references, and representations, while advancing a specific legal argument and course of action. Therefore, when we think about law and market economy we focus our attention on the relationship between our skills of interpreting and creating meaning, and the way in which these meanings can influence or facilitate particular allocations of resources.

In law we do not simply write or tell stories – our words have consequences that go beyond mere story-telling. Our words may sentence a man to death, or spare him from that fate. Our words may allow a grandchild to enjoy an inheritance, or permit the development of a multi-million dollar mall or office building, or assure a disabled child's access to medical treatment. Legal words and legal texts exist in a market context and they shape the distribution of resources within society.[36] The structure of these "texts" or semiotic signs can also facilitate the process of economic growth and wealth formation.

Law can be used to help shape the distribution of resources in society by the way in which it indexically "frames" the issues, questions, facts, consequences, and interpretive environment of the disputes and

---

[35] See NOTH, HANDBOOK ON SEMIOTICS; BERGER, SIGNS; HODGE & KRESS, SOCIAL SEMIOTICS; ECO, THEORY OF SEMIOTICS; ECO, SEMIOTICS AND THE PHILOSOPHY OF LANGUAGE.

[36] See MALLOY, LAW AND MARKET ECONOMY 136–65.

exchanges to be mediated. In simple terms, familiar to all lawyers and law students, indexical framing or shifting of interpretive reference involves positioning or characterizing our situation in a manner that most favors an advantageous outcome. For example, if my client is injured because a new lawn mower he purchased was defective, I might consider framing the claim for recovery as one in contract, for breach of warranty, or as one in tort or products liability. Shifting from contract to tort law allows for different remedies and requires different elements of proof. It also involves a moving away from the idea of a fully informed and consensual exchange between market participants to a concern for underinformed or non-consensual exchange. Similarly, one can often reframe a long-term land sales contract as a lease relationship, or as a constructive conveyance subject to an implied or equitable mortgage.[37] Reframing the situation works to change the meaning of the exchange relationship and implicates different elements of substantive and procedural law. It also raises issues related to resource allocation, as the different parties to the exchange will seek an interpretive frame or reference that is most favorable to her or him.

This framing and referencing process includes the ability to create value opportunities from innovations in structuring tax planning, real estate transactions, financial investments, and other exchange relationships. Generating "loopholes," developing new financing techniques, and creating other legal devices involves careful and insightful use of language, communication, and interpretation skills.[38] In these, and numerous other ways, legal actors generate and capture value through the interpretive process.

There are also important moves to be made in framing the manner in which the legal system itself is understood. This involves the framing of underlying assumptions about the legal system that inform us about the kinds of moves or categories that are available.

To understand this point, just think of a time when you may have visited a different country or culture, or even just a family from another neighborhood, and discovered that they did not do everything the way that you did. They had different customs, and different assumptions about the roles of women and men, or about shaking hands, bowing, or eating. Perhaps you discovered that in this other country or place, it is unheard

---

[37] *See e.g.* MALLOY & SMITH, REAL ESTATE TRANSACTIONS *supra* n. 28, at 813–46 (discussing examples related to mortgage substitutes, disguised mortgages, and installment land contracts).

[38] *See* MALLOY, LAW AND MARKET ECONOMY 43–49, 78–90, 106–35.

of that a private person can own a lake or a beach, or that a woman would question the authority of her husband in public. What one discovers in these situations is that certain basic assumptions are so fundamental to a system of social organization or cultural-interpretive hierarchy that they are not even made visible until someone challenges them in a direct or indirect way, or in an intentional or unintentional way.[39]

This is also true when we think about the relationship between legal and economic systems. In the United States, for instance, we are accustomed to validating private property ownership and to keeping detailed records to protect title to valuable land holdings. These records are based on land descriptions. Under Marxism, however, land had no value except to the extent that labor was applied to the land. Consequently, the Russian legal system, under the Soviet Union, did not keep records of land ownership but rather focused its attention on recording the ownership of buildings and improvements to the land.[40] The underlying frames and references resulted in a different approach to legal action.

The Russians developed institutions and values based on reference to improvements to land, whereas countries such as the United States developed institutions focused on the land itself. In a similar way, we have a number of competing interpretive frames, references, and representations at play in our own legal system. We have liberal and conservative views of law, feminist and critical race views of law, and a variety of other conceptions each competing for authoritative influence over the way in which we interpret and understand law. Each of these interpretive frames, references, and representations seeks to influence, through law and legal institutions, the allocation of scarce resources and the access to decision making authority. Each attempts to indexically frame and influence the process of interpretation, and thereby the process of social/market choice.

Standard market models and concepts are also important because they function as interpretive frames and references for justifying and validating standards and criteria used in the allocation of resources and access to decision making authority.[41] For example, legal concepts such as fairness, justice, and reasonableness can be given meaning by reference to ideas or signs of "competition" and "market opportunity." Likewise, legal outcomes can be justified by reference to various economic concepts such as

---

[39] Hom & Malloy, *China's Market Economy*.

[40] Conversation with Ivan Velev of Land and Real Estate Initiative (LARI) Group of The World Bank, Washington, DC, April 10, 2001.

[41] *See* SEN, DEVELOPMENT AS FREEDOM; Sen argues for a variety of measures of economic well-being because different measures focus on different information and criteria.

efficiency, externalities, transactions costs, and other interpretive devices. In a similar manner, legal and cultural mechanisms embrace interpretive frames, references, and representations that give substantive form to market development. These may include reference to transparency, stability, liquidity, reciprocity, accountability, diversity, and tolerance. All of this is important to the form and structure of persuasive legal argument, and to the way in which law and legal institutions generate value-enhancing opportunities.

The form of legal argument

This section of the chapter relates the three-step or triadic form of legal argument to Peirce's three modes of logic. As indicated, Peirce referred to these modes as firstness, secondness, and thirdness. All argument forms can be understood within these three modes.[42] *Firstness* involves basic elements or the facts of a relationship. Firstness is experience-based.[43] *Secondness* involves the referencing of the facts to a cultural–interpretive referent, model, theory, or convention.[44] It is reflective, comparative, and indexical (meaning it points to or references). *Thirdness* is the bringing together of firstness and secondness to form an argument, a plan of action, or conclusion.[45]

The relationship between these modes is continuous. Thus, the conclusion reached in thirdness influences the further understanding of a first. Likewise, these modes are dynamic. As an example, let us consider the simple process of using precedent in law. Let us assume that our client was just involved in an automobile accident at a busy intersection. We can proceed to question the client and any witnesses about what happened. In doing this, we are gathering and establishing the "experiential" facts of the exchange as a mode of firstness. Then we go to our office and compare these facts against statutes and earlier cases. This indexical referencing process involves secondness. Finally, after determining the rules applied in earlier cases and applying them to our facts we put together an argument for a particular result. This argument operates as a mode

---

[42] The relationship between these three modes involves semiosis. *Semiosis* is the process of "synthesis" between Peirce's three modes of logic and it is continuous. NOTH, HANDBOOK ON SEMIOTICS 39–47. Peirce uses a complex triadic structure to analyze the relationship of signs, *id.* at 39–47; SHERIFF, CHARLES PEIRCE'S GUESS AT THE RIDDLE 31–47; LISZKA, A GENERAL INTRODUCTION TO THE SEMEIOTIC OF CHARLES SANDERS PEIRCE 18–52; HOOKWAY, PEIRCE 106–74, 272; REASONING AND THE LOGIC OF THINGS (Ketner, ed.) 68–150; PHILOSOPHICAL WRITINGS OF PEIRCE (Buchler, ed.) 74–119.
[43] *See* MALLOY, LAW AND MARKET ECONOMY 29–36, 57–77.
[44] *Id.*   [45] *Id.*

of thirdness. Notice that we took our facts then referenced precedent and reached a conclusion. We might just as easily have proceeded by gathering basic rules on car accidents (legal precedents), as a mode of firstness, and then referencing our facts to these rules, in a mode of secondness, to reach our conclusion. Furthermore, in each instance the initial conclusions drawn, as a mode of thirdness, actually operate to focus and shape our consideration of the first.[46] Simply put, our initial conclusions lend guidance and further refinement to our interpretation process. They help us identify and justify which facts and which rules are most important for any given or particular purpose. In this way we are always refining and reading back into our analysis as we move between these modes. In other words, we do not have simple dualistic or binary relationships. We have integrated webs of triadic relationships.

In moving through these modes, we employ a number of semiotic devices. We make reference to logic, metaphor, analogy, and story.[47] We construct a beginning, middle, and an end as we tell the story of what happened on the fateful day when our client became involved in the car accident. We use metaphor when we explain how the rain falling on the road that day left the surface as slick as ice causing our client to lose control of the vehicle through no fault of her own. We use analogy when we explain how these road conditions and our client's response are just like the facts in an earlier case and that the court should therefore follow the decision of that earlier case. We are descriptive and persuasive in our narrative. We appeal to logic in setting up the premises of our case and ask others to follow us through to the logical and favorable conclusion we seek. We also employ references to a variety of other quasi- and non-legal sources such as statistics on car accidents, engineering and design information on cars and road intersections, insurance tables and costs. All of these devices rely for success upon our ability to master the skills of constructing persuasive arguments. This means that they rely upon our ability to understand and to shape the way in which others interpret the facts, the rules, and the contextual environment surrounding the accidental exchange involving our client.

More generally, we can create value as well as redistribute resources by inventing and transforming legal convention – by creating new

---

[46] It is the relationship between the modes of logic that is significant and not that a particular one must be first in the process of semiosis. SHERIFF, CHARLES PEIRCE'S GUESS AT THE RIDDLE 37–47; KEVELSON, LAW AS A SYSTEM OF SIGNS 253 (according to Peirce, anywhere is a place to begin).
[47] See MCCLOSKEY, RHETORIC OF ECONOMICS; MCCLOSKEY, IF YOU'RE SO SMART; BEYOND ECONOMIC MAN (Ferber & Nelson, eds.).

grammatical forms, styles of discourse, and representations of property. Developing cultural-interpretive skills, therefore, is important for anyone interested in being an effective lawyer or legal actor. In a world of diverse and multi-valued interpretive communities, one must be able to understand exchange with reference to multi-factor references and intermittent framing variables. It is no longer sufficient to simply rely on knowledge of traditional legal categories sounding in contract, property, or tort, for example. To be competent one must be able to understand the meanings and values of exchange from a variety of legal, market, and cultural positions.

Peirce's triadic theory of signs helps us to better understand these complex relationships. It also provides a useful method for understanding the way in which particular approaches to exchange facilitate more extensive, creative, equitable, and wealth-promoting relationships.

In a similar manner, semiotics helps us to understand better the strategic and representational function of legal concepts as cultural-interpretive signs. Consider, for example, the idea of property.[48] In semiotic terms, property is not a bundle of sticks – property is a representational sign referring to a particular web of exchange relationships. This distinction is important because property rights do not exist as independent sticks or objects of coherent investigation in the absence of an interpretive web of relational exchange.[49] The idea of property functions as a cultural-interpretive referent and operates to organize exchange relationships in accordance with particular conventionalized interpretive hierarchies. Property, in other words, organizes social status, defines power over semiotic space, and allocates resources according to conventionalized rules.[50]

---

[48] See, e.g., Kevelson, *Property as Rhetoric*; Williams, *The Rhetoric of Property*; Brion, *The Ethics of Property*.

[49] Law and market economy examines exchange systems, and the scientific method of inquiry used in semiotics to understand exchange systems reveals that they are like a "web" with indefinite boundaries. See PHILOSOPHICAL WRITINGS OF PEIRCE (Buchler, ed.) at xii. This is also a point raised in general chaos or complex systems theory. See KAUFFMAN, AT HOME IN THE UNIVERSE 270–87 (discussing co-evolving webs in complex systems). In studying these webs of exchange it is important to investigate and understand discourse across a number of conventionalized boundaries. See, KEVELSON, PEIRCE, SCIENCE, SIGNS 11, 63, 78, 109, 131; KEVELSON, PEIRCE'S ESTHETICS OF FREEDOM 27–28, 62–64.

[50] See generally, KEVELSON, LAW AS A SYSTEM OF SIGNS 181–93. "From this point of view, the legal idea of Property is taken as the name of the game of a certain set of moves and countermoves for the purpose of bringing about, or realizing, continually changing social-status significances," Kevelson, *Property as Rhetoric*, at 203. And significance is related

Property law, in a semiotic sense, functions in a representational capacity and allows us to deal with relationships in abstract terms. For instance, a leasehold estate and an interest in air rights are representational. Such property interests organize exchange relationships between owners, landlords, and tenants in the one case, and between surface, subsurface, and above-surface interests in the other case. These concepts tell us something about the characteristics of exchange and the infrastructure of exchange. They also inform us about the distribution of power, authority, and the allocation of resources between the parties to an exchange. A leasehold estate or an air right, however, is not something that one can physically put in a box and move. Leaseholds and air rights are representational signs that convey meanings and values about the relationships between people, places, and things.

Using Peirce's triadic approach, the physical object of property, a specific parcel of land, for instance, stands as a mode of firstness. In its physical sense the property is of quality and stands for itself as a specific item of property, and at the same time stands for and represents similar categories of property more generally. The abstract legal devices we create to represent interests in property, such as recordable deeds, leases, and air rights, are in a mode of secondness. These devices refer to the physical object in some way and allow us to capture and create value by enhancing our ability to use property as collateral and as an item of exchange. Thirdness involves the various meanings and values that can be generated from the legal conventions linking property to its various representative forms.

Understanding the function of representational signs in the process of exchange is important because it is central to an appreciation of the way in which ideas and categories evolve, and to the way in which they are borrowed and transferred between communities. The cultural-interpretive representation of a legal right is not, in other words, the same as the idea or the right itself. Consequently, understanding exchange and market economy as a human practice involves a communicative study of the networks and patterns of exchange. Furthermore, it involves an appreciation of the central function of indexical referents in shaping resource allocations. While there are numerous ways of working through the interpretive process of exchange, the point of law and market economy is that one needs to start by recognizing the semiotic connection between law,

to the *result* or consequences of the sign's relation to its final or ultimate interpretant. LISZKA, A GENERAL INTRODUCTION TO THE SEMEIOTIC OF CHARLES SANDERS PEIRCE 80.

markets and culture.[51] This is the key starting point for understanding exchange as a process of meaning and value formation, and of developing a multi-valued framework for imagining more extensive, participatory, equitable, and creative social arrangements. It is also the starting point for understanding the way in which institutions of language, communication, and interpretation can be used to create new value.

Moreover, semiotics informs us of the changing nature of *value* in social understanding. Value is not simply based on labor inputs or on consumer preferences: *value arises from the continuous expansion and transformation of ideas through exchange.* By informing us about exchange systems, semiotics reveals that all such systems involve a continuous process of substitution and permutation, and since, in a semiotic sense, there are no perfect substitutes, all substitutions or exchanges generate the potentiality of new meaning and new value.[52]

Thus, law and market economy investigates exchange because an understanding of the networks and patterns of exchange is important. Furthermore, exchange is not so much concerned with efficiency as it is with the idea of facilitating accessible, extensive, transparent, reciprocal, and participatory market and sign systems. In this regard, interventions or redistributions may be desirable in order to change or alter certain conventionalized networks and patterns of exchange. This may be an important element in dealing with people or groups that find that they are continually excluded from important market activities such as access to housing and mortgage markets. It may also be important for helping people "trapped" in intergenerational dependence on welfare, or in the criminal justice system. Problems of exclusion, intergenerational dependence on the welfare system, and involvement in the criminal justice system affect many people from all walks of life and all types of backgrounds. Mapping exchange relationships and using these maps as a starting point for law and public policy reform is important because it helps us develop a better assessment of the people and issues involved.

---

[51] *See, e.g.,* REPRESENTATION 1–2 (Stuart Hall, ed.).

[52] KEVELSON, PEIRCE'S ESTHETICS OF FREEDOM 8: "[B]ut even the mere repetition of a sign is a new sign which creates a new dimension of meaning that holds within itself a cumulative meaning and value of all that which preceded it and which it represents in each successive 'here and now,'" *id.* at 198. "[W]e cannot observe the same thing twice, and not only that we cannot observe a given thing exactly as someone else claims to observe it or can be shown to have observed it," KEVELSON, CHARLES S. PEIRCE'S METHOD OF METHODS 7. "[A] semiotic methodology will assume that a mark of a mark is not a 're-mark' but an Interpretant, or new potential subject," *id.* at 8.

In this approach to the relationship among law, markets, and culture, a primary function of law involves the mediation of conflicting claims to interpretive authority, and the objective of this mediation process is not so much one of achieving efficiency, or some abstract notion of justice, as it is to facilitate convergence toward the successful pursuit of common goals and purposes within and between competing interpretive communities. Understanding this mediation process also means appreciating the way in which legal actors create value through the development and transformation of cultural-interpretive frames and references.

Having provided a broad sketch of the general foundations for an interpretive framework on the relationship between law and market economy, this chapter proceeds by discussing some additional examples.

Some basic examples of mapping exchange relationships

Law and market economy positions the market as a place of meaning and value formation. It contends that choice involves a cultural-interpretive process, and that this process influences the generation and allocation of resources. To understand better the relationship among law, culture, and markets, law and market economy "maps" exchange relationships.

The mapping process involves the identification of basic exchange relationships with reference to Peirce's triadic approach.[53] This involves examining legal disputes from a variety of cultural-interpretive perspectives to gain a better "picture" or "map" of the contested facts and values. This approach can be used to examine problems of choice, two-party exchanges, multi-party exchanges, commons problems, Coase problems, public goods problems, agency, and externality problems, among others.[54]

To gain a better sense of this process, two introductory examples are discussed. The point is to stress the need for taking an exchange relationship apart to explore its constituent elements, and "map" alternative understandings. Peirce's triadic method is helpful here because it directs our

---

[53] Peirce was very interested in the idea of mapping. *See* KEVELSON, PEIRCE, SCIENCE, SIGNS 12–14. Peirce thinks of maps as attempts to represent our experiences of the real world – to present the real in ideational form, *id.* In an open-ended and dynamic universe these ideas or representations are always provisional and limited by the constraints over boundaries of the interpretive tools we use, *id.* at 1–42. Thus, our models and theories are by definition always partial, incomplete and provisional. In a logical and scientific community they are always open to revision, correction, and fallibility.

[54] *See, e.g.,* MALLOY, LAW AND MARKET ECONOMY 90–99 (Coase), 99–105 (public choice), 144–46 (efficient breach).

attention to the possibility of experiencing and understanding exchange in a variety of competing ways. Below, I present two specific exchanges for discussion: an exchange for sexual favors,[55] and an exchange involving automobile sales.[56]

First, however, I offer some simple "mapping" diagrams for thinking about the exchange relationship between a patient and her doctor. These simple diagrams are presented to illustrate a way of beginning to understand the mapping process. As one becomes more comfortable with the approach of this book, the diagramming will be more like map making in that it will reflect the drawer's deeper understanding of the alternative interpretive positioning represented by the diagrams.

To illustrate a way to approach the mapping process let us assume that we have a fact pattern involving some sort of liability or conflict issue between a patient and her doctor. As we examine the facts of the dispute we can set different frames and focus on a variety of reference points in addressing the situation. Some ways of diagramming the exchange are drawn below.

(1)   Patient ⟷ Doctor
                        (consumer)   (provider/seller)

In this mapping, the relationship is explored as a simple two-party exchange between a consumer and provider of a service. There is easy feedback between the two participants. We can do a legal and market analysis of the relationship looking only at variables relative to these two primary parties.

(2)   Patient ⟷ Doctor

                        Insurance co.

In sketch (2), we add a third party to the exchange relationship. Now the exchange recognizes that the patient pays premiums to an insurance company and the insurance company pays most of the doctor's bill. The patient typically pays only a small co-payment with each doctor visit. This is a more complicated exchange relationship because there is an indirect feedback loop between consumer and provider. The party paying most of the cost is not the one receiving the care. This reduces the power of the

[55] *Id.* at 140–41 (I develop this example in more detail here than in my earlier book).
[56] *Id.* at 40–41 (I develop this example in more detail here than in my earlier book).

consumer in the transaction. It also raises agency problems in that the insurance company and the doctor both act as agents for the patient in terms of working to determine what is best for her. The expanded map of the exchange relationship creates additional variables and references for both the legal and economic analysis of the relationship.

(3)

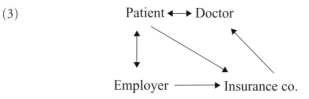

In sketch (3), the employer is introduced into the picture. In many cases a person has insurance as a result of an employment relationship. The employer contributes to the insurance cost in some proportion, and generally enters into a particular cost containment (saving) arrangement with the insurance company and the doctor/providers. The employer may enter into agreements that save money but that constrain and restrict patient choice. The insurance company may constrain or restrict doctor options, or create incentives and disincentives for particular procedures. The agency relationships become more complex, and the information and feedback loops become more problematic.

(4)

Sketch (4) is even more complex. It starts to include the public in recognition of the fact that certain costs of healthcare are covered by the public, and certain benefits of good health flow beyond the individual patient to the public. The diagram also adds the hospital and government regulators. Doctors have privileges and constraints in establishing a professional relationship with a hospital. Patients generally must go to hospitals where their doctors have privileges such that choice is again limited. Government regulators are also involved in the process as they administer programs and guidelines covering a number of healthcare matters. In this diagram the relationships are shown as more connected and multi-directional. This diagram could be expanded and made even more complex. The point is that the legal and market analysis changes as one develops a more complex set of exchange relationships to explore. Things that are cost effective or efficient in one framing of the relationship are not in another.

Similarly the assumptions about good information and voluntary exchange are more meaningful in one scenario than another.

In each of the above diagrams, additional mapping can be done, not only in terms of adding to the diagram but also in terms of situating the relationships within the diagram. For instance, the race, gender, class, income, or age of the patient or doctor may have some implication for the exchange relationship – for example, how they relate to each other or understand each other. The exchange, and the legal and market factors may also be different based on the position from which one views the situation. Thus, the viewpoint of the doctor may be very different than that of the employer, the hospital, and the government regulator, as well as from that of the patient. We must also consider the potential legal categories that might be raised with respect to each relationship in our mapping process. For example, some of the relationships may best be addressed under rules of professional responsibility, some under labor or employment law, some under contract law, some under agency principles, and some under tort law. Likewise, the relationships may be understood differently from an interpretive viewpoint within different approaches to understanding legal and market theory. For example, the relationship may be understood differently as between a neoclassical law and economics scholar and a critical race or critical feminist scholar.

To improve legal reasoning skills, one must work at expanding the number of ways in which to understand an exchange relationship. One must learn to imagine and to map alternative networks and patterns of exchange. Once a number of maps are worked out, the lawyer or legal actor must select a specific strategy from among the sets generated. The mapping strategy that best advances the interest of a client or a constituent should be selected. Then arguments must be developed to justify the various frames, references, and representations to be used.

The idea of mapping is that it draws attention to the complexity of the human practice of exchange. Market analysis helps us to better understand this complexity. It also gives us a way of discussing the relationship and analyzing responses to tensions within the system. Because the potential approaches to the problem are many, however, economics is not going to provide a simple calculus for resolving disputes.

The role of the lawyer, in this process, involves gaining a sound and well-developed understanding of the exchange relationship and of the dispute at hand. The lawyer needs to understand the market context of the relationship and must develop multiple frames of analysis. The lawyer must then identify a set of potentially good resolutions to the problem.

In the end, economics can assist in this process but the lawyer (judge or other legal actor) must make a normative judgment about the best course of action. This judgment must then be supportable and justifiable within a reasonable and recognizable discourse of jurisprudence. This jurisprudence now includes a variety of economic concepts that have been recognized as useful and authoritative. This book prepares the reader to use and understand these concepts so that they can be used effectively in advancing the interests of clients and of the public.

Two examples

In this section I provide two narrative examples to illustrate some basic framing and referencing problems. The key is to appreciate the flexibility of both the economic and legal analysis when examining law in a market context.

Example (1): sexual favors

Let us consider the question of legalizing transactions for sexual favors.[57] More specifically, consider the idea of legalizing prostitution. At first glance, the exchange itself, as a mode of firstness, seems to be a simple two-party exchange, but we can quickly show how it becomes more complex when we seek a better understanding of the exchange relationship by applying different frames, references, and representations as a mode of secondness, to the facts.

If we address our inquiry to only the immediate parties to the transaction, we might conclude that the seemingly voluntary and consensual nature of the exchange of money for sexual services is a wealth-maximizing move. Under such a scenario, an efficiency-driven legal economist, as a mode of thirdness, might argue for the legalization of prostitution. If, on the other hand, we change the frame of our investigation and look at the way in which these activities affect third parties, we might reach a different conclusion.

Assume that we include estimates of the "cost" impacts of this activity on the families and friends of the participants, the communities they live in, and the potential for extended health-related consequences across multiple communities. By including these third-party costs we change our efficiency calculations and, thus, we might reach a different set of

---

[57] *See also* MALLOY, LAW AND MARKET ECONOMY 140–41 (the example here is more developed than in my earlier book).

conclusions. Thus, the way in which we frame an exchange relationship raises the problem of what and whom to count. Should we even worry about accounting for externalities, and if we do, then how should we decide on where to draw the line between impacts that count and those we deem too far removed from the transaction to be relevant? Depending upon how we chose to define the relevant frame of exchange, as a two-party or multi-party transaction, our conclusions will vary even if we profess a desire to operate at the most efficient point.

Still further problems can be raised when we consider alternative ways to measure the third-party impacts of these exchanges. How should we quantify such things as health, and emotional, esthetic, and family values, for instance? Slight variations in pricing estimates, or in assessing distributive implications, may lead to significantly different outcomes.

Similarly, we can introduce additional referencing problems when we consider the position of each party to our investigation. Perhaps the market under investigation reveals that actions of the parties are not based on consent. Maybe there is historical, cultural, or institutional bias in the exchange, or some personal considerations that result in the woman feeling compelled to participate. Seen from the reference point of the woman, this transaction may have very different dynamics from those presumed under an assumption of rational consent theory. A change in referencing might, once again, change our conclusion.

An important point here is to appreciate the power of being able to influence the interpretive frames, references, and representations applied in an indexical mode of secondness, as used to analyze this exchange relationship. The authority to set the legally applied frames, references, and representations can determine the meaning and value of the exchange. For example, from a male-centered point of view, the transaction might be considered consensual, but from a female-centered point of view, it may be viewed as socially coerced. Likewise, viewed as a two-party voluntary exchange it might be considered efficient, but viewed in terms of third-party costs and externalities, it might be considered otherwise. Furthermore, these alternative references may be grounded in potentially contestable ideas with respect to the meaning of "appropriate" female sexual behavior or "family values," and externalities may be positive or negative.

In a complex system like the market exchange process, alternative frames, references, and representations reveal degrees of freedom and suggest, as illustrated above, a number of potential transactional influences. Consequently, we need to focus more attention on the dynamic nature of the networks and patterns of exchange that are being observed. We need to develop a better understanding, for example, of the way in which men, women, families, and communities interact. We need to transform our point of reference from one of concern for calculating economic efficiency to one that investigates the nature, scope, dynamics, and consequences of particular exchange relationships.

We need, in other words, to inquire as to the manner in which prostitution affects the social and market exchange *process* and not merely as to the efficiency of making it legal. We also need to ask about other ways of understanding these exchange relationships, and the ways in which they can best advance positive ethical and esthetic values. This involves a process of mapping – a process of seeking to understand the exchange relationship from multiple frames, references, and representations, as illustrated in the above example. This process facilitates a better basis for pragmatic and informed decision making than one that is focused on a calculus of wealth maximization.

Example (2): car sales

As a second example, let us consider the market for automobile sales.[58] This example also illustrates the use of shifting interpretive frames and references. First, assume that we have collected basic data about the market for automobile sales – a mode of firstness. Our data indicate that product offerings are essentially the same across brands, prices for similar products by different manufacturers are close to identical, and purchase or lease terms are virtually the same. The raw data that has been collected makes up a Peircean mode of firstness – it is basic information about the nature of the thing or product itself. In the process of interpreting the data so that we can draw a conclusion or response, we frame our investigation and make a reference to an interpretive or indexical mediator which functions as a Peircean mode of secondness. The mediating point of interpretive reference is important because it shapes our economic and legal conclusion in a mode of thirdness. For instance, if one reviews the data through a "Chicago School" lens of neoclassical economics he may very well conclude that the data reveals the presence of a perfectly competitive market. In such a market, no seller has the power to set terms but must, instead, take its terms from the marketplace, and as a consequence we would expect to find close similarity between product lines, prices, and sales terms. Such a competitive market makes the consumer the "king" or "queen" while the producer acts as servant. The conclusion, as to the meaning of the data, functions as a Peircean mode of thirdness and

---

[58] *Id.* at 40–41(this example is better developed than the one in my earlier book).

further informs our interpretation of the market as we use it to re-examine the data in light of our newly achieved understanding.

Now, to better understand this process, imagine reviewing the data through an alternative interpretive frames, references, and representations. From the point of view of some positions in critical theory, for example, one might conclude that the data reveal strong corporate power in a market where sellers band together to set terms of exchange in a way that leaves the consumer helpless. The signs of uniformity between products, prices, and terms, are interpreted as evidence of market power rather than as indications of market constraints. In other words, rather than concluding that there is a competitive market, one might readily conclude just the opposite.

Interpretation of the data, in a mode of thirdness, is important because our conclusions about the meaning of the exchange process will implicate particular responses. If we believe, for instance, the Chicago School interpretation, we have no need for concern because we have a voluntary and consensual exchange process in which consumers are protected by competition. In such a setting, consumers receive exactly what they want. Therefore, we would reject any proposed intrusion by government into the marketplace. On the other hand, if we reach the opposite conclusion based upon the use of an alternative interpretive frame or reference, we may advocate a need for government regulation to protect consumers and to break up the power of corporate dominance in the marketplace. Importantly, the point is that the facts themselves (the raw data as a mode of firstness) tell us little without the mediation of those facts through an interpretive frame and reference (a mode of secondness). The conclusions drawn from this indexical mediation process function as a mode of thirdness and implicate a course of action or inaction. They also serve as a "touch stone" for further investigation and analysis of the "facts." In this way, they effect the continuity of semiosis in moving from firstness to secondness and thirdness, and back to firstness in an on-going process. Moreover, we see that the conclusions reached in the mode of thirdness shape and influence the allocation of resources between producers and consumers.

The point of this example is not to show the real world of exchange as unknowable or completely indeterminate. It is to illustrate the process of mapping the exchange relationship, and to show that people positioned in alternative interpretive communities use different interpretive frames and references. Thus, different people understand the world in different and sometimes conflicting ways. Therefore, we must be aware of a variety of cultural-interpretive perspectives as they influence the direction of law and social policy. Consequently, we must understand the relationship between law, markets, and culture, and we must realize that by shifting interpretive perspectives we can alter authoritative influence over the interpretation process. Furthermore, we must appreciate the need to develop and address comparative sources of information that will advance legal mediation of conflicts between people situated in competing interpretive communities.

Clarifying the cultural-interpretive approach

Beyond clarifying some basic semiotic terms and concepts, there are two main objectives to this part of the chapter. The first objective involves explaining Peirce's understanding of meaning in the relationship between the real world of exchange and the cultural-interpretive signs we use to understand the real. This involves a discussion of exchange and of the limits of interpretation. This is important because it helps clarify the extent to which there are subjective and objective elements involved in understanding law in a market context. In challenging the objectivity of applying economics to law, for instance, I am not arguing that law is hopelessly subjective and indeterminate, or that law is merely the product of social construction. The relationship is more complex. The discussion of this relationship involves an examination of Peirce's idea of *abductive logic* and *speculative rhetoric*.[59] The second objective of this part of the chapter involves an examination of the normative foundation for using market concepts in legal reasoning. The focus of this discussion is on explaining that the use of economics in law does not eliminate the need for normative decision making. In this discussion, particular reference is made to Peirce's idea of the normative sciences, including esthetics, ethics, and logic.

Exchange and the limits of interpretation

In this section I clarify the use of cultural-interpretation theory in understanding law in a market context. To a certain extent some readers may misunderstand the framework developed in this chapter by thinking that it challenges the objectivity of an economic analysis of law for the purpose of replacing it with a subjective model of social construction. This is not the argument. As will be explained, the argument is one that is based on a dynamic relationship between objectivity and subjectivity. Both

---

[59] *See* Liszka, A General Introduction to the Semeiotic of Charles Sanders Peirce 53–77; Peirce Vol. II, 299 (abduction described).

are simultaneously present in the relationship among law, markets, and culture.

In order to understand better this idea we need a more detailed discussion of social meaning in exchange. According to Peircean semiotics social meaning in the exchange process emerges out of an original state of chaos or indeterminacy.[60] This is a state of pure chance, nothingness, or ambiguity that becomes real with the emergence of a habit and the formation of a pattern(s) of regularity.[61] The tendency toward habit and pattern formation is normal according to Peirce and, thus, potentiality always gives rise to an actuality.[62]

In market theory we can see this connection when we think in terms of simple cost and benefit analysis.[63] From the chaotic activities of numerous independent market actors emerges a set of patterns that formulates a habit and results in a temporary equilibrium.[64] The information provided by the equilibrium is useful and influential in thinking about extending the meaning/consequences of that relationship to the next exchange. Current prices influence, or inform, thinking about alternative investment trade offs, for instance. At the same time, new information is constantly emerging in the marketplace and chance, surprise and other factors all play a part in destabilizing the observed equilibrium. As a consequence, a new pattern emerges and a new equilibrium is located. This new equilibrium once again provides meaning for market actors and once again stands ready for revision in the dynamic interplay between conventionalized regularity and chaotic indeterminacy. The same process happens in law. The common law, for example, with its case-by-case analysis continually revises the meaning of legal rules. Continuity is preserved by reference

---

[60] SHERIFF, PEIRCE'S GUESS AT THE RIDDLE 8–16.

[61] Id.; KAUFFMAN, AT HOME IN THE UNIVERSE 277–79. (Complex systems have a tendency to move from chaos to sets, patterns, habits, redundancy, and replication. This tendency is similar to that ascribed to Peirce's theory of signs.)

[62] SHERIFF, PEIRCE'S GUESS AT THE RIDDLE, "The possibility evokes the actuality," id. at 9.

[63] MALLOY, LAW AND MARKET ECONOMY 29–42.

[64] SHERIFF, PEIRCE'S GUESS AT THE RIDDLE 9–59. Also note how this idea of a pattern arising out of chaos corresponds to chaos theory (see GLEICK, CHAOS; KAUFFMAN, AT HOME IN THE UNIVERSE); and it corresponds to Hayek's theory of spontaneous social order. KEVELSON, LAW AS A SYSTEM OF SIGNS 167–92. ("The freedom to interpret and reinterpret leading principles is antithetical to closed societies, but such indeterminate review constitutes the basis of a free marketplace, in the context of what Hayek refers to as the 'spontaneous order' of the open society," id. at 168.) HAYEK, LAW, LEGISLATION, AND LIBERTY, VOL. 1, 35–54 (discussing spontaneous social order related to law and social cooperation); MALLOY, PLANNING FOR SERFDOM 1–60 (general rules and spontaneous social order with reference to Hayek).

to precedent and legal doctrine, yet endlessly variable fact patterns give rise to constant extensions and revisions of meaning.[65] Chance and indeterminacy work toward diversity and freedom, while regularity and habit work toward continuity and convention.[66] The synthesis of these states, or modes of being, results in the continuous creation and recreation of meanings and values in an infinite process of referential and substitutional exchange.

This continuous synthesis is referred to as the process of *semiosis* and it is present in all systems of exchange:

> Since every sign creates an interpretant which in turn is the representamen of a second sign, semiosis results in a series of successive interpretants *ad infinitum*. There is no "first" nor "last" sign in this process of unlimited semiosis . . . thinking always proceeds in the form of dialogue . . . every thought must adhere itself to some other . . . this endless series is essentially a *potential* one. Peirce's point is that any actual interpretant of a given sign *can* theoretically be interpreted in some further sign, and that in another without any necessary end being reached. The exigencies of practical life inevitably cut short such potentially endless development.[67]

Importantly, depending upon the point of inquiry, the positional designation of firstness, secondness, and thirdness may change or shift:

> [T]herefore a part of every thought continues in the succeeding thoughts. Every sign is interpreted by a subsequent sign or thought in which the-relation-of-the-sign-to- its-object becomes the object of the new sign. Not only does a sign refer to a subsequent thought-sign that interprets it, it also stands *for* some object through a previous thought-sign . . . Meaning, then, lies not in what is actually thought [immediately present], but in what this thought may be connected with in representation by subsequent thoughts; so that the meaning of a thought is altogether something virtual. Meaning exists only as the dynamic relation of signs. To the degree that life has meaning, it is a train of thought.[68]

---

[65] *See generally*, GLEICK, CHAOS 140 (complex systems raise the prospect of infinite points of possibility within a limited space).

[66] SHERIFF, PEIRCE'S GUESS AT THE RIDDLE 9.

[67] NOTH, HANDBOOK ON SEMIOTICS 43 (defining the idea of unlimited semiosis).

[68] SHERIFF, PEIRCE'S GUESS AT THE RIDDLE 37, 33–47. Eco provides a similar interpretation of Peirce. *See, e.g.*, ECO, LIMITS OF INTERPRETATION 60, 28–30:
> The idea of interpretation requires that a "piece" of ordinary language be used as the "interpretant" (in a Peircean sense) of another "piece" of ordinary language. When one says that/man/means "human male adult," one is interpreting ordinary language through ordinary language, and the second sign is the interpretant of the first one, as well as the first can become interpretant of the second. (*Id.* at 60.)

In the simplest of terms, this idea can be expressed with reference to the age-old question of the chicken and the egg. As such, one might understand this semiotic approach as not so much concerned with determining whether the chicken or the egg came first but rather with investigating the relationship between chickens and eggs in an on-going process of evolutionary change.

Focusing on dynamic relationships over time, however, does not mean that meanings and values are completely indeterminate. For example, Umberto Eco explains that Peirce's idea of unlimited semiosis does not mean that there are unlimited meanings to a text or a sign.[69] While there are multiple ways to interpret a sign it does not follow that a sign or a text can mean anything a reader wants it to mean.[70] To a certain extent signs, like texts, are anchored in convention, and the community constrains the individual's ability to interpret meaning.[71]

This point is also discussed by Carl R. Hausman. Hausman explains that Peirce was not a radical anti-realist.[72] Peirce offered a theory of a dynamic process but the process was not completely subjective nor was it simply the product of social construction. According to Hausman, Peirce believed in real dynamical objects that existed independently of our opinion about them. Peirce, he argues, was concerned with a search for an external permanency that was discoverable in the reality of science.[73]

In making his argument Hausman suggests that Peirce was a *pragmatic evolutionary realist.*[74] By this term he means that Peirce was committed to a belief in an independent reality as a semiotic sign or cultural-interpretive idea, but he also understood that this reality was itself dynamic and evolutionary, and thus unattainable.[75] The idea of the real, however, is important. This is because the idea of the real constrains us even if it is dynamic and evolutionary. Likewise, the idea of the real causes us to question and doubt our theories, models, and interpretive frames, references, and representations as we continually measure our own experiences against various interpretive conventions. We come to doubt, for instance,

---

[69] Eco explains that Peirce's idea of unlimited semiosis does not mean that there are unlimited meanings of a text or a sign, ECO, LIMITS OF INTERPRETATION 57. Peirce's semiosis is constrained by a community of inquirers and a final judgment of meaning emerges as habit or convention, *id.* at 37–42. There is an objective meaning in a contextual, fallible, dynamic and revisionary sense, *id.* Unlimited semiosis is not, therefore, the same as hermetic drift, *id.* at 27–32. Unlimited semiosis means that there are multiple ways to *read* a text but *not* that a text can mean anything a reader wants it to mean, *id.* at 148–49.

[70] *Id. See also* ESSENTIAL PEIRCE VOL. 1, at 63.   [71] *See supra* n. 69.

[72] *See* HAUSMAN, CHARLES S. PEIRCE'S EVOLUTIONARY PHILOSOPHY 194–225.

[73] *See id.* at 140–225.   [74] *See id.* at 140–225.   [75] *Id.* at 194–224.

theories of rational choice, or theories of creationism when our experiences diverge from the expectations generated by these conventionalized beliefs – our experiential encounter with the factual world (firstness), diverges from the expectations of our indexical reference (secondness), and causes us to have doubt (thirdness). This doubt creates *semiotic resistance* to conventionality and leads us to revise our current conventions (conclusions and ways of thinking and reasoning).[76]

In seeking to mediate this semiotic resistance (or cultural-interpretive dissonance), we engage in a form of reasoning that Peirce identified as *abductive reasoning* or *speculative rhetoric or logic*.[77] Abductive reasoning involves the development of new theories and explanations in an effort to mediate resistance and reclaim convergence between our experience of the real and our semiotic representation of the real.[78]

Hausman offers an example to help explain this idea. In the example, Hausman makes reference to C. G. Prado in explaining the idea of a reality independent of language.[79] He does this to explain Peirce in relation to radical anti-realists.[80] The point is to explain that while language may

---

[76] Charles Sanders Peirce believed that our experience with doubt, inquiry, and interactive exchange in community could cause a shift in view and reframe our interpretive reference points or *ground*. *See* HOOKWAY, PEIRCE 119–25 (experience as a subjective ground); PHILOSOPHICAL WRITINGS OF PEIRCE (Buchler, ed.), at 8–12 (on shifting views); ESSENTIAL PEIRCE VOL. II, at 336 (doubt is the starting point for critical inquiry). *See also*, LISZKA, A GENERAL INTRODUCTION TO THE SEMEIOTIC OF CHARLES SANDERS PEIRCE 53–77; HAUSMAN, CHARLES S. PEIRCE'S EVOLUTIONARY PHILOSOPHY 194–225.

[77] *See* LISZKA, A GENERAL INTRODUCTION TO THE SEMEIOTIC OF CHARLES SANDERS PEIRCE.

[78] Market theory stands in reference to, as an interpretive sign of, the real world but it is not, itself, real. "Ultimately we do not know this phenomenal world of which we are part. But we do know or are capable of knowing that which we construct as a means of knowing better and more fully the unknowable, ever changing circumstances of existence," KEVELSON, LAW AS A SYSTEM OF SIGNS 269. In this respect the market, as idea, stands as a referential mode of secondness. It helps us to interpret the real world that *is*, in all its evolving potentiality, which is positioned as a mode of firstness. The conclusions and meanings to be drawn from this relationship are, in the process of semiosis, a mode of thirdness. *See also* HAYAKAWA & HAYAKAWA, LANGUAGE IN THOUGHT AND ACTION 13–21. Likewise, our market models and theories are symbols and sign systems *of* but are not the real social/market exchange process. Adam Smith made a similar observation with his metaphor of a clock. *See* MALLOY, LAW AND MARKET ECONOMY 41–42. Adam Smith describes the face of the clock as attracting our attention but its internal structure remains hidden, remains invisible and the subject of speculation, *id*. This he said was also true of the universe in general, *id*. My point is similar.

[79] *See* HAUSMAN, CHARLES S. PEIRCE'S EVOLUTIONARY PHILOSOPHY 198–200.

[80] *Id*. at 140–225.

not be able to fully capture the real, and may constrain our ability to understand the real, it does not follow, in a Peircean sense, that there is no real beyond our language or opinion. As applied to understanding law in a market context, this means that while using economics does not make law objective, the lack of complete objectivity does not make law entirely subjective and indeterminate.

This point is important because it tells us that even if our models, theories, and representations of the market are incomplete, partial, or problematic, they are not useless. Similarly, the idea that we can take deliberative and thoughtful action to influence the market exchange process does not mean that the market can simply take any form or meaning that we desire. The market is neither the purely subjective and biased construction of social organization as suggested by some critical theorists, nor is it the objective, neutral, and scientific process seemingly suggested by some traditional advocates of law and economics. There is both regularity and irregularity in a complex system such as the market. Reaching a deeper understanding of these relationships requires us to move beyond simplistic binary approaches. Interpretation theory, and the relationship among law, markets, and culture are not simply objective or subjective. In a Peircean sense, they are simultaneously subjective *and* objective. There is a dynamic synthesis between the objective and the subjective that reveals itself in a "third" – a synthesis of the two.

Turning to Hausman's example, he explains:

> In explaining the "linguistic turn" in philosophy, C. G. Prado argues that the pre-Copernican seamen who found that they did not fall off the earth where its flat surface was supposed to end could have revised the way they were willing to talk and believe. And they could have continued to insist that the world is flat if they had "readjusted their beliefs to allow for odd events" . . . It must be kept in mind, however, that the initial condition that supposedly prompted the seamen to change or adjust their ways of speaking was not itself a change in the language, or in belief. The initial condition that they encountered was expressed as a resistance to their accepted language and belief. It was a resistance to expectations. The initial condition of their resistance was not language, even if its interpretation takes place in inescapable language or vocabularies. The seamen would have found it increasingly difficult to stick by their adjusted beliefs as they gained more experience. Their adjustments would not have been arbitrary.
>
> The constraints given with resistances (the surprises and discoveries) do not guarantee that specific sentences are true or false, although they do function negatively to prompt the abandonment or modification of what were regarded as "true," or as justifiable and acceptable. What such constraints do is prompt

changes that bring about evolution in thinking and language. What justifies the kind of changes is continued growing agreement, or at least the expectation that if the changes seem to be anomalies, they will eventually be reconciled – in future situations in which networks of beliefs or sentences fit together.[81]

Hausman's example of the relationship between experience and constraint has useful applications for taking an interpretive turn in understanding law in a market context. It helps us appreciate the constraints of law (conventionalized rules and standards, for example) and the relationship between these constraints and our experiences. It provides a framework for understanding the importance of addressing the way in which people, as social beings, experience the relationship among law, markets, and culture. These experiences are important because they can confirm or undermine the normative foundation of law and of market economy. These experiences inform the contested meaning of markets and of law in a market context.

Hausman's example also implies that the market is an idea open to deliberate and thoughtful influence while being simultaneously constrained by real boundaries – boundaries that are more than mere social constructions. In working through the mapping of exchange, as discussed in the earlier part of the chapter, law in a market context affirms a need to take an interpretive turn away from the "objective" and "heroic spectator" view of traditional economic approaches to law and market theory. At the same time it acknowledges a constraint on individual and communal subjectivity.[82] Consequently, market relationships can be viewed from a variety of perspectives and subject to alternative frames, references, and representations, but the meanings and values of these relationships are not purely self-referencing, nor are they without an anchor in the real world.

The normative sciences of esthetics, ethics, and logic

In this section I further clarify the relationship between subjectivity and objectivity in understanding law in a market context. I explain, with

---

[81] *Id.* at 199.
[82] *See* HAUSMAN, CHARLES S. PEIRCE'S EVOLUTIONARY PHILOSOPHY 224:
Peirce's picture recognizes what is vital to those who have taken the linguistic turn . . . It affirms the need to turn away from a spectator view, but without abandoning something valuable in that view: the acknowledgment of constraints on our communal and individual habits, constraints that "we" do not make. (*Id.* at 224.)

reference to Peirce's idea of the normative sciences, that economics can not eliminate the normative aspects of law and legal reasoning. Some people may wish for law to be transformed into a legal science by addition of economic analysis, but this is not possible. Economics and market theory can help us reach a deeper understanding of law and legal institutions but they can not spare us from the very real and important task of exercising our normative judgment.

Interpretation theory can help us understand the limitations of using economic "science" to solve complex socio-legal problems. The problem is that the market exchange process can not be fully captured by an economic calculus. More importantly, while economics may provide a useful logic for promoting a particular end, it is ill-equipped to address, in the first instance, fundamental questions of framing, referencing, and representation. Selecting the appropriate interpretive frames, references, and representations involves normative analysis outside of the scope of traditional neoclassical economics. Questions of interpretive framing, referencing, and representation are normative ones that come within Peirce's idea of the relationship between esthetics, ethics, and logic.[83] Therefore, this section of the chapter provides a brief definition of Peirce's use of the terms esthetics, ethics, and logic. It then explains the relationship between these concepts and the idea of understanding law in a market context.

Peirce developed a theory for normative analysis making reference to the traditionally recognized categories of esthetics, ethics, and logic.[84] The meaning Peirce ascribed to these categories was not completely traditional.[85] For Peirce, *esthetics* was not to be understood in terms of beauty because the beautiful and the ugly were categories within esthetics.[86] Instead, esthetics has to do with establishing the criteria and process for determining that something is either beautiful or ugly.[87]

In the framework of understanding law in a market context esthetics involves the process by which meanings and values are formed and reformed in the clash between people positioned in different cultural-interpretive communities. While specific outcomes may be judged by

---

[83] POTTER, NORMS & IDEALS; ESSENTIAL PEIRCE VOL. II, at 196–207 (discussing the normative sciences as including esthetics, ethics, and logic).

[84] POTTER, NORMS & IDEALS 8–51. In Peirce's triadic theory of signs esthetics is of feelings and is a mode of firstness; ethics is of action and is a mode of secondness; logic is of thought and is a mode of thirdness, *id.* at 19.

[85] *Id.* at 31–46. Peirce used these terms because they were close enough to what he wanted to discuss and it was useful in terms of directing the attention of his audience, *id.* at 31.

[86] *Id.* at 32–33.   [87] *Id.*

conflicting standards as between these cultural-interpretive communities, a Peircean approach would favor a process of open inquiry and exchange. This would be an esthetic of cultural-interpretive, or semiotic, democracy wherein the sign making process – the continuous production and extension of meanings and values – is accessible to a wide variety of people and groups.

In a similar way, Peirce did not believe that *ethics* was about what is right.[88] He thought of ethics in terms of the criteria for determining that one's aims were directed at the accomplishment of an esthetic end, or objective.[89] In the framework of law in a market context, ethical action involves the deliberate selection and justification of a particular conclusion. It involves the justification of a given set of frames, references, and representations used to advance a particular conclusion and course of action.

Finally, for Peirce, *logic* involved thinking as a deliberate activity, and this activity was directed at evaluating ways to achieve an end – an end that is admirable.[90] Thus, in our context, logic concerns the process of working through the various maps and alternative patterns of argument that might be available for defining and addressing a given exchange relationship.

This process can be directly related to the idea of understanding law in a market context. At the outset, esthetics is involved in questioning the process used to establish and conventionalize a particular cultural-interpretive hierarchy. Normative justifications must also be identified to support or challenge the conventionalized patterns of framing, referencing, and representing. And, with expanding networks of exchange and trade (including globalization), the legal system must be able to mediate between people positioned in a variety of cultural-interpretive communities. In this context the esthetic argument is designed to persuade us to support or reject the major value choices that underlie a given form of social organization – ethical argument does this with respect to the means of achieving our esthetic objective, and logical argument does this with respect to our definition and examination of the exchange relationship.

An example

The use of the normative sciences (just discussed) and the limitations on interpretation (as discussed in the earlier section) can each be made more understandable with an example. Therefore, let us assume that we work in

---

[88] *Id.* at 31–34.   [89] *Id.*   [90] *Id.* at 32–41.

a large hotel. Imagine that we have been instructed by the hotel manager to prepare a large ballroom for a meeting that will be taking place later in the day.[91] We are instructed to go to the room, examine the various pieces of furniture, and to arrange the room in the most efficient manner. When we get to the room we are confronted with a space of a given size and shape, with particular lighting fixtures, and other characteristics. We also take note of a variety of furniture, including chairs and tables of various styles and shapes. The physical characteristics of the room can not be changed (size, shape, etc.) and we are instructed that none of the furniture can be taken from the room.

In this situation, the nature and characteristics of the room and the furniture operate as constraints on the ways in which the room can be arranged. In other words, there are real-world constraints to the way we can "socially construct" the relationships within this particular room.[92] At the same time, however, there are also numerous ways in which we might exercise some influence over relationships in the room by virtue of our authority to re-arrange the furniture. The arrangement of the furniture by itself may signal important meanings, as in identifying important people with a head table, or it might shape conversation or influence physical movement based on the spacing we use around and between tables. An important problem from the outset, however, involves our ability to determine the most efficient arrangement of the furniture in the absence of a predetermined use for the room. If the room is to be used for a lecture we may want to arrange a head table or podium with all the other tables and chairs, facing the "front." If, on the other hand, the room is to be used for a round-table discussion, or for a job fair, we might arrange the room differently. Likewise, if the room will be used for dancing we will need to push tables and chairs to the side so that ample space can be left open for the activity. In short, the idea of efficiency can be ambiguous in the absence of a predetermined goal or objective.

Once we are clear about the use of the room, we can begin to make progress at identifying plausibly good alternatives for arranging the room in a useful way – or, in other words, once a normative decision is made

---

[91] See MALLOY, LAW AND MARKET ECONOMY 147–48 (in this article I use a much more developed version of the example); DEELY, BASICS OF SEMIOTICS 42 (using a home furnishings example to discuss semiotic relationships signaling different meanings even as the contents of the room remain constant).

[92] This is an illustration of the idea behind Peirce's theory of speculative rhetoric. Interpretation is a dynamic process yet it is constrained by the real world. In other words, the world is not simply the product of social construction.

with respect to our given objective we can then seek to achieve that goal in a more cost effective manner.

Relating to our earlier discussion, the physical constraints of the room are like the real-world constraints in Hausman's example. Even with these physical constraints, however, there is still an opportunity to influence the organization of the room. Within these constraints there are probably several good ways of setting up the room for any particular purpose. While some of the arrangements might be awkward or inappropriate, it is quite possible that several different arrangements could be equally suitable. Experience and experimentation will help in the decision making process – they may also trigger ideas for the future construction of different types of rooms.

This example can also be related to our discussion of the normative sciences. For example, esthetics guides our normative determination and justification of the use of the room – including the process by which these determinations are made. Logic helps in mapping out the alternative ways to arrange the room for the given purpose. Ethics is involved in selecting a particular arrangement from the various options available.

The problem of arranging furniture in our hypothetical room is, of course, a metaphor for law. In the real world of human interaction and exchange there are always numerous "rooms" to arrange. In seeking to arrange these rooms we are constrained by convention and by physical limitations, yet we must not be misled into thinking that we have no power to influence the understanding of these rooms and their contents. We can influence these understandings and facilitate favorable arrangements (outcomes) by carefully and strategically using market concepts in legal reasoning. To do this, we need to understand economic terms and concepts while appreciating their primary semiotic function as elements of secondness in the structure of legal argument – we need to understand them as tools for advancing particular ends, and not as ends in themselves.

Therefore, the point of this example is that it illustrates the need to exercise normative judgment when integrating economic terms and concepts into law. Without normative decision making in the first instance (deciding on how to use the room), we can not make sense of the request to arrange the room in the most efficient way. Similarly, in the real world, economics does not provide law with an objective calculus capable of freeing us from the challenge and opportunity of exercising normative judgment. Economics can help illuminate the constraints that we confront, and it can help us develop useful maps of potentially good courses of action. Economics can not help us identify the optimal course of action, but it can help us understand problems in new ways and provide us with a useful "language" for analysis.[93] Moreover, economics does not make law purely objective, and it does not substitute for more traditional jurisprudential reasoning. Consequently, while there are limitations to our ability to shape specific outcomes (there are problems of scarcity, for example), there is still plenty of room to "arrange" law and legal institutions to advance particular normative values – even when economic analysis is incorporated into legal reasoning.

An outline of basic tools

Up until this point, the book has generalized about the idea of using frames, references, and representations in understanding law in a market context. It is now time to be more specific so that a set of "tools" can be assembled for practicing the process of mapping, and the process of developing better legal reasoning skills. Thus, this section of the chapter is designed to offer a way to categorize and characterize elements of legal argument for understanding law in a market context.

As with any attempt to outline or identify particular tools for legal analysis and reasoning, this list is not offered as complete or definitive. Instead, this list is offered as a helpful starting point for organizing the many ideas and concepts to be developed in the remaining chapters of the book. I have found that these tools have been very helpful for people unfamiliar with doing the complex interdisciplinary work of law and market economy. This work requires one to become familiar with work in the fields of law, economics, and culture. It also requires one to deal with interpretation theory. Therefore, this basic outline of "tools" is offered to assist the reader in going from the materials covered up to this point to the materials in the remaining pages of the book.

The primary purpose of these tools is to provide a useful mechanism for approaching legal analysis. For example, one should read a case decision, law review article, or other work and think about the framing of the legal question and the types of references and representations used in developing the line of argument offered to support the conclusion. This should be coupled with use of the three-step process identified in figure 3.3, earlier

---

[93] *See* MALLOY, LAW AND MARKET ECONOMY 137–48. *See generally,* KAUFFMAN, AT HOME IN THE UNIVERSE 248–62, 268–69. It is impossible to optimize a course of action in a complex system – one can only hope to make a reasonable compromise within a wide range of constraints, *id.* at 268–69.

in the chapter – first, identify the basic facts of the exchange relationship; second, identify the organizing patterns of socio-legal argument; and third, identify the justifications offered to support the conclusions.

The outline presented here includes frames, references, and representations.[94] I explain what I mean to include in each of these categories and provide the reader with a general indication of the location in the book where particular ideas are covered more specifically.

Frames

In analyzing and developing legal arguments it is helpful to think in terms of several types of frames. This outline breaks framing devices into two groups. These groups include general market frames and paradigmatic market frames.

General market frames

General market framing devices are used to set the basic market context of transactional or exchange analysis. These frames focus attention on the costs and benefits of legal action. They direct our attention to the economic consequences of law and legal institutions while simultaneously indicating the market constraints on law and legal institutions. There are two types of general market frames: scaling frames, and cost and benefit frames.

Scaling (chapter 4)   Scaling frames involve setting the scope of the exchange. In general, this means setting a focus on either a two-party exchange or some form of a multi-party exchange. Scaling can be thought of as similar to the work of a photographer in selecting the appropriate lens and setting for a picture. A zoom lens highlights the individuals, or the two primary parties to an exchange, whereas a wide-angle lens includes third parties, externalities, and a broader community context. Changing the lens, or the scale, brings different information into view. By changing the scale of an exchange relationship, one can influence the meanings and values of the relationships.

---

[94] I am aware of the fact that scholars of interpretation theory may find the distinctions between frames, references, and representations to be ambiguous but I have found that these distinctions are very useful for introducing people to the approach of this book. Users of the book can also add to or modify these "tools" in such a way as to more directly integrate their own ideas about alternative frames and references that can be generated using different political, ideological, or theoretical schools of thought.

Cost and benefit analysis (chapter 5)   This framing requires law and legislation to account for economic and market consequences. In evaluating a particular legal action or inaction, it requires consideration of the costs and the benefits that are likely to be involved. Therefore, it assumes an ability to measure and to define the relevant costs and benefits. This framing also involves a comparison between alternative allocation methods, including a comparison among those methods discussed in Chapter 1. These methods generally involve allocating resources based on one of three simple approaches, including first-in-time, highest bidder, and lottery.

Paradigmatic market frames

There are a number of standard narrative patterns, or what I call paradigms from economic analyses, that are applied to particular fact patterns in law. The six major paradigms described in this book are frequently observed in legal analysis. Being able to identify these paradigmatic frames is important because they frequently shape the contours of legal analysis. These frames include:

(1) The tragedy of the commons, and the related problem of public goods (chapter 4)
(2) The prisoner's dilemma (chapter 4)
(3) The Coase Theorem (chapter 5)
(4) Public choice and Arrow's Impossibility Theorem (chapter 5)
(5) The efficient breach (chapter 5) and
(6) The non-profit organization (chapter 6).

In the remaining chapters these paradigmatic frames will be explained. There are also problems at the end of the relevant chapters that provide fact patterns giving practice in using these framing devices.

References

References function as interpretive devices within frames. References have a more narrow scope than a frame.[95] For example, once a cost and benefit frame or a Coase frame is selected, there are still a number of issues to contend with in the frame. We have to determine the valuation method and the discount rate to be used in calculating the various costs and benefits, for instance. We also have to think in terms of the boundary line to be set for externalities or spillover costs that will count or not count within

---

[95] See the discussion of references in chapter 1 for additional guidance on this point.

a Coase analysis. And we have to select from among multiple definitions of efficiency and other variables. Thus, while selecting a frame constrains some of our choices, it still leaves room for alternative arguments based on the use of different referencing devices within the frame. Certain frames may implicate the relevance of particular reference criteria more than others.

Common references used in understanding law in a market context include a variety of economic terms and concepts. Most of these are explored in chapters 4–6. The partial list set out below identifies some of the common references that will be defined and illustrated in this book. At this point, the list that follows should be used to signal the need to think of these terms as referencing devices when they, and other such terms, are encountered in this book.

- Externalities
- Transaction costs
- Opportunity costs
- Out-of-pocket costs
- Valuation methods (market methods: comparable sales, replacement cost, income flow; hedonic valuation, contingent valuation)
- Pareto efficiency
- Kaldor–Hicks efficiency
- Asymmetrical information
- Adverse selection
- Wealth effects
- Rent seeking
- Moral hazard
- Accounting and economic profits
- Opportunistic behavior
- Path dependent
- Endowment effect
- Present value, time value of money, discount rate
- Transactional misbehavior
- Marginal utility

Once a particular frame has been selected it is important to use appropriate referencing tools to advance a given legal argument. It is also important to develop a sense of flexibility in moving between and using various referencing tools. Keep in mind that different referencing tools, like alternative frames, facilitate different outcomes.

Representations

In order to make something the subject of market exchange, in an economic sense, it must have a legally identifiable form. The law must provide a representation that permits commodification. For example, a deed is a representation of an interest in property. The deed is not the property but a legal representation of the ownership of a given property interest, and this ability to represent the abstract interest in a legal form permits easy exchange. It also enables the owner to use the property interest as security (collateral) for a loan. Thus, the deed facilitates exchange and the ability to put the property to work as collateral for further economic activity. In a similar way the protection of intellectual ideas is furthered by creating representations through copyright and patent law. Likewise, emissions' trading, wetlands' banking, and transferable development rights are made possible by laws that give "name," definition, and meaning to the interests involved.

While informal representation is possible, it is of much less importance because it is legal representation that offers a stable, predictable, and transparent framework for exchange beyond a very local community. Economist Hernando DeSoto makes this point in his best-selling book, *The Mystery of Capital: Why Capitalism Triumphs in the West and Fails Everywhere Else*.[96] DeSoto explains that "dead capital" is transformed into active capital through the institutions of language, communication, and interpretation, in the form of *legal representations*. He explains how the "west" has developed complex interpretive representations for capital that permit individuals to connect to a broad and extensive marketplace. In the "west," legal representation facilitates extensive and positive network externalities. Less-developed countries (LDCs) have failed to take full advantage of these interpretive devices. In some developing countries, for instance, a person may physically possess a home on a given piece of property but may remain unable to acquire full and formal recognition of his ownership. Without a deed to *represent* his ownership, and in the absence of a secure place to record or register that interest, the property becomes an element of *dead capital*. The property has value in its physical sense, but it is unable to produce additional capital:

> In the West, by contrast, every parcel of land, every building, every piece of equipment, or store of inventories is represented in a property document that is the visible sign of a vast hidden process that connects all of these assets to the rest of

---

[96] DeSoto, Mystery of Capital.

the economy. Thanks to this representational process, assets can lead an invisible, parallel life alongside their material existence. They can be used as collateral for credit. The single most important source of funds for new business in the United States is a mortgage on the entrepreneur's house. These assets can also provide a link to the owner's credit history, an accountable address for collection of debts and taxes, the basis for the creation of reliable and universal public utilities, and a foundation for the creation of securities (like mortgage-backed bonds) that can then be rediscounted and sold in secondary markets. By this process the West injects life into assets and makes them generate capital.[97]

Third World and former communist nations do not have this representational process. As a result, most of them are undercapitalized, in the same way that a firm is undercapitalized when it issues fewer securities than its income and assets would justify. The enterprises of the poor are very much like corporations that cannot issue shares or bonds to obtain new investment and finance. Without representations, their assets are dead capital.[98]

As DeSoto notes, market exchange is facilitated by the ability to legally represent assets. This means that various interests need to be legally definable and transferable. And it means that the owner of the interest should be able to exclude others, and to enjoy the economic benefits of the interest.

In working to improve one's ability to work with a cultural- interpretive approach to understanding law in a market context one must practice identifying common frames, references, and representations in legal and public policy arguments. Case opinions, law review articles, legislative histories, policy statements, and political speeches are among the types of communications that can be deconstructed and better understood by categorizing and characterizing their essential elements in terms of the tools outlined in this section of the chapter.

As one proceeds through this book it is helpful to keep these basic organizing tools in mind, and to return to them periodically.

Understanding law in a market context is difficult because it involves interdisciplinary work in law, economics, and culture. It also requires an understanding of interpretation theory. Consequently, it is useful to work with some simplifying tools. This outline should be used as a guide to assist the reader in organizing the discussion of terms and concepts into manageable categories. Organizing them into categories makes it easier to begin applying the terms and concepts to an understanding of law in a market context. Thus, one should practice reading a case, for example, by examining it in terms of its identification of the basic facts (firstness),

---

[97] *Id* at 6.   [98] *Id.*

its discussion of organizing patterns of legal argument (secondness), and its justification for a particular conclusion or course of action. Likewise, the case should be examined in terms of the way it is framed, and for its selection and use of references and representations.

As one becomes more comfortable with the process, new organizing principles may be developed and added to this set of suggestions.

Conclusion

This chapter set out a way of understanding the relationship among law, markets, and culture, and it developed a basic three-step model of legal argument. It indicates that economics can help us understand law in a market context but economics can not eliminate the need to engage in the exploration of the meanings and values of worthy human objectives. Likewise, it can be concluded that even though we operate and make decisions within a world of constraints, we also have an ability to influence and facilitate the values and meanings of social organization. Thus, we can improve legal reasoning and public policy making by paying more attention to the human experience of exchange, by expressly recognizing the need for esthetic and ethical references in legal decision making, and by using a basic set of tools to examine the relationship among law, markets, and culture.

Problems

(1) Explain the idea behind the expression, "the map is not the territory." Discuss the way in which this expression relates to legal argument and the use of economic analysis. Think of a case or an example to illustrate your point.

(2) This chapter provided two introductory examples involving an exchange for sexual services and an exchange in the automobile market. Go back to those examples and map out the various frames and references that you can identify. Also think about the way in which the human body, men, and women, are represented in various approaches to the fact pattern involving the exchange for sexual services.

(3) In a long-awaited settlement of an aboriginal-related land claim between Native Americans and New York State, the State has agreed to turn over 550,000 acres of land to recognized Indian nations within the Six nations of the Iroquois: The Mohawk, Oneida, Onondaga, Cayuga, Seneca, and Tuscaraura. At issue in the return is the question of how the

land should be returned. Tribal Chiefs and leaders want the land returned to the tribes to be held in common by all of the members. The lands will be used for a variety of purposes such as for housing, hunting, fishing, grazing, and agriculture. There is an internal dispute about the desire of some members to use land for certain commercial purposes. In fact, a small but vocal group of individuals complains that common ownership is inefficient and does not empower them to make decisions for themselves. They want a tribunal setup that will recognize individual claims to return of land, and allow individual fee ownership of a pro rata share of land for each member.

Assume that in all there are 10,000 recognized members of the Indian nations. Some of the individual members say that the Chiefs do not, and can not, know how to best use these lands for all of the people. The Chiefs say that tradition is against individual ownership and that this talk is merely the influence of White European values – it reflects greed and selfishness rather than community and interdependence. The State says that it will not finalize a deal until this dispute is resolved.

What frames, references, and representations can be used to understand the nature of the problem in this situation? Can you construct responses to each of the competing groups and explain the basis for a workable resolution?

(4) Education cost and opportunity varies by location within the state of New Europa. There are publicly funded schools and private schools. Many schools, located in low-income neighborhoods, are poorly funded under the state funding formula. The formula makes local residents carry the majority of costs for local education. Schools in the low-income communities tend to have poor quality and test scores are low. Furthermore, students graduating from the public or state-supported primary and secondary schools find that they are not welcome at some of the most prestigious colleges and universities in New Europa. The elite colleges and universities tend to favor students from private schools, even when public school students perform better on standard entrance tests. In an attempt to correct some of these problems, New Europa seeks to even out the cost and opportunity of primary and secondary school by implementing a school privatization and voucher program. The program would seek to improve schools by fostering competition and by funding increased school choice. The program would dramatically reduce public funding and require all students to pay tuition. For students and families without ample financial resources, targeted funding would be provided to assist them in attending the school of their choice. The program would award

every family a $3,000 voucher per child to pay toward school tuition at any primary school through the end of secondary school (grades K-12 in the United States). In addition, the plan calls for add-on vouchers worth up to $2,000 per child with certain certified special needs or a disability, and up to an additional $3,000 per child for families whose income is less than 60 percent of the median household income in the local district of their residence within the State. Local school districts would be responsible for funding busing/transportation for children to any school within an area reachable by bus within two hours. The proposal has a number of supporters who believe that competition will be good for schools and for the education of their children. A number of parent groups want this pro-choice school option. At the same time, there is a great deal of opposition to the proposal.

Explain the market for education as a two-party exchange and then as a multi-party exchange relationship. Identify different ways of measuring the costs and benefits of success or failure in the system. Explain how the proposed changes might work, and how different people in the community might experience them. For example, explain the differences that age, race, gender, class, and culture might have on such a program.

(5) As a variation on problem (4) above, consider a similar situation except that New Europa is addressing college and university education. Traditionally, college and university education has been publicly financed in New Europa with individual students paying a very small fraction of the cost of their education. In an attempt at making higher education more efficient, and in an effort to make those who acquire the benefits of the education pay, New Europa passes a law to privatize all colleges and universities.

Pronouncing the benefits of private markets in other areas of life, New Europa projects many social benefits from its new legislation. It believes that this will cause students to pursue more useful fields of education since they will need to pay for it themselves or take out loans. As a result, colleges and universities will need to respond to community needs and train students for jobs, rather than spending time and resources on ancient history and dead languages. Furthermore, the new system will be more equitable since it makes the people who benefit from higher education pay the cost.

A second topic of new legislation is the ending of life tenure and job security for faculty members. New Europa's politicians say that they must continually face re-election, and everyone else faces the uncertainty of life in the global and competitive marketplace, so why should professors be free from competitive rigor? While many professors argue about the need for independence and free inquiry, the truth is that many professors use tenure to avoid updating their courses. They use tenure as a means of insulating themselves from the need to stay current and fresh in their research, or as a shield to hide behind when they are bad teachers. New Europa declares that faculty, as well as students, must face the open and competitive market, and all of its citizens will be better for the change.

Explain the market for college-level education as a two-party exchange and then as a multi-party exchange relationship. Identify differences between college-level education and the primary and secondary education addressed in the earlier problem. Identify different ways of measuring the costs and benefits of success or failure in the system. Explain how the proposed changes might work, and how different people in the community might experience them. For example, explain the differences that age, race, gender, class, and culture might have on such a program.

4

Market concepts of exchange

This chapter begins to analyze law and legal relationships in terms of the networks and patterns of social/market exchange. It discusses a number of basic framing devices. While it can not provide an exhaustive analysis of potential exchange relationships, it does offer a useful set of examples. These examples cover common exchange relationships that one is likely to deal with in law. In covering these examples, the chapter discusses a variety of transactional arrangements including: single-party or individual choice; the two-party transaction; externalities; the multi-party transaction; and transactional arrangements involving public goods and problems of common ownership. Chapter 5 expands on the discussion in this chapter – offering additional framing tools along with an explanation of many commonly used economic concepts and referencing tools.

Single party or individual choice

Traditional approaches to market analysis focus on the individual. Much time is spent thinking about how individuals make decisions and make choices. This is an important element of human behavior but one must also think about the fact that exchange takes place within a community context. What we do and how we shape and express our preferences is informed by the community(ies) in which we are situated. What we exchange, the terms we exchange on, and who initiates an exchange are all community-based. Likewise, the language we use to carry on or describe an exchange is community-based.

When individuals make choices, they seldom affect only the individual. Take, for example, the claim of the motorcycle rider who insists that she has a right to decide for herself about whether or not to wear a safety helmet. When she is in an accident and suffers a brain injury that could have been prevented by wearing a helmet, society will have to take her to the hospital and provide care. If she is rendered incapacitated or if she dies, her death has an impact on her family, relatives, friends, and work associates. Society may have to provide for children that are left behind without adequate financial support. Her choices, therefore, have social implications that go beyond the idealized notion of the individual as an autonomous and atomistic persona of a hypothetical market actor. Thus, even though individuals exercise a right of choice, these choices are seldom, if ever, free of *spillover effects* or community impacts.

We also know that individual choice will be influenced by knowledge of social efforts to reduce the impact of bad choices. For instance, when our motorcycle driver understands that society will provide medical care and other benefits to her if she is injured, she is less likely to provide for her own insurance and perhaps becomes less cautious in her conduct. She will be more careful when she is aware that she must absorb all losses herself. This reaction is known as a *moral hazard* in economics. It is important for law and public policy because it cautions us to consider how some well-meaning legislation may in fact encourage some people to engage in the very types of behavior or choice making processes that we might be hoping to discourage. In other words, it may foster an incremental increase in risky or unsafe behavior even though the goal is to reduce the negative consequences of such conduct.

Two-party transactions

The most basic model of market exchange involves a two-party transaction. This is typically a simple exchange between a buyer and a seller. When the exchange is voluntary or consensual, as in buying a car or new home, we generally think of it in terms of contract law. On the other hand, a coercive or unplanned exchange might involve a car accident or other type of tort action, or it might involve a theft covered by the criminal law. All of these situations involve exchange relationships, and in thinking about law in a market context we need to think about the norms and laws that govern or facilitate different types of exchange. We also need to think about how we use law to define certain exchanges as voluntary and others as coercive. To a large extent, this issue turns upon the rules for defining property ownership and the rules that govern the transfer and manipulation of property.

For example, I may own a car that you would like to use. Under a given set of property rules my ownership allows me to exclude you from use of the car. If you want to use the car you can negotiate with me over a rental fee or perhaps contract to buy the car. This involves a voluntary and consensual exchange. On the other hand, you may decide to sneak over to my driveway one night and "hot wire" my car so that you can take it for a "joy ride." In this situation, you violate my property right of exclusion, and you may be found guilty of a tort action for conversion as well as for a crime related to auto theft. The initial property rule and the rules for legitimate transfer implicate the tort and criminal law consequences. That is, property rules assign ownership to me and allow me to exclude others, and tort law and criminal law help to enforce compliance with the property rule. The tort rules generally allow for private-party enforcement whereas the criminal law creates a mechanism for action in the name of the "people" or public. In each case, however, the consensual or coercive taking of the car involves an exchange because each involves the allocation of scarce resources – control over the car.

In our situation involving the use of my car by another person, consider how one might further look at the market context of the exchange. Would it be relevant that the car was not taken for a joy ride but that the taker was a poor neighbor with a very sick daughter? He had asked repeatedly to have his daughter driven to the hospital but the car owner said, "no." On the night in question, the daughter appeared to be dying so the car was taken. Should this make a difference and, if so, why should it make a difference?

Also consider a situation in which the property rule might be different. Assume that we are in a developing country where very few people own a car. The property rule permits car ownership by individuals but obligates individuals to provide emergency transportation to others in the community. This would be similar to saying that a lawyer has a property right in her license to practice law and earn an income from that practice but she also has an obligation to make her skills and services available to members of the public who can not pay. Our goal in looking at law in a market context is to explore how different rules implicate different relationships, and to investigate how different relationships simultaneously implicate different rules.

With our two-party transaction we can also ask, as we did with the example of single-party or individual choice, if the transaction is truly private. Does the transaction involve only the immediate and readily apparent parties? While many legal economists focus only on the buyer and seller when they consider a sale of something such as an automobile, should this be the sole or primary focus when considering the purchase and sale of heroin or nuclear weapons? In other words, we must once again determine the extent to which given transactions have a public dimension as well as a private one. We must also think about the ability of the individuals to reflect or represent the public interest in their "private" exchange. Furthermore, we must ask how we justify calling some transactions legal (the car sale) and others (the drug sale) illegal. These types of questions carry over into a variety of areas. Why do we make the criminal sanction for some drugs (crack cocaine), used more frequently by certain identifiable segments of our population, greater than the sanction for other drugs (powder cocaine) used by a different segment of our population? We are also left to question the ability of the law to define differences between exchanges involving informed and voluntary consent as opposed to those that are not voluntary or consensual.

Externalities and spillover effects

The questions raised above concern a problem of defining and distinguishing the idea of the private and the public. The difficulty involves the impossibility of separating private and public interest. They are related, and this relationship involves a need to mediate the intersections of private interest and public interest so as to promote the pursuit of the common good. Therefore, considering law in a market context involves working out these relationships, and mediating the tensions between private/self-interest and the public interest so that a common interest can be identified and facilitated.

As previously discussed with the example involving the decision to wear a motorcycle helmet and the sale of drugs or nuclear weapons, some transactions have costs or implications for a community that may not be fully captured by the individual's pursuit of his or her own self-interest. This simply means that a perfectly competitive market is not always at work, and there are problems involving transaction costs or of accessing information that prevent individuals from fully assessing all of the costs and benefits of their exchanges. Stated differently, not all of the costs of the exchange can be fully internalized by the parties, and thus they pursue exchanges that look good to them primarily because they do not account for the actual cost of their actions. This means that they impose costs on others and these costs are known as *externalities or spillover effects*.[1] For example, I may operate a factory that discharges smoke and dust onto your adjoining property. This discharge causes bad health effects and makes your home dirty. If I do not have to pay you for this impact I am

---

[1] *See e.g.* Demsetz, *Toward a Theory of Property Rights* (property rights and transaction costs); Coase *Problem of Social Cost*; Regan, *Problem of Social Costs Revisited.*

not internalizing the full cost of my actions. This is a negative externality. Thought of differently, I am getting an *equitable servitude* over your property for free.

Not all externalities are negative. For example, perhaps we are neighbors and I enjoy gardening and plant thousands of flowers every spring and summer. You get great pleasure from my flowers and experience a free benefit. This is a positive externality in that you receive a benefit for which you do not pay. On the other hand, what if you have severe allergies and the flowers make you feel awful; would you be able to justify treating my gardening as a negative externality in the same way as the factory pollution in the above situation? Would or should there be a difference between the factory pollution, that may be considered a negative externality generally, and the flowers that create a harm only because of the allergy problems of a particular person?

Externalities raise several key issues. First, to the extent that one seeks to internalize the costs of externalities to a transaction, one must know where to draw the line between externalities that count and ones that are too distant to be included. Second, one must agree on a mechanism to measure the cost of the externality and a way to enforce the cost on the transacting parties. Third, one must be able to identify the source of the externality. For example, several factories may discharge various chemicals into the same body of water. It can be difficult, therefore, to assess the specific responsibility of each factory. Finally, one must deal with an important rhetorical use of externalities. As a rhetorical strategy, externalities can be used to set aside, change, or interfere with the process of private or individual choice or exchange. The search for and identification of externalities, just like transaction costs, can become a game of undermining every individual transaction. Every transaction that looks voluntary or reasonably beneficial to one or both of the private parties may be recharacterized as against the public interest by raising concerns for externalities – third-party costs for which the private parties have not accounted.

Multi-party coordination transactions

As more parties become involved in a transaction, the coordination problems become more complex. Transaction costs go up and information problems become more acute. It also becomes more difficult to account for externalities. These complexities are evident in a typical real estate transaction where the buyer of a home must coordinate with a seller plus a lender, broker, title insurance company, home insurance company, surveyor, and others.

In thinking about law in its market context, therefore, one should begin by mapping out the exchange relationship. It is then possible to consider the legal and economic implications raised by the relationship under investigation. For instance, one can look at a two-party transaction such as the buying and selling of an automobile. In so doing, one might examine, from the perspective of both the buyer and the seller, the terms of the exchange, the ability to bargain, the setting of the bargain, the formalities of the contract, the market expectations, and other variables relevant to this exchange. After this initial step, one might expand the investigation by shifting focus, as if one were controlling a zoom lens on a camera. When this is done one might start mapping out, for example, the way in which the purchase and sale contract implicates other parties and interests. Perhaps one would look at the production process that made the car available to the consumer, the financing arrangements for the dealer's inventory, and the safety issues presented by putting this or any other particular car on the road. This expanded focus might also lead to further considerations such as insurance costs. As more and more connections are made to the initial transaction, one might begin to see more and more intersections between law and economics. Mapping the exchange relationship, therefore, facilitates thinking about the complexity of law in its various market contexts.

One can also use this process to gain a better understanding of other types of exchanges. For instance, consider a health care situation as a prototypical three-party exchange. The patient goes to the doctor but an insurance company pays the doctor. The patient may or may not contribute a nominal amount toward the cost of the insurance or make a co-payment when visiting the doctor. Because the patient does not experience the full cost of visiting the doctor, she is likely to demand more service. At the same time, the doctor gets most of her money from the insurance company so she is less interested in her patient/customer than she may be in keeping the insurance company satisfied. This changes the doctor/patient relationship. At the same time the insurance company is trying to make a profit, so it has an interest in keeping costs down. The insurance company might, therefore, pressure the doctor to cut costs while the patient has an incentive to over-demand services. In order to reduce patient demand for services, the doctor must impose more costs on the patient, and this may involve making it more difficult for the patient to come in for a visit.

Now consider the way in which this three-party exchange maps out when a drug prescription, or some other service, is brought into question. An agency issue arises as both the doctor and the insurance company exercise some control over what drug will be prescribed for the patient. How will they exercise their agency in determining the best course of action for the particular patient? As this issue is considered, a new variable enters the picture. Drug companies begin to advertise on television and in the popular press so as to directly reach end consumers. This puts them in a new position that differs from the prior practice of simply focusing on advertising to doctors. The drug companies do this in an attempt to push demand for their products by having consumers request specific drugs rather than to simply accept the prescription worked out by the doctor and the insurance company. Again, our analysis of the exchange relationship helps us to better understand law in its market context.

This type of exchange can be further investigated once it is remembered that health care is a *quasi-public good*. That is, some of the benefits of good health care are captured by the individual while some are captured by the public. Thus, the "public" enters as an additional party with an interest in the exchange relationship. There are also externalities and other factors to consider. All of this further complicates our legal and economic analysis and opens up ever-increasing opportunities to reframe the matter. In learning to understand these issues as exchanges involving the intersection of law and economics one becomes better skilled and better informed with respect to the way in which human relationships are influenced by law.

Multi-party transaction issues also arise in other ways. For instance, there is a tendency when doing traditional law and economics to reduce complex organizations such as the corporation to a single unit. This means that the corporation is often treated as a single microeconomic actor seeking to maximize its wealth. In reality the corporation is a complex entity with many subparts. There are internal incentives and costs that motivate people in various parts of the firm to act in ways that may make sense to them but which may be inconsistent with the best interests of the organization. For example, as a young attorney in the corporate legal department you may be more concerned with pleasing the boss and getting a promotion than with the long-term and abstract idea of the corporation's best interests. Similarly, managers and executives may be more interested in securing their jobs and big paychecks than in the long-run estimates of return to stockholders. The corporation, like other organizations, is a vehicle for coordinating market exchange activities, but in so doing it reflects complex multi-party transactional dynamics that can not be captured by thinking of the entity as a single market actor.

Another multi-party problem arises when one deals with matters of *agency*. The employees and managers of the corporation, for example, make decisions as agents for the owners of the company, the stockholders. Likewise, the public and parents make curriculum and other decisions for children attending school. In these multi-party transactions we need to ask how the law can, or if the law should, worry about bringing the interests of the agent and principal into equivalence. We also have the problem of thinking about whose interests the law should focus on. Should the law take primary notice of the stockholder's interest because the stockholder is an owner of the company, or are there other interests besides that of legal ownership that should be considered? Should the law consider the economic interests of stakeholders rather than, or in addition to owners and, if so, who are these stakeholders and what interests should the law protect? In our corporation example, stakeholders might go beyond stockholders and include employees, union members, managers, and the communities where corporations are located. All of these stakeholders may have claims or expectation interests that the law should protect, but one must be aware of the economic implications of expanding the nature and scope of protected interests.

Finally, when investigating exchange relationships, one must keep in mind that there are almost always alternative ways for controlling access to resources. For example, in the above healthcare situation, should access to drugs and doctors be controlled by price? This would allocate them to the highest bidder (wealthiest bidders)? Should access be by rationing and waiting in line for service? This would allocate resources to the people that get there first and who have the time to wait in line. In the alternative, should access be granted by random drawing? This would simply allocate resources on the basis of luck. Each allocation method produces its winners and losers because scarcity means that people can not have all that they might demand. Thus, one is ultimately left to unravel the complex exchange relationships at work, and to justify the consequences of the methods used to shape the transactions. By studying law in its market context, one can gain insight into problems of law and public policy, and can learn to use economic concepts and market models to justify and rationalize the social discourse concerning the fairness and justice of particular methods of allocation and distribution.

Public goods and commons problems

Additional transactional issues arise when one considers the concept of public goods and the problem of the "commons." First, this section addresses the idea of public goods and then it explains the problem of the commons.[2]

A *public good* is one that displays two key characteristics. First, it is a good that can be enjoyed by many people without reducing the pleasure or enjoyment of others. For instance, the fact that I enjoy a sunny day or listening to an outdoor concert does not take away from the fact that someone else can get similar enjoyment from the same things at the same time. This is unlike allocating a single piece of cake where my enjoyment from eating it means that you will not be able to enjoy it. The second characteristic of a public good is that it is difficult to exclude others from it. Thus, it is difficult for me to exclude you from enjoying the sunshine or from hearing the outdoor concert. It is not so difficult for one of us to exclude the other from enjoying the piece of cake.

Public television (PBS) is an example of a public good. The fact that I do not contribute to PBS does not prevent me from watching it, and the fact that you enjoy watching does not diminish my viewing pleasure. This problem of difficulty in excluding the non-paying party from the activity is sometimes referred to as the *free rider* problem. Since it is difficult to exclude people from public goods, they tend to be under-produced. This is because it is difficult to capture the full return on your investment when you lack the ability to exclude and control access.

Some exchanges involve a mix of private and public goods. For example, education provides a private benefit to the student by building his human capital. This will make the student more employable and able to earn more money. At the same time, education provides a public benefit by enhancing citizenship and providing a more informed and productive work force. Thus, education benefits the entire community.

---

[2] *See* COOTER & ULEN, LAW AND ECONOMICS 42–43 (defining aspects of public goods); NON-PROFIT ORGANIZATIONS IN A MARKET ECONOMY 23–78 (Hammack & Young, eds.) (explaining public goods issues and examples in the role of non-profit organizations); PUBLIC GOODS AND MARKET FAILURES (Tyler Cowen, ed.); HEAD, PUBLIC GOODS AND PUBLIC WELFARE; ROSEN, PUBLIC FINANCE 55–58; GEUSS, PUBLIC GOODS, PRIVATE GOODS.

A *commons* shares a characteristic with a public good.[3] With respect to each, it is difficult to exclude someone. This is true for the commons because there are either no rights of exclusion or property rights are unclearly defined or enforced. An example of a commons can be a lake that is owned by all of the people. In such a situation the lake will be over-fished. It will be over-fished because everyone will have an incentive to fish as long as there is one unit of net gain from fishing even if there is so much fishing that the fish population is ultimately destroyed. The logic is that I do not want to be the "chump" and sit back while everyone else gets some free fish, so I join in as well. All of us fish to get what we can out of the lake. In effect, we impose negative externalities on the lake and others by over-fishing but we do not have to fully account for this cost.

Let us think about it in a different light. You and three friends order a pizza that you all agree you will share and you each chip in $3 to cover the $12 cost. When the pizza is delivered it is cut into 12 pieces so that each of you could have three pieces if you shared it equally. One of your friends, however, eats really fast and gets away with eating six pieces, leaving only two pieces each for the rest of you. This is a sort of commons problem because once the initial cost is paid for by a participant, each has an incentive to get as much as possible out of the commons (the group pizza). The problem is one of defining and enforcing a property right to the pizza. For instance, after the same routine takes place several times, you and your friends wise up. When the pizza is delivered you immediately divide the pizza and put three pieces on each of four plates and allocate one plate to each person, rather than leaving all of the pieces sitting in the center of the table as a commons.

Public goods and commons raise important issues for law and markets.[4] One initial problem is that the idea of a commons or of a public good is informed by a contested discourse regarding the boundary line between *the self and the other; between what is mine, yours, theirs, and ours.* The idea of a commons or a public good raises issues of definition and of exclusion, and it also challenges our image of the isolated and detached individual as he appears in the standard economic narrative. Consequently, we need to think carefully about how we define rights and how we allocate access

---

[3] *Id.*
[4] *See* Hardin, *Tragedy of the Commons*; HARDIN & GARLING, THE IMMIGRATION DILEMMA; SWANSON, THE ECONOMICS OF ENVIRONMENTAL DEGRADATION; BARNES & STOUT, LAW & ECONOMICS 28–34. *See generally* Heller, *Tragedy of the Anticommons* 621, 634.

Table 4.1

# Fishermen	Size of catch	Total catch	Marginal gain
1	7	7	7
2	9	18	11
3	8	24	6
4	7	28	4
5	6	30	2
6	5	30	0
7	4	28	−2
8	3	24	−4
9	1	9	−15
10	−1	−10	−19

to resources. We need to appreciate the nature of boundary line disputes and the way in which these boundary lines relate to the concerns of people situated in alternative cultural-interpretive positions. We need to inquire as to the relationship between any given boundary line and a particular set of characteristics such as those related to race, gender, nationality, religion, class, education, income, age, and geography, among others.

Commons problems are often associated with legal disputes over the environment. The air, for instance, is a commons as are many waterways, forests, and minerals. Ocean fishing and mining rights also raise commons problems because of the difficulty of exclusion. Likewise, many problems connected to urban sprawl relate to the inability of urban communities to stop or control the inflow of new residents. And, issues related to commons problems also arise in the context of dealing with the relationship between co-tenants in a tenancy in common under property law. In all these situations problems arise from the difficulty associated with defining rights and with being unable to exclude others. In economic terms a commons gets over-used and depleted because individuals do not experience the full cost of the impact of their actions. The individual's cost, in other words, is less than the total social impact related to the given course of conduct.

To better understand the *commons problem*, let us consider an example of fishermen working a small lake. The lake and its fish resources are a commons open to everyone who wants to fish. Table 4.1 provides information about fishing the lake. The first column on the left identifies the number of fishermen working the lake. The next column indicates the number of fish each fisherman catches at each given level of fishermen.

The third column identifies the total catch or total social benefit from the given number of fishermen. The last column on the right identifies the additional or marginal gain to the community from each given number of fishermen.

In this situation, we can see what happens when everyone pursues his own self-interest. With a commons, each individual considers only the gain he will receive by fishing the lake. Under the above facts, nine people will fish the lake. This is because each fisherman, up to and including the ninth, receives a positive benefit from working the lake. The tenth fisherman gets a negative benefit from working the lake; it costs him more to fish than he makes from fishing. Thus, nine people will work the lake with the ninth person imposing −15 value on the community, but gaining one for himself. The table also indicates that as more and more people work the lake, each catch, after the first few fishermen, contains fewer fish. This is a typical problem with natural resources.

When we look at the table from the point of view of the community or the public interest, we find that the optimal number of fishermen is different from the number that will be drawn to the lake in pursuit of self-interest. We see that with five fishermen, there is a social gain of two, and when the sixth fisherman joins in, the social gain falls to zero. Every additional fisherman, after the sixth, generates more costs than benefits for the community. From the interest of society, the maximum number of fishermen should be no more than six.

The technical problem in the commons situation is measuring the impact of additional use on a natural resource. The legal problem is taking the information that we have and developing legal tools to direct private action toward a socially optimal level of activity.

In our example, consider the result in a situation where one person has exclusive ownership of the lake and its fish. In this case, the owner would act to optimize the value of the resource and make sure that fishing was limited to no more than six people. She might issue fishing permits or licenses to limit the number of people fishing the lake. In this way, private interest would be brought in line with the public interest. This means that we might gain from clarifying legal rights in the lake and the fish. In this way private ownership and self-interest would be coordinated to promote the public interest. We might also obtain this result even if the lake is owned in common, provided that the group has full information and one decision maker determines the level of fishing. Here we rely on legal rights to access information and on the ability of a decision making process to mimic that of an individual.

Another way to approach our problem might be to develop legal rules that impose liability or impact fees on each new fisherman. Let us assume, for instance, that each new fisherman must pay each prior fisherman for any loss of fish to them as a result of working the lake. In this situation fisherman 1 pays no fee and likewise for fisherman 2. Fisherman 3 enters the market and benefits by eight fish but in so doing, imposes a catch reduction on 1 and 2. Where 1 and 2 previously took home nine fish each, they now take home only eight. Fisherman 3 must pay one to each of fisherman 1 and 2. Thus, fisherman 3 gets a benefit of eight and pays two for a net benefit of six. Fisherman 4 joins in and the catch falls to 7 each. So fisherman 4 must pay three (one to each of fisherman 1, 2, and 3). Fisherman 3 still has his impact fee to pay as well. If we follow this through, we see that fisherman 6 gets five fish but has to pay five fish for no net benefit. When we get to fisherman 7, we see that his work will get him four fish but our liability or impact fee rule will cost him six; thus, the optimal number of fishermen would be no more than six. In this way we see that the use of a legal liability rule or impact fee regulation can also lead us to the socially desirable result.

As a further example, consider the problem of urban growth. Some cities are growing in population at a rate that exceeds their present infrastructure for public services and utilities. They have, for example, inadequate schools, roads, firehouses, water, and sewer facilities. In spite of this they have a high demand for real estate development. Population pressure is increasing and the local government feels a need to do something. This requires them to understand the problem they are confronting so that they can develop a logical and rational approach to growth management. This means that they need to develop a land use plan that will be able to coordinate future population growth with the concurrent expansion of needed public services and infrastructure.

We can understand this growth management problem better when we see it as a commons problem. Since people, under the US Constitution, can not be excluded from moving to a given city, the city functions as a sort of commons. The city is in a similar position as the lake in our above example. The problem is that more and more people keep moving into the city because they experience an individual benefit from the move that is not the same as the impact they cause on others by their move. Eventually, so many people move into the city that the quality of life is degraded for everyone.

To keep this example simple, refer back to the table that we set up for the fishing example (table 4.1). Assume that the column identifying the number of fishermen now represents the number of people in the city. For ease of understanding you can look at this as a very small town of one–ten people, or for a more realistic feel you can imagine that the numbers stated in the column are in hundreds of thousands (this means that one represents 100,000 people and ten represents 1 million people). The second column (size of catch) would now represent the personal benefit of moving to the city. This would include the benefit of getting a job or of enjoying warmer weather, for instance. The third column (total catch) would now be a measure of the overall quality of life for the city, or the social benefit of adding population. The last column (marginal gain) would now reflect the marginal gain in quality of life from the additional population increase.

We see that, at the outset, in the increase from one to two people, the benefit to each individual increases. This can be from having someone else to talk with, from getting better use of underutilized facilities, or from enhancing the business climate. They say, for example, that a town with one lawyer does not have a lot of legal business but when you add another one, things pick up. This basic idea holds for many market ideas.

Using the same table as the fish example (table 4.1) we can go through a similar analysis. Without any growth management controls we would expect people, following their own self-interest, to keep moving in until the population reached nine. This is because the ninth person is the last person that experiences a positive benefit from moving. From the point of view of society, however, the maximum population should not exceed six. This means that we should be thinking about a growth management program that will move us in the direction of a population that does not exceed six, given our current ability to provide public services and infrastructure. As in the fishing example, one way to achieve this goal is to use impact fees and assessments that make newcomers pay for the impact they cause. If these impact fees and assessments are properly placed, the cost of moving to the city will change in such a way as to have self-interest converge with the public interest in just the same sort of way as explained in the fishing example.

The important thing about this example is that it does more than simply make the problem comprehensible and translatable. It provides the foundation for the legal justification of impact fees and assessments. In the land use area such fees and assessments can not just be arbitrarily imposed. There must be a demonstrated *nexus* between the fee or assessment and the goal to be achieved. Likewise, the law requires that any such fees or assessments bear some *rough proportionality* to the cost imposed by the person being assessed. Integrating this table with the law permits one to show both the *nexus* and the *rough proportionality* because it offers a coherent and justifiable link between the government action and the translation of the problem.[5]

We can use this same type of analysis in a variety of situations including the assessment of impact fees and user fees in the areas of environmental, fishing, and air rights law. Whenever we have a resource that is subject to inadequate legal definition or which is subject to an inability to exclude, we have a commons problem. We can think of a global commons problem, for example, when we are trying to deal with the protection of copyrighted material that is made freely accessible and able to be downloaded off of the Internet.[6] This can include the sharing of music and video files that infringe the copyright value to the creators and producers of such works. By thinking creatively about the implications of the above examples concerning fishing of a lake, and of urban growth management, we can understand the commons problem as it emerges in a variety of settings.

One case that illustrates the commons problem is *Fred F. French Investing Co. v. City of New York*.[7] This case offers a representative example of the kind of background legal tension at work in several areas of law. These areas include: matters of real estate development, land use, and growth management; air quality and emissions trading schemes; development of natural resources; and the protection of sensitive bio-diversity habitats including schemes for wetlands banking.

The *French* case involved a review of a New York City zoning and land use scheme. It was one of the earliest court challenges to the concept now commonly known as *transferable development rights* (TDRs). In this case, French Investing held certain interests in a real estate development called Tudor City. The Tudor City development was a four-acre residential complex built on an elevated level above East 42nd Street, across First Avenue from the United Nations in mid-town Manhattan.[8] The development consisted of apartment buildings, brownstone buildings, a hotel, and two private parks.

---

[5] These requirements (for a nexus and for rough proportionality) relate to a number of issues in the land use area and are of specific importance in takings law. *See, e.g.*, Nollan v. Calif. Coastal Comm., 483 U.S. 825 (1987), and Dolan v. City of Tigard, 114 S. Ct. 2309 (1994).

[6] See Ghosh, *Merits of Ownership* (commons); Ghosh, *Turning Gray Into Green* (Napster); Ghosh, *Gray Markets in Cyberspace*.

[7] Fred F. French Investing Co. v. City of New York, 39 N.Y. 2d 587, 350 N.E. 2d 381 (Ct. of Appeals N.Y., 1976), *appeal dismissed*, 429 U.S. 990 (1976).

[8] *Id.*

The immediate dispute in this case arose when plans were announced for building a new fifty-storey tower on the property. Certain members of the public responded adversely to the plan for the tower. In response to the situation the city rezoned the property denying permission for the tower at that location and requiring the opening of the private parks to the public. In return for the imposition of these restrictions, the property owner was awarded TDRs in the airspace over its current buildings.[9] These air rights could be transferred to other areas of the city and sold to property owners seeking to obtain development rights for buildings exceeding the height restrictions in their own location.

In addressing this dispute, the court upheld the validity of TDRs but found the scheme for actual transfer to be lacking in legal infrastructure. Because the regulatory guidelines for TDRs were, in a sense incomplete, it was unclear that a real market existed for the successful economic transfer and relocation of the air rights. In other words, the regulations were insufficient to establish a well-functioning market. These uncertainties left the property owner with little if any real economic value, and thus the regulation was held to be an improper infringement on the property rights of the developer.

The significance of *French*, and other cases of this type, is in understanding the way in which law attempts to create value and promote exchange by commodifying abstract property rights. Instead of permitting surface land owners to freely claim and develop an unlimited amount of airspace, the law can "sever" the airspace from the surface in the same way that the law creates the potential for both surface and subsurface estates. The idea of creating a property right in airspace, and in an ability to transfer air rights between and among various properties, involves a complex abstraction. The idea of a TDR is a legal representation of that abstraction.

Significantly, TDRs and other related concepts create value, assuming the proper legal and technical infrastructure for a functioning market in these rights. They can also function to prevent over-development and exploitation of the airspace by eliminating a costless use of additional space. In a situation like that of the *French* case, for example, there is a tendency to over-use airspace (to build taller and taller buildings), in part because the full cost of using that airspace is not internalized by

---

[9] For a similar case about air rights *see* Penn Central Transp. Co. v. City of New York, 438 U.S. 104 (1978) (the US Supreme Court upheld a similar scheme using TDRs to compensate a property owner for not being able to replace Penn Central Station with a new high-rise building).

the developer. Taller buildings generally mean that more people will be attracted to the property for work, living, or entertainment. This will impose costs on surrounding properties resulting from increased vehicle and pedestrian traffic and noise. It will also increase the demands on public utilities and will have an esthetic impact on the broader community. One way of understanding this problem is in terms of the Commons Problem.[10] When such things as airspace, fishing rights, hunting rights, or water rights are undefined (or poorly defined) we can expect to experience over-use in the way predicted by the tragedy of the commons. Using regulation to better define rights in these valuable resources and creating markets for their exchange organizes their use in a way that brings convergence between private and public interests.

Cooperative exchange problems

We often deal with market exchanges that require cooperation as well as the coordination of information and activity. Many of these exchanges in our modern marketplace take place between distant parties or entities, or between parties that are simply unfamiliar with each other. The more impersonal these cooperative efforts, the more the parties may have trouble implementing an optimal strategy for cooperation. The problems of implementing an optimal or efficient strategy relate to each party's concern that the other party may "cheat" on the deal. The common example of this involves the situation of the *prisoner's dilemma*. The fact pattern usually has two people picked up by police, separated, and charged with a crime. Each party is individually offered a deal whereby cooperation with the police (cheating or snitching on the partner) will result in no jail time for him or her but considerable jail time for his or her partner. If both parties "rat" on each other, they get a reduced sentence with each of them serving some jail time, and if both remain silent (a cooperative strategy with his or her partner rather than the police), both walk free, without any jail time. They walk free because there is not enough evidence to convict either one unless someone confesses. The outcome of the example is that the fear of the other party cheating drives each individual to snitch on the other, and as a result both do jail time. This is a rational and self-interested strategy but it is not an optimal one for the arrested parties.

---

[10] Another way to understand this type of problem is in terms of the paradigmatic Coase frame to be discussed in chapter 5.

Table 4.2

	Tiffany cooperates	Tiffany cheats
Hannah cooperates	3, 3	1, 4
Hannah cheats	4, 1	2, 2

The prisoner's dilemma illustrates an important point. In traditional approaches to law and economics, transactions are often framed as two-party exchanges with the individuals pursuing their own self-interest and seeking to optimize the value of their relationship. The prisoner's dilemma offers an alternative frame indicating that individuals, pursuing self-interest, will not in fact achieve an optimal outcome (no prison time, in this example). Thus, as with using the framing device of the Commons Problem we see that private coordination can be readily argued to result in a lack of equivalence between self-interest and the public interest.

To understand this problem better, let us look at the cooperation issue in a simple fishing example. Assume that Tiffany and Hannah both fish out of a small lake. They are the only two people on the lake and they agree that it is important not to over-fish the lake. They understand that they will both be better off if they cooperate in limiting their fishing to an amount that will continue to allow the fish population to sustain itself. Therefore, they enter into an agreement that limits fishing to a six-hour period during the day. Since the lake is small they both feel it will be easy to observe compliance with the agreement during daylight hours, but each has some concern about the other cheating on the deal during the night when it will be more difficult to observe the other's actions. Tiffany and Hannah believe that if they cooperate, they will each have a benefit of three and this will produce a total benefit of six. They also believe that if one party cheats, that party will get a benefit of four and the non-cheating party will obtain a benefit of one for a total benefit of five. They also know that if they both cheat on the agreement they will quickly over-fish the lake and each will receive a benefit of two for a total benefit of four. In this situation, the best social outcome is when each party cooperates because we get the most value from the fish in the lake. Self-interest and the concern over cheating will, however, lead each party to cheat and that will give us the least desirable outcome. Table 4.2 shows the above options.

The outcome, as in the standard prisoner's dilemma, is not efficient because we end up with less value being created. The problem for law is to figure out how we can identify these types of exchange situations and to implement rules that will help us avoid this outcome. In this situation, the parties need to be able to monitor their transaction and they need to have some ability to enforce the deal by imposing costs on a party that cheats. Thus, we can think in terms of different types of damages and penalties that might be available and different means for checking on fishing activity or production. Central to this issue is the need for law to provide a framework for enforcement that will make cooperation or trust more likely.

The cooperation problem illustrated here is one that is relevant to a variety of situations. Consider, for instance, the pumping of oil from an underground oil field. Subsurface oil reserves do not match up with the artificial property lines that people trace upon the surface. Thus, multiple surface owners may have rights to pump oil from the common field, and they may seek to cooperate in the way they use the resource so as to get the most out of the field. They face the same type of problem as discussed above. How do they enforce cooperation and reduce the incentive to cheat? The same problem arises with agreements on fishing rights, use of air space, lumber cuts, and long-term contracts.

The prisoner's dilemma may also function as a social narrative confirming a sort of detached and self-interested existence, as projected in traditional economics. The idea behind the dilemma is one that rationalizes feelings of distrust and betrayal between individuals. It tells us not only that cooperation is difficult, but also that advantage may occur to a "cheating" party. In this way, the prisoner's dilemma confirms the old adage that "it's every man for himself."

Discrimination in exchange

"Discrimination" has become a very socially charged word, but we need to think more carefully about what discrimination means in terms of markets and exchange. We discriminate all of the time and in the vast majority of cases, no one thinks anything of it. We discriminate when we prefer chocolate ice cream to vanilla, when we decide to read a book rather than watch television, when we hire a non-smoker over a smoker, when we select members of the basketball team, when we give out scouting merit badges, when we give grades on a final examination, and in almost every choice that we make. Discrimination involves the way in which we choose but it is not always bad, irrational, or even illegal. In a market context we need to think about discrimination in terms of rational and irrational discrimination, and in terms of legal and illegal discrimination.

In market terms, we can think of discrimination as either rational or irrational. Irrational discrimination has no basis in fact. An example of irrational discrimination might involve not hiring people of nationality "*X*" because I believe that everyone of "*X*" background is a vampire. On a more practical level, we might think of irrational discrimination as being based on misinformation. This might occur when we are asked to make decisions about people from a different culture or background that we are unfamiliar with and do not understand. For example, during the early years of Christianity some people believed that Christians were cannibals because they practiced a ritual in which they "ate the body of Christ and drank His blood." In this situation, some people made discriminatory decisions about Christians because of incorrect information with respect to their religious practices. This type of irrational discrimination can generally be corrected when information is accessible and widely disseminated.

Rational discrimination raises a different set of problems. Rational discrimination has a basis in fact. For example, people that are greatly over-weight have more health problems than people who are not over-weight, and people known to be at a higher risk of health problems cost more to insure. Therefore, insurance companies would want to discriminate by charging more for health insurance to people that are greatly over-weight. Likewise, employers who pay for worker health insurance may not wish to hire people who are greatly over-weight. These are rational economic decisions. Here, weight functions as *a proxy or sign* of the underlying issue – health problems and health costs. Based on the correlation between the proxy and the cost, the choice to discriminate makes sense.

We see the same type of rational discrimination when we look at law firm hiring practices. Generally, firms are looking for bright, creative, and hard working people. They want associates that will be able to make them money. The difficult problem is in discovering the identity of the potentially good workers. It is too costly for a firm to interview thousands of people, so a firm makes some key initial choices based on rational discrimination. A firm may decide, for instance, to interview only at certain schools with exceptional reputations in given areas of practice, and it may decide to interview only students in the top 10 percent of the class who are also on law review. The firm may have found these criteria to be good indicators of basic intelligence and of a strong work ethic. The firm knows that some of the people within the *proxy or profile* will not in fact be good hires, and it knows that some really good people are not going to fall within the proxy. Thus, it may wrongly select or exclude people and end up making an *adverse selection*. It may use the proxy or profile, however, because its use greatly reduces search costs and the firm has found, from experience, that the proxy generally provides it with an adequate pool of interview candidates. This selection screening process involves discrimination and the discrimination is economically rational.

Even though some forms of discrimination may be rational, we may not want to permit the use of certain criteria, proxies, or profiles that support a given discriminatory practice. For instance, if it turns out that there is a strong correlation between people of "X" nationality and the characteristic of being greatly over-weight, we may want to prevent weight from being a criteria in the pricing of health insurance by an insurance company. We may also be concerned about law firm hiring practices if people from "X" nationality disproportionately fail to appear in the group of students that have grades in the top 10 percent and participation on law review. The important issues here involve our ability to generate and understand good statistical analysis and our ability to justify the reasons for not permitting economically rational discrimination.

Similar issues arise when we think about using profiles or proxies in screening passengers at airport security. The same concerns emerge when police departments decide to use certain racial profiles to stop African-American and Latino males when they are observed driving late-model luxury cars. Likewise, when Italian-Americans are singled out for different treatment based on the false assumption that many of them are connected to organized crime. And, similarly when native speakers of English are sometimes treated differently than others when in Quebec or France. Is this rational discrimination? Should this be legal discrimination?

We should also remember that some programs, considered by many to be socially desirable, such as affirmative action and the use of diversity guidelines, involve the use of profiles. Fitting a profile in these programs can be beneficial to the individual. Thus, the law does not typically hold that all profiles impose costs – some profiles are used to award benefits. Again, we should ask – is it rational, and is it legal? Consequently, profiling and discrimination are very complex areas, but we can begin to address these issues by thinking carefully and by mapping a variety of alternative perspectives.

We should also be prepared to question the statistical validity and justification for any particular profile or proxy, and then ask if the discriminatory nature of the proxy or profile is one that can or should be tolerated. Likewise, we should examine the cultural context and history related to a profile or proxy so as to understand the potential bias that might be embedded within it.[11]

Generally, rational economic discrimination makes logical sense and enjoys some presumption of validity. Therefore, in order to deny this form of decision making we should develop arguments that undercut the validity of the proxy (as in arguments that assert that standardized tests are biased and not good predictors) or that demonstrate a correlation between the proxy and a conflict with other important social objectives. Even if we do this, we still have the question of who should bear the cost of promoting certain social policies. For example, should the insurance company have to suffer a loss if forced to insure all greatly over-weight people at the same rate as people that are not over-weight? More insurance risk means more costs to the company so it either has to take a cut in profits or pass the cost on to others. Is it fair to have the people who are not over-weight pay more than is needed for insurance so as to subsidize the insurance rate for the greatly over-weight people? Should the government provide a subsidy or a public insurance program for these over-weight people? As can be seen, rational discrimination raises a number of policy questions. Irrational discrimination, on the other hand, serves no legitimate purpose and if we can identify it, we should try to have law work to eliminate it. It can do this by promoting information or by simply prohibiting certain irrational discriminatory practices.

Conclusion

In thinking about law in a market context, we need to consider the nature of exchange and of social relationships. It is important to start by trying to characterize the type of transactions involved. It is also important to consider the exchange relationship with reference to the hypothetical model of perfect competition. While no transaction is likely to rise to the ideal assumptions of a perfectly competitive market, these traditional market assumptions provide us with a valuable framework for analyzing important elements of social and market exchange, and for considering the mediation of private and public interest.

---

[11] *See e.g.* MORRISON, RACING JUSTICE; HIGGINBOTHAM, IN THE MATTER OF COLOR; BELL, AND WE ARE NOT SAVED; RACE, RIGHTS, AND REPARATION (Yamamoto, Chon, Izumi, & Kang, eds.); BROWN, BURY MY HEART AT WOUNDED KNEE.

Problems

(1) Ted and Louise are in business together. They operate out of a blue van in various locations within a six-block radius of downtown. Ted and Louise provide drugs and sexual services to customers. They have customers of all races and both genders. All of their customers are age eighteen or older. The business employs twelve people from the neighborhood that is an area of high unemployment. The employees can make anywhere from $3,000–$6,000 per month depending upon what they do. Ted and Louise make a great deal of money from the business and some of their money is used to sponsor a local basketball league and to upgrade a local park for neighborhood children. They also make occasional grants of money to elderly people in the area.

One night, as part of the conclusion to a long-term police investigation, Ted, Louise, and seven of their "employees" are arrested. In defense of their position they ask you to explain what is wrong with their business. They simply provide goods and services to consenting adult consumers. They employ people and they give back to the neighborhood. In economic terms, how is what they do any different than any other business? They ask, don't chemical companies, gun manufacturers, and tobacco and alcohol companies hurt more people, and no one prevents them from operating? If economics is concerned with market activities and not with morality, how can the economist distinguish Ted's and Louise's business from that of any other small enterprises? How and why should the law make such a distinction?

(2) North American Free Trade Agreement (NAFTA) countries and the European Union (EU) countries agree to a proposed limit on tree cuts in an effort to better manage forest resources. The agreement is designed to protect the future of lumber production in managed forest areas and at the same time strike an eco-system balance to help preserve forest habitat. With a successful forest management plan, each party to the agreement expects to receive $5 billion in benefits over the life of the agreement. Without a successful agreement, each party anticipates only $2.5 billion in benefits over the same time period.

One concern that arises in the negotiation process involves the establishment of a proper mechanism for enforcing the management restrictions under the NAFTA/EU agreement. Globally rising demand for lumber products has created incentives for lumber companies to over-harvest for short-term gains. These incentives would encourage harvesting at levels above the agreed amount.

Both of the entities signing the agreement for NAFTA and for the EU feel confident that none of their own Member States will cheat on other Member States, but there is suspicion as between NAFTA and the EU. A primary concern about cheating on the agreement arises from some comments in an economic report prepared for the negotiations. The report identifies the potential for either group to earn $6 billion in the time period by simply harvesting 15 percent more than the agreement calls for, provided the other party sticks to the agreed amount. If either party unilaterally exceeds the harvest management guidelines, the other party will find its total benefits reduced to $2 billion over the time period. If both parties cheat this is treated the same as not cooperating and each party earns $2.5 billion.

(a) Discuss the likely strategy concerns at issue in this exchange relationship. (Assume that it is a one-time exchange agreement between the parties.)
(b) What steps might you recommend, from a legal institutional point of view, to enhance cooperative compliance with such an agreement?
(c) How might the dynamics change if the parties participated in numerous or repeat exchange relationships?

(3) Oil companies from several countries, the United States, Canada, and the United Kingdom, are competing to develop oil resources in a newly discovered area on the floor of the Atlantic Ocean. Economic and ecological studies have been done on the reserves and the potential drilling and pumping operations. In this area of the ocean, there is presently no clear set of property rules to govern ownership of the oil resources that have been identified. The reports presented to your consulting group contain the following information. It identifies a number of oil companies, each operating one well. The report also identifies the benefits (in dollars) to each from operating a given number of wells. For each identified number of operating wells, the value of pumping is stated in the bracket: 1 (9); 2 (12); 3 (10); 4 (8); 5 (5); 6 (3); 7 (2); 8 (1); 9 (-2); 10 (-3).

(a) Explain how many wells are likely to operate in the absence of a clearly defined property rule.
(b) Identify the socially optimal number of wells.
(c) Explain how many are likely to operate if a liability rule is used to protect people.

(d) Discuss problems in and possible approaches to deciding on an original allocation right to drill, assuming that a property system is set up
to limit the number of wells. In other words, how should the law make
an initial allocation of well locations available to particular operators?
(For some ideas look back at the example in chapter 1 with respect
to basic justifications of property and basic allocation rules.)
(e) Discuss methods that could be employed to facilitate cooperation
between multiple owners, and explain what they are likely to agree
on in terms of a legal arrangement between them.
(f) Discuss how you will deal with access and transfer issues, if at all,
once an original allocation of property rights has been made.

(4) The city of Townsville is studying ways to use local zoning and
land use regulations to help it preserve its parks, schools, and quality of
life. The city has done three studies over a period of several years and
has held four public meetings in the last year. Currently, Townsville has
a population of 100,000 people but there is a major economic boom in
the region that is putting pressure for growth on the city. The city seeks
to manage growth as development pressures would result in a lot of new
residential and commercial construction as well as a need for additional
roadways and other services. In particular, Townsville is concerned about
potential loss of open space, park space, and rapidly increasing demands
on schools as the school-age population rises with new residential
development.

The city has done a detailed assessment of the capacity of its current
parks and schools. Currently, there is some excess capacity in these key
areas, so some growth may actually lead to a more optimal use of the
resources. The city has also used a State study developed for the use of other
towns and cities similar to Townsville to assist in its growth management
efforts. In assessing the quality of its schools and parks with reference to
different levels of population, the city made use of the State Quality of Life
Index system that compares population statistics and projections against
various fixed elements of schools and parks. This provides a Quality of
Life Score that can be used in developing a land use plan. The fixed
elements include such things as acres of park space, acres of open or green
space, square feet of school building space, and number of classrooms per
building.

Using this index system the city, with its current population of 100,000
people, earns a Quality of Life Score of 8. Using the information from
its studies and the Index, the city concludes that a population of 200,000
people would result in a Quality of Life Score of 9; 300,000 people would

result in a Quality of Life Score of 7; 400,000 people would result in a Quality of Life Score of 5; 500,000 people would result in a Quality of Life Score of 3; 600,000 people would result in a Quality of Life Score of 1; and 700,000 people would result in a Quality of Life Score of 0.

On the basis of its studies and calculations, the city is seeking to develop a set of zoning provisions that will facilitate the best or optimal population related to the Quality of Life for its current school and park utilization. Based on these considerations and the stated information, the city has asked you to comment on three specific points.

(a) Identify the optimal population for the city given its current situation.
(b) Identify and explain the likely population if there is no growth management restraint and people simply pursue their own self-interest in deciding to move into Townsville.
(c) Explain how an impact fee might be used to create an incentive structure for individuals to shape their behavior in a way that would move them to the same total population point as the city determines to be socially optimal. Also briefly note a justification for establishing a supportable connection between population growth and such an impact fee arrangement.

5) Below are five profile strategies ((a)–(e)) now in use for various purposes. Read and consider each of these profile strategies and then prepare a response. First, explain in economic terms the purpose, objective, and social value promoted by each profile. Second, as to each of the five profiles, provide a justification and rationale for either upholding or rejecting the identified proxy.

(a) Oxbridge College in the United Kingdom has developed a new profile system to help diversify its student body. For a number of years Oxbridge College has been admitting students based on their individual test scores on national examinations. As a general rule Oxbridge admits only students scoring in the top 10 percent on the tests. The college simply looks at the test results, rank orders the scores from highest to lowest, identifies the students earning scores that place them in the top 10 percent, and then draws a cut-off line. No one below the line is offered admission. Typically this results in admitting about 110 students.

Recently the college has come under public pressure to do more to encourage diversity in its student body. In response to this pressure, Oxbridge has implemented a new policy called "population norming." The idea behind this concept is that the college first decides on a program of diversity. It has, for instance, selected a formula based on achieving diversity in the geographic location of students that it admits. It will then take test results and divide them into groups based on the diversity mix it has identified. Once scores are separated by group, the college will rank order scores from highest to lowest within that group, and select the top 10 percent of test score earners in each group, rather than the top 10 percent of test score in any absolute sense.

This year Oxbridge has set up group profiles for student applicants identified as being from Canada, Australia, Wales, Scotland, Ireland, England, and other European Union (EU) countries. The number of test takers from each group are: Canada 50; Australia 100; Wales 100; Scotland 150; Ireland 100; England 650; other EU countries 50. When the scores are reported, Oxbridge separates them by profile and then selects the students that are in the top 10 percent from each group. For purposes of illustration assume that the test results include the following in absolute terms: The top twenty scores were earned by test takers from Canada, the next twenty-five were all by student applicants from Scotland, and the bottom fifty scores were all from students in the profile for other EU countries. Under the old system, Oxbridge would have admitted all of the top twenty students from Canada and all of the top twenty-five students from Scotland. It would not have admitted anyone from other EU countries. Under the new system it admits 10 percent (or five) of the students in the Canada profile; 10 percent (or fifteen) of the students in the Scotland profile; and 10 percent (or five) of the students in the EU profile. Under this system Oxbridge achieves the desired diversity and still publicly asserts that it has not changed its admission standards, as "all students admitted are in the top 10 percent." Assuming success with its new program, Oxbridge plans to implement some new "population norm profiles" in future years. It will develop profile and admission categories for state school students, gay and lesbian students, and for diversity based on gender and race.

How might such a profile system be received and used in Canada, the United States, or elsewhere?

(b) A suburban police department in the Bay area of California has established a profile for use by its officers on patrol. The stated purpose of the profile is to aid in the reduction of car thefts from local residents. The suburb is an upper-middle-class area with a population identified as 65 percent Asian and 35 percent white. The profile tells officers to pay extra attention to any late-model high-end (expensive) vehicles being driven by young to middle age black or Latino males. The profile suggests targeting such drivers for increased "routine" traffic stops.

(c) A suburban police department in the Atlanta metropolitan area has established a profile for use by its officers on patrol. The purpose of the profile is to prevent violence and racially motivated incidents before they happen. The suburb is a residential community primarily composed of high-income and young professionals. The local population is 75 percent African-American, 20 percent Latino, and 5 percent white. The profile tells officers to pay extra attention to any pick-up trucks displaying an image of the Confederate flag, sporting a rifle rack, and being driven by young white males, with extra special attention if the males are also "skin heads." The profile suggests targeting such drivers for increased "routine" traffic stops.

(d) The Hot Shot Consulting Company is engaged in world-wide consulting on issues related to accounting, law, and financial and strategic management. In making hiring decisions Hot Shot uses a recruiting profile. The profile is designed to enhance selection of the candidates most likely to succeed at Hot Shot. The profile focuses on students who are in the top 10 percent of the class, who have been recognized for leadership in a major academic organization such as a law journal, or as leaders of student government, or as leaders in a graduate honor society, and who had a high-level work experience while undertaking their studies. Hot Shot has a strict policy of denying interviews to all candidates that do not fit the profile, unless the job applicant is over age twenty-six or has served on active duty in the armed forces of his or her country of citizenship.

(e) North American and European Security Forces have established a profile to use in screening passengers at all airports. The profile is designed to aid in the reduction of the probability of a possible terrorist attack. The profile informs all airport personnel to pay extra close attention to men who look to be of an origin that expresses itself in facial characteristics that Americans traditionally identify as Middle Eastern, who are traveling alone, and who have either no checked baggage or are traveling without a round-trip ticket. People fitting the profile are to be taken aside for additional questioning. Does it make a difference if the profile form advises security personnel to randomly select a number of people for "cursory questioning" that do not fit the profile? What if this is suggested so that statistics will show a broader group of people being considered, even when the actual target group is narrower?

5

Additional economic concepts for law in a market context

This chapter provides additional background and discussion of common concepts and terms that are useful in understanding the relationship between law and market analysis. These concepts and terms function as additional interpretive tools in the process of framing, referencing, and representing exchange relationships in law and market economy. These terms and concepts are not presented as part of a positive theory of economics. To the contrary, they are presented to further explain the vocabulary of economics as used in law and legal reasoning. Therefore, this chapter continues with the work commenced in chapter 4, and it introduces a variety of additional concepts that are important to understanding law in a market context.

A key point that needs to be kept in mind as one proceeds through this chapter is that economic concepts provide tools for facilitating and enhancing the mapping and understanding of exchange relationships. For example, when one talks about doing a cost and benefit analysis, or about trying to develop a land use policy that promotes a rational or efficient use of property, one is talking about framing a legal concept in economic terms. Likewise, when a court seeks to protect a private landowner's reasonable investment-backed expectations, the court is using economic concepts to interpret exchange relationships.

We can use law to define rights and to represent rights, but economics functions as a primary interpretive vehicle for representing legal rights in terms of market variables. Economic concepts function as framing tools and as tools for referencing and representing exchange relationships. In understanding these concepts one can better analyze law in a market context. This will enhance the ability to engage in the development of useful and authoritative legal reasoning, by extending one's ability to identify, construct, and deconstruct patterns of legal argument using economic concepts to support given conclusions.

With this in mind, discussion now turns to some central market concepts used in legal reasoning.

Scarcity

A fundamental principle of economics is that there is *scarcity*. In economics scarcity reflects the unlimited nature of human *wants*, but this should not be equated with an inability to get what one needs. That is to say, we can think of more goods and services we would like than we can actually afford, or need. On a personal level scarcity simply means that a person has to make choices. For example, with an annual income of $30,000 Dana may want to buy a three-bedroom home, buy a BMW sports car, go to a movie once a week, eat out three times a week, and send $10,000 per year home to her sick mother. Doing this, however, might actually require an annual income much greater than $30,000. Consequently, her resources are scarce and she just can't do everything that she wants to do on a $30,000 income. She must order her preferences between these choices and allocate her resources as best she can. At the same time Dana should consider how much she needs in order to be comfortable. Perhaps she can get along with a cheaper car, a smaller house, or less entertainment. The point is that *wants* and *needs* are not the same and choices have to be made at both the individual and at the group level.

The Federal Government has a similar problem related to scarcity and resources. This results when it takes in, for example, $300 billion in tax revenue but wants to spend much more than that on military equipment, homeland security, welfare benefits, health care, education, space exploration, dam and road building, and a variety of other programs.

The easiest way to understand scarcity in our everyday lives is to simply realize that time is scarce. We must make choices concerning how we spend our time. We can not be in two different classrooms at the same time; we cannot go to the movies, the football game, and the grocery store at the same time. The existence of scarcity means that choices must be made, i.e. if you can't do everything on your dream list, but can do some of it, what do you choose? The "what" you choose is related to how you choose, and this involves arranging *preferences* (preferences are discussed later in this chapter). At the group or community level, we have the added issue of organizing competing and conflicting individual preferences. In other words, we need to address the matter of whose preferences count the most, and we need mechanisms for mediating the tension between competing claims.

Law and legal institutions deal with scarcity issues in the market by regulating access to and control over resources. For example, *property law* defines rights over resources, and the concept of ownership generally includes a right to use and possession; the right to exclude others; the right to transfer or destroy an interest; and the right to enjoy the economic benefits of the resource. *Contract law* generally comes into play as a way of providing the legal infrastructure for trade and exchange of various ownership interests. In a corresponding manner, *tort law* and *criminal law* regulate and provide remedies or penalties for violation of ownership rights, and of transfer rules.

From the point of view of law and market economy, we must consider the way in which scarcity is *experienced* by different individuals and identifiable groups within and between communities. We need to explore the way in which access and control over resources varies by a number of characteristics including race, gender, age, class, education level, income level, and geographic location, among others. We must also consider the way in which scarcity is used in socio-legal argument. It is often used to describe an inability to respond to particular demands for such things as increased spending on healthcare and education – as when a politician says, "we would like to provide everyone with a free education and with healthcare insurance but, due to scarcity, we just do not have the resources." In this regard we can understand "scarcity" as a cultural–interpretive reference used by people in authority to "mask" unwillingness to address spending and distributional preferences. While there is some absolute sense of scarcity, politicians, and others, often use the term 'scarcity' when the real issue involves their unwillingness to address the ranking of social preferences.

Rationality

Rationality means that in the choice process confronting people, because of scarcity, people will act in a way that they interpret as giving them the best combination of desirable results, given the confines of their resources.[1] Rationality provides a basis for prediction of economic behavior and economics assumes that rational people will act to maximize their

---

[1] While rationality is generally assumed, there is evidence that it is sometimes difficult for people to accurately assess certain information such as that related to low-probability events. This makes the rationality assumption problematic in some situations. *See generally*, JUDGMENT UNDER UNCERTAINTY (Kahneman & Tversky, eds.); Ulen, *Rational Choice*.

own self-interest. This means that the rational economic actor is assumed to maximize gain or profit, but it is also possible to think of the rational economic actor as acting to achieve a gain, even if not to maximize that gain at the expense of others.

The *rational economic person* is possibly analogous to the *reasonably prudent person* in law in the following sense: for economic theory to have relevance and to be a good predictor we do not need to know that every person is always rational in the economic sense as long as most people will act rationally much of the time. Similarly, in law we can assume a standard based on what a reasonable person would be expected to do even if we know that everyone does not always and everywhere act according to the assumed standard. The assumption provides a general basis for policy analysis and human prediction. In this sense, it doesn't affect our general ability to make predictions even though we know that some people are self-destructive, under the influence of drugs or mind control, or otherwise irrational in the common understanding of the term.

The assumption of rationality is important because it forms the basis for believing that law makes a difference in human behavior. If people are rational they should respond to incentives and disincentives created by law – for example, fines, penalties, and damages will be considered in making a rational decision. Likewise, legal rules requiring specific conduct, if normatively accepted, should result in predictable responses when people act rationally.

Law focuses on rationality in a number of areas. For instance, we look for *mens rea* in the criminal law, and we punish intentional acts more harshly than accidental wrongs.[2] We also provide an alternative to criminal sanction for those unable to act rationally, such as in allowing someone to plead not guilty by reason of insanity. This makes sense if we want to deter people from doing bad acts because they must be able to understand the connection between action and penalty. We also assume rationality in tort law where we distinguish between negligence and intentional torts, and in contract law when we look for the reasonable meaning or intentions of the parties.

Significantly, the rationality of any given course of action does not depend on the actual choice made but rather on the process by which the choice was made. Therefore, it is entirely possible for two individuals to make different choices, and yet for each individual to be acting rationally.

---

[2] *Mens rea* involves the appropriate level of intent that makes one criminally responsible.

Example: "*A*" and "*B*" both have $30,000, and each would like to buy a new car and a new boat this year. In their world of car and boat sales, a full-size car costs $30,000, a smaller car costs $15,000, and a boat costs $15,000. "*A*" buys the full-size car for $30,000 and "*B*" buys the smaller car and the boat for $30,000. Have both "*A*" and "*B*" acted rationally?

Yes. "*A*" values the full-size car more than the smaller car and the boat combined. Many people own extremely expensive cars even though buying a cheaper car would allow them to buy other goods and services. Maybe a full-size car is important to "*A*" for prestige or to impress clients, or "*A*" does a lot of long-distance driving, or "*A*" was previously a victim of a serious car accident in which the other driver in a small car was killed and "*A*" is convinced that he was saved by virtue of being in a full-size car. "*B*," on the other hand, has a different set of preferences. Both "*A*" and "*B*" act rationally because they each set out to obtain what they felt was the best return for their investment.

It should also be noted that a person's choice may be rational even though the actual choice made may seem irrational, immoral, or frivolous to someone else. Rationality is a behavioral and interpretive concept. As such, it may vary with cultural context. Moreover, the idea of rational action, even when linked to the pursuit of self-interest, does not mean that optimal outcomes can be calculated. The concept of rationality can help us imagine sets of plausibly good choice opportunities, or assist in identifying lower-cost methods for achieving particular normative objectives, but rationality is limited by a number of factors including cognitive ability. Studies have shown, for instance, that many people have trouble in dealing with certain types of information. Many people seem to believe that spending $1 on a chance at winning $100 is better than spending $100 on a chance to win $10,000. Rationally the risk is the same and people should be indifferent, but there seems to be cognitive difficulty in processing this information. An even better example is the willingness of people to spend $10 on lottery tickets for a one in 200 million chance to win a million dollars while perceiving this to be a better deal than spending $10 on a one in 200 chance of winning $100. Other cognitive problems also exist. Thus, the assumption of rationality is useful but it is limited.

Rational ignorance

Sometimes, particularly when discussing public choice (addressed later in this chapter), economists speak of rational ignorance. The idea of *rational ignorance* is that it sometimes makes sense not to be well informed. Our time and resources are limited so we can not be fully informed on all of the issues that confront us in our daily lives. We have to make choices about what issues to invest in or to be informed about. In this process of screening out less important issues we act rationally in choosing to be less informed or more ignorant as to a great many issues. There are, for instance, numerous bills and proposals before Congress every day that we could learn about, but we choose not to educate ourselves about all of these issues. We choose instead to be ignorant of many issues even when information may be readily available. This is a rational economic choice.

As relates to public choice and the political process, rational ignorance concerns the difference between the average person and a member of a special interest group. For example, consider the situation in which I am a member of the Florida Bar and the State of Florida is considering legislation that would dramatically change the requirements for having a license to practice law. As a person that will be directly and perhaps substantially affected by the proposed legislation, I have a high incentive for being informed about this topic even though a lot of people in the broader community have no particular reason to be as well informed. The benefits or detriments imposed by legislation in this area will have a greater degree of impact on me than on the average person. In such a situation, the people with a special interest have a strong motivation to lobby and influence the political process while the vast majority of people remain rationally uninterested in, or ignorant of, the issues. This raises questions about the political process and its ability to respond to or represent the public interest. In as much as the political process is actively influenced by people pursuing a special interest, it is difficult to determine the degree to which legislation reflects an adequate concern for the public interest.

It is also important to consider the ways in which law might respond to the matter of rational ignorance. In as much as we know that it can make rational sense for an individual to remain uniformed about matters of public interest, we may want to require regulatory oversight or encourage consumer "watchdog groups" to be actively involved in the legislative process. For a similar reason it might be helpful to have a diversity of cultural-interpretive viewpoints reflected in the legislative process, and in the oversight and judicial review process. These and other measures may help to bring a broader public interest into the process of law and public policy making.

The idea of rational ignorance provides a cultural-interpretive reference for exploring lack of public participation in the political process, and for shifting discussion to a concern for the influence of special interest groups.

Opportunity cost

The concept of scarcity mean that we must make choices, and when we make choices we must give up some opportunities. When "A" in the previous example decides to buy the full-size car, "A" has an opportunity cost of giving up the boat – an opportunity cost of $15,000. In simple terms, opportunity costs ask us to consider our next-best option. This is a comparative or indexical reference that gives particular meaning to the individual's choice process.

A discussion and comparison of the salaries of professors in various schools or departments of major American universities provides a good example of opportunity cost analysis. On one level, when I decide to go into law teaching I must weigh the opportunity cost of giving up private practice to teach. I am willing to take less pay teaching in exchange for more control over the projects I work on and for flexibility in determining the hours and days in which I do my work. On a second level, the reason many argue that law school and medical school professors make twice the salary of history professors is that history PhDs have less in the way of alternative job opportunities outside of the university setting. Because job prospects and salaries are less promising in history than in law, the history professor has less opportunity cost in choosing teaching, and thus competent history professors can be hired and retained at lower salaries than law professors. This raises the question of how we structure compensation. Should we pay people based on market-related opportunity costs or should we pay them based upon certain non-market criteria such as number of students taught, teaching evaluations, and publications? Using non-market criteria changes the pay differential between the typical law professor and the typical history professor.

In the United Kingdom and Australia, for example, market references are not used as a primary basis for salary differences between professors in different fields. Professors are paid on a more or less uniform scale across disciplines based on particular academic, rather than market, criteria. Whether or not a system incorporates market references will influence the way in which resources are allocated between competing claimants. Thus, selecting rules that incorporate certain market assumptions influences the ultimate allocation of resources. It also challenges us to justify the fairness of the references we use in any given system of allocation.

Accounting profits and economic profits

The concept of opportunity costs also plays a role in distinguishing *economic profits* from *accounting profits*. Accounting profits are measured by the return you earn on an investment. For example, if you invest in an apartment building (become a landlord), you may make a 4 percent return on your investment after taking into account all of your expenses. Such a return would be your accounting profit. Economic profit, however, considers opportunity costs. That is, if an investor can put money into a different market, say computer software instead of rental housing, and if that alternative investment carried the same risk but returned a 15 percent accounting profit, he would have an opportunity cost (economic loss) of 11 percent from investing in rental housing, even though rental housing returned a 4 percent accounting profit.

Given similar risks, investors should prefer the types of investments that return higher accounting profits. This observation means that attempts to regulate such things as rental housing must be sensitive to more information than pure accounting profits. For example, to impose costs on a landlord that might reduce the rate of return from 15 to 4 percent may seem "fair" because it still leaves the investor with an "adequate profit." The problem is that investors might feel that they are taking an economic loss relative to other investment opportunities. As a consequence, they may seek to exit the rental housing market even though it provides them with a 4 percent return. Alternatively, they may stay in the rental housing market and attempt to further reduce their costs by providing fewer services or lower-quality housing in an attempt to indirectly raise their economic returns. Because both types of profit are important factors in setting regulatory policy and predicting the potential consequences of regulation, economic analysis of such issues should take both types of profit into account.

Furthermore, the idea of opportunity costs implies a concern for understanding the nature of opportunity differences between people positioned within different cultural-interpretive communities.

The idea of thinking in terms of opportunity costs and in terms of the distinction between accounting and economic profits is important. These factors come into play, for example, when trying to establish the *reasonable investment-backed expectation* of a property owner – a fundamental concern of takings law jurisprudence.

For example, in the case of *Penn Central Transp. Co.* v. *City of New York*, the US Supreme Court dealt with the issue of a taking of private property

without just compensation under New York City's Landmarks Preservation Law.[3] The owners of the property commonly referred to as Grand
Central Station sought to grant lease rights to a development company
to build a high-rise office building over the Terminal. The Landmarks
Preservation Commission refused to approve the project. The owner,
Penn Central, subsequently sued for the taking of its property without
just compensation. In the analysis of the case the Court reasoned that the
law required it to consider the economic impact of the regulation on the
property owner and in particular to consider the way in which the regulation might interfere with the "distinct investment-backed expectations"
of Penn Central.

Likewise, in *Lucas v. South Carolina Coastal Council,* the US Supreme
Court addressed a takings claim in terms of considering the investment-
backed expectations of the property owner, and the beneficial value of
the property relative to a regulation that prohibited all development of
certain lands within an identified coastal zone.[4] Lucas was a developer who
acquired two lots for development on the coast prior to the regulation.
These lots were of considerable value for residential development. The
coastal zone regulation was put in place and prohibited development of
all lots in the area where Lucas had his property. In evaluating Lucas' claim
the Court considered a number of factors that went into evaluating the
investment-backed expectation of Lucas in acquiring his lots. It went on
to hold that it was a *per se* taking of private property when a government
regulation deprives the owner of all beneficial value in the land.

The key point in each of these two cases, *Penn Central* and *Lucas,* is in
recognizing the significant role of economic argument and the distinction
between accounting and economic profits when discussing reasonable
investment-backed expectations. The need to identify land value and a
property owner's investment-backed expectations relates not only to matters of fixing compensation but more fundamentally to the substantive
issue of determining a taking in the first instance. This thus means that
we need to know something about the way in which one establishes the
value of property and the reasonable investment-backed expectations of a
property owner. And a starting point for understanding how to proceed is
in knowing something about the opportunity costs of the property owner,
and also being able to work with alternative measures of profit and loss
relative to accounting and economic calculations.

---

[3] Penn Central Transp. Co. v. City of New York, 438 U.S. 104 (1978).
[4] Lucas v. South Carolina Coastal Council, 505 U.S. 1003 (1992).

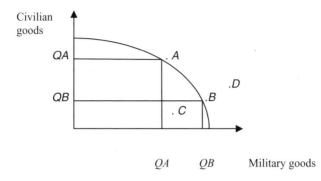

Figure 5.1

Production possibility curve

Some of the concepts discussed so far can be brought together in the visual context of the *production possibility curve* (PPC).

The classic example of the PPC trade off is to consider the scarcity issue for the United States as creating a social choice between expenditures on civilian goods as opposed to military goods. The curve in figure 5.1 illustrates the limits of our resources at any given time when operating efficiently, and thus there is a trade off between civilian and military goods. In order to buy more civilian goods, we must give up some military goods and vice versa. According to economics, we operate efficiently at points along the curve (at points along the curve we are getting the most for our investment). Thus, both points "*A*" and "*B*" represent efficient use of resources even though each involves a different mix as between civilian and military goods.

If we are at point "*C*" we are operating inefficiently. Point "*C*" represents bureaucratic mismanagement that pays $1,000 for a $.05 cent screw at the Department of Defense. Point "*D*" represents an unattainable combination. Point "*D*" can be reached only if we are able, over time, to develop new technologies or resources that make us richer or more productive. This would gradually shift the curve outwards and if the economy expanded enough, we would be able to reach point "D."

Figure 5.1 can also be used to represent an individual's choice between spending and saving, with the position of the curve being determined by the individual's income and the points along the curve reflecting the trade off between alternative mixes of goods and services.

The PPC is important for law because it provides a reference point for understanding that law and legal institutions operate to influence the nature of the trade offs that we make. Law controls the formal framework for making choices and it defines the objects/subjects of trade. Furthermore, if we are concerned with using law to facilitate the efficient use of scarce resources we must pay attention to ways in which to discourage or deter waste. We must also think about how law can enhance the environment for creativity and discovery so that the PPC curve can move outward and expand the pie of opportunity.

The PPC focuses our attention on the idea of scarcity and reminds us that we operate in a world of constraints. We can not have everything that we demand or desire. If, for example, law requires too much to be spent on marginal increases in automobile safety, or some other good, there will be fewer resources available to address other worthy matters. Therefore, law must guide us in understanding and making choices about the many trade offs that confront us.

In the context of law and market economy, we must also consider the process by which choice is exercised in determining the particular trade offs between, for example, healthcare and military goods, or between education and oil production. We must also inquire as to the way in which the trade offs and production possibilities are identified, shaped, and understood by different segments of our community. Arranging these trade offs involves preference ordering and we need to be aware of the "invisible hands" of power that influence and present us with the trade off choices to be considered.

Substitute goods

In considering scarcity and the need to make choices, we need to introduce another idea that is relevant to the rational economic person, and that is the notion of *substitute goods*. Substitute goods are important in getting the best use of your resources. An example of substitution occurred in many factories in the Northeastern United States during the oil crisis of the 1970s. The dramatic rise in oil prices throughout the 1970s led many companies to switch their factory power plants from oil to natural gas or coal. They substituted one good for another based on changing prices and expectations. The changes were not cost-free, but were undertaken anyway because of an overall cost savings, even after figuring in the cost of substitution. The main point is that the availability of substitutes helps one adjust the particular goods consumed based on changes in relative prices.

In thinking about substitute goods, we must also consider that law helps to define and regulate substitution. For instance, nuclear power is also a substitute for oil but law can regulate and restrict this substitution option. Likewise, high-sulfur coal and low-sulfur coal can be used as substitutes for one another in various industrial settings. Law can restrict this substitution, however, by constraining the use of high-sulfur coal on the grounds that its use does more to degrade air quality than does the use of low-sulfur coal. Restricting the use of high-sulfur coal has implications that need to be analyzed. High-sulfur coal is more abundant in the eastern United States where coal mining is generally more labor-intensive and more unionized. Low-sulfur coal is more abundant in the western United States. Thus, a legal policy on coal substitution affects more than coal; it has other political and socio-legal implications. It has implications for labor and union groups, and for job locations as between the eastern and western United States.

Substitutes are also important in other ways. For example, when we try to control the use of a certain pesticide in agriculture we might do a cost and benefit analysis of the given product. We might compare the health risk of use to the benefits of use. It is important when evaluating a particular pesticide to ask if the regulation requires or permits analysis to include substitutes for the product. The consideration of substitutes may change the outcome of a cost and benefit calculus regarding the original pesticide. We should also ask if the law should require or permit consideration of allowing no pesticide use as a substitute. These substitution questions come up repeatedly in dealing with a variety of legal areas including environmental regulations, real estate development in sensitive habitat areas, and the approval of new food and drug products.

Substitution is also a concept relevant to certain types of remedies. For example, in the real estate area if a home burns down during the executory contract period of a purchase and sale contract, the insurance proceeds may "substitute" for the value of the house. Likewise, under contract law we may ask about the availability of substitute performance. The lack of a ready and fungible substitute can give rise to an action for specific performance in both property and contract law.

Constructing the simple economic model: supply and demand

A key market framing device in law involves the use of cost and benefit analysis. The basic idea behind this framing device centers on the relationship between supply and demand. Therefore, we must have a basic idea of the concepts of supply and demand when we think about law in a market context.

Supply or cost curve

The cost or supply curve represents the amount of goods that will be supplied to a market at a given price. It also can be used to illustrate the effect on market behavior when perceived social, psychic or other costs raise the cost of a certain activity.

Five important factors about the supply (cost) curve are:

(1) Quantity supplied of a good depends on the price of *that* good.
(2) Quantity supplied of a good depends on the prices of *other* goods. This refers to relative price. For example, if the price of soybeans goes up, the supply of corn may go down as farmers begin to shift their production from corn to soybeans.
(3) Quantity supplied depends on the costs of *factors of production.* For example, if law school tuition were to rise significantly, fewer people might decide to attend law school, thus decreasing the supply of attorneys.
(4) Quantity supplied depends on the *state of technology.* (The cheaper it is to produce "chips" the more affordable computers and calculators become.)
(5) Quantity supplied depends on the *goals of the suppliers.* For example, if it is more prestigious or socially acceptable to produce chemicals for healthcare than war, maybe people will be more willing to supply healthcare needs.

Do not forget that cost also means cost as we discussed with respect to opportunity costs. That is, as a producer you are confronted with choices of what to produce (you can also choose not to produce at all and merely invest your money elsewhere). As a consumer you are confronted with choices of what to buy. Remember that not doing anything or merely passive investment is always an option. These choices, as I said, involve a system of scarcity and preference shaping. Thus, any choice necessarily forecloses another opportunity and that is a cost.

An important concept in understanding supply is *marginal cost.* Marginal cost is the increase in cost required to increase output of some good or service by one unit. Although marginal cost may fall at first, it must eventually rise with increased output because of the law of diminishing returns. An example of the law of diminishing returns can be seen in the production of oil. Although the cost of producing each additional barrel of oil may decrease at first, eventually it will cost more to produce each additional barrel of oil because of additional exploration costs and more expensive drilling to tap deeper wells. Therefore, the supply or cost curve is upward sloping.

Demand or benefit curve

The demand curve represents the amount of goods that consumers will be willing to buy at any given price.

Six important factors affecting demand are:

(1) Quantity demanded of a good depends on the price of *that* good.
(2) Quantity demanded of a good depends on the prices of *other* goods. If goods are *substitute goods* (say, oil and natural gas) then an increase in the price of one will result in an increase in demand for the other and a decrease in the price of one will result in a decrease in demand for the other. If goods are *complementary goods* (e.g. gas and automobiles) then an increase in the price of one will result in a decrease in demand for the other and a decrease in the price of one will result in an increase in demand for the other.
(3) Quantity demanded varies with the *tastes or preferences* of the members of society (e.g. hula hoops, bell-bottom jeans, etc.).
(4) Quantity demanded depends on the *level of income* of the average household. A poor population spends much of its income on basics, and a rich population not only buys more but buys a different mix of goods and services.
(5) Quantity demanded depends on the *size of the total population,* although just having more people is not sufficient; they must have purchasing power.
(6) Quantity demanded depends on the *distribution of income* among households. Distribution of income affects the market – take, for example, an oil-rich country with high average income but with 90 percent of the income in a few hands. Such a distribution results in a different type of product mix than if wealth is more evenly distributed among the general population.

Thus, quantity demanded depends on (and changes with) average income, population, distribution of income, the price of the commodity, and the price of other commodities.

We can set up a demand curve much as we can a supply curve. The whole demand curve is a representation of the complete relation between quantity demanded and price, other things held constant. The supply or cost curve involves marginal cost. Now we need to discuss *marginal utility*.

Marginal utility is the additional utility a person receives from consuming one additional unit of a good. This can best be illustrated by an example.

Example: It is a hot sunny day and John is very thirsty. John arrives at a soda stand. John's first glass of Coke is very good and of great value to him. In fact John may be so thirsty that he would be willing to pay $3.00 instead of the asking price of $1.00. John's second, third, and fourth glasses of Coke are less and less valuable as he is now cooled down and is no longer as thirsty. John may not want another glass even if offered for 50 cents, or half price.

The Coke example illustrates the principle of *diminishing marginal utility* and thus the demand curve is downward sloping.

Like a supply curve, a demand curve can also shift. The causes of shifts of demand curves include:

(1) *Changes in taste* (people decide they like Pepsi more than Coke – so less is sold at every price)
(2) *Increases or decreases in population* (more or fewer people to buy Coke or to demand alternative products)
(3) *Redistribution of income* (more people with lower income may prefer water or generic-brand cola – or more people with higher income may prefer Perrier)
(4) *Changes in average household income* (if average household income increases, more families can afford Coke)
(5) *Changes in markets of substitute or complementary goods* (change in cost of other colas, non-colas, fruit juices, or water, will affect demand for Coke).

The basic model

Now we are ready to put the basic economic model together by combining the concepts of supply and demand. The basic model serves as a model for general predictions of behavior and is depicted in figure 5.2. When we put these two elements together, we are creating a cost (supply) and benefit (demand) model. This basic model is used to "identify" and "represent" the efficient outcome in economics.

On this simple diagram, the supply (cost) and demand (benefit) curves intersect at "*A*." For this market, then, "*A*" represents a *market equilibrium*. That is the point at which marginal cost (*MC*) equals marginal utility (*MU*). This is the point at which all goods supplied are just enough to meet demand. At prices greater than *Pa*, sellers will be willing to supply more than *Qa*. Supply will exceed demand and as sellers' inventories pile

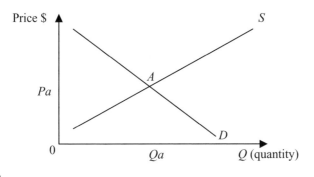

Figure 5.2

up with unpurchased goods, sellers will cut back on their production. At prices less than *Pa*, suppliers will be willing to supply less than *Qa*, and buyers will wish to purchase more than *Qa*. Additional sellers will enter the market in order to realize the profit that can be made as long as price is greater than *MC* (which is represented by the supply or cost curve), and the price will be driven down to *Pa*, with *Qa* being the resulting quantity sold and purchased. An *equilibrium* is where there is no tendency for change and therefore a market equilibrium is where the separate plans of the buyers and sellers mesh exactly (quantity supplied = quantity demanded).

The *cost and benefit model* is used to *represent* the idea of a market, and of the possibility of achieving a finite point of equilibrium. This idealized *representation* promotes the cultural-interpretive position that suggests an efficient and wealth-maximizing point can be calculated and translated into public policy through law. The goal of the model is to find a balance between costs on the one hand and benefits on the other. Ideally we should try to minimize costs while advancing the benefits. Even if the model could make this calculation possible, we should note that it tells us little about the distribution of the various costs and benefits. It also tells us little about the underlying cultural-interpretive hierarchy that conventionalizes the preference rankings being measured by the model. Furthermore, the model assumes an ability to quantify a number of factors that may be difficult to quantify, and it operates under conditions where all other factors are held constant. This means that it is basically a static rather than dynamic analysis, constructed upon contested and ambiguous assumptions.

Even with its weakness, however, the model can help us organize fragmented information and help us construct a contingent yet comprehensible hypothesis for advancing legal inquiry and legal reasoning. It can not, however, reveal the optimal course of action to take in developing law and legal policy. Such a predictive outcome is impossible. As explained in earlier chapters, there are multiple frames, references, and representations that can be used to construct different cultural–interpretive understandings of market "facts" and responses to those "facts." Furthermore, we must remember that the model is grounded on particular assumptions (discussed in chapter 2) that are highly contested. Therefore, the model should be understood as a useful tool for organizing information and facilitating speculative inquiry. It serves as a baseline for mapping various frames, references, and representations, and not as a scientific equation for calculating precise answers to complex socio-legal problems.

A classic case for illustrating the idea behind a cost and benefit analysis is *U.S. v. Carroll Towing Co.*[5] This case, with the opinion written by Judge Learned Hand, has become famous for its simple formulation of a cost and benefit approach to liability for damages caused from failure to take appropriate caution to avoid injury. The case involved the docking of various barges off a pier along the North River in New York Harbor. While undertaking to maneuver a particular barge other barges broke adrift and were carried by the tide and the wind until the barge "Anna C" hit a tanker. The impact with the tanker resulted in a hole in the "Anna C" caused by the tanker's propeller. Ultimately the "Anna C" sank and the lawsuit involved a claim for damages related to the lost cargo and for the expenses in salvaging the cargo and the barge.[6]

In addressing the conduct of the various parties Judge Hand set out a three-part formula for determining an owner's duty to provide against resulting injuries. His formula provided for liability where the burden of preventing the harm (B) is less than the probability of the event occurring (P) multiplied by the amount of the injury caused (L).[7] Thus, if $10 worth of precaution could prevent a 25 percent chance of losing $100, the person failing to use such precaution should be held liable for the resulting loss. In other words, the benefit associated with taking precaution (avoiding $25 of harm) outweighs the cost therefore ($10) and we should encourage the person to take precaution.

In a negligence action such as that illustrated by the case of *Carroll Towing*, the determination of the appropriate level of precaution and of liability is determined on a case-by-case basis. Sometimes, however, the law will address liability on a broader and more generalized basis.

---

[5] U.S. v. Carroll Towing Co., 159 F. 2d 169 (2d Gr. 1947).   [6] *Id.* at 171.   [7] *Id.* at 173.

For example, the law may impose strict liability against one party in a given exchange relationship. This may be reasonable when one party has superior information, is better able to control particular aspects of the relationship (as in the production process for commercial products), and is better positioned either to insure against the risk of loss or to spread the cost of a loss over numerous transactions. In such situations a known potential risk, as a by-product or externality of a useful undertaking, may be assigned to the least-cost avoider (the party best able to cover or control the risk). In this way, a strict liability rule attempts to internalize the full cost of an enterprise or activity while avoiding a case-by-case cost and benefit analysis under the rule announced in *Carroll Towing*. Thus, a generalized cost and benefit analysis, used to justify the strict liability approach to a broad category of exchange relationships, replaces the particularized calculation of costs and benefits in the circumstances of a specific exchange.

Cost and benefit analysis is also used in a number of other type of situations. For instance, it is frequently used to make generalized legal standards more specific and concrete for legal analysis. Two examples of this type of use follow in the discussion of *Vande Zande v. Wisconsin Dept. of Admin.*,[8] and *Samperi v. Inland Wetlands Agency of West Haven.*[9]

In *Vande Zande*, Judge Richard Posner cites Hand's formula from *Carroll Towing* when addressing the meaning of the statutory requirement of providing "reasonable accommodation" to an employee under the Americans with Disabilities Act (ADA).[10] This Federal law is designed to reduce discrimination in the workplace and to make the marketplace more accessible to people with disabilities. In clarifying the meaning of reasonable accommodation, Judge Posner explains that the cost of accommodation should not be disproportionate to the benefit. He hastens to add that this need not be a precise calculation. Nonetheless, the cost and benefit calculation must be accounted for in two different ways when analyzing a question of reasonable accommodation. Posner explains that the employer should have "an opportunity to prove that upon more careful consideration the costs are excessive in relation either to the benefits of the accommodation or to the employer's financial survival or health."[11] This means that the cost and benefit analysis is done in relation to the actual needs of a particular employee and then given a second review relative to

---

[8] Vande Zande v. Wisconsin Dept. of Admin., 44 F.3d 538 (7th Cir. 1995).
[9] Samperi v. Inlands Wetlands Agency of West Haven, 628 A.2d 1286 (Conn. 1993).
[10] Vande Zande, *supra* at 542.   [11] *Id.* at 543.

the financial health of the employer. Thus, a particular accommodation might be reasonable when considered in isolation from the firm's financial situation and yet be held unreasonable in light of an employer's overall financial picture. The legal standard, therefore, requires a comprehensive market analysis.

In the context of this particular case Judge Posner addresses a number of accommodations that have been made for the plaintiff, Vande Zande. One of the plaintiff's claims relates to the failure of the employer to alter the design of a sink and countertop in a kitchenette provided for in the work area of the building in which Vande Zande is employed. Vande Zande uses a wheelchair and the sink and countertop are too high at a height of 36 inches from the floor. The requested accommodation was to lower the sink and countertop to a height of 34 inches from the floor. This would make them fully accessible to the plaintiff. Citing to the availability of a sink in a bathroom on the same floor of the building, Judge Posner concluded that the $150 expense of resizing the sink and countertop was greater than the benefit.[12] Thus, the resizing was not required under the reasonable accommodation standard of the ADA.

In another illustration of a cost and benefit approach let us consider the *Samperi* case. This case involved a challenge to a development permit issued to a real estate developer by a state agency in Connecticut. The permit was granted pursuant to a statute regarding the protection of wetland habitat. The state statute was "designed to protect and preserve the "indispensable and irreplaceable but fragile natural resource" of inland wetlands "by providing an orderly process to balance the need for economic growth of the state and the use of its land with the need to protect its environment and ecology."[13] In achieving this goal and deciding on the issuing of a development permit, the local inland wetlands agency is required to make a determination that "no feasible and prudent alternative to the proposed development exists."[14]

The case deals with the meaning of "feasible and prudent alternative" to a proposed development project. In addressing the meaning to be given to this legal standard the court looks to prior decisions in which it interpreted similar language under the Federal Environmental Protection Act (EPA). It concluded that a feasible and prudent alternative standard must meet two requirements. First, alternative ways of doing a project must be sound from an engineering standpoint. Second, they must be "economically reasonable in light of the social benefits derived from the

---

[12] *Id.* at 546.   [13] *Id.* at 1294.   [14] *Id.*

activity."[15] Thus, a number of alternative ways of doing a project may be sound from an engineering perspective and yet a developer need not pursue them if the cost of protecting the environment outweighs the benefit to be achieved.

In each of the above cases we see examples of the way in which the law is informed by market analysis, and we see how important it is for the lawyer to understand basic economics. The economic concepts are central to the legal discourse and mastering the appropriate economic concepts and terms is essential to being an effective lawyer. Importantly, it must be noted that the modern-day requirement for cost and benefit analysis can be much more complicated than it first appears to the uninitiated lawyer. While sounding rather simple, the process can actually be very complex as one realizes that a proper cost and benefit analysis may include reference to many other market concepts such as those related to risk, valuation, opportunity cost, externalities, alternative measures of efficiency, and the complexities of the commons, among others. It also requires the lawyer to be aware of the many values that can not be readily quantified in a cost and benefit analysis. Environmental values, and consideration of esthetic and human values, are often difficult to quantify, thus they get under-valued or ignored when doing a cost and benefit calculus.

Making out a favorable cost and benefit calculus requires an ability to understand and manipulate many of the terms and concepts discussed in this book. These skills are also required for one to have a clear understanding of how to read earlier case decisions for precedential value. The reasoning employed in such cases is interconnected to the use of economic concepts, and thus its full meaning and value can not be understood when approached with ignorance of the framework in which the reasoning is developed and articulated.

Competition

Competition deserves a little further comment. Competition is an idea that mimics democracy and pluralism. In the market context, just as in the political one, it is believed to be advantageous to have multiple decision makers and decentralized power. In the market context it is not always easy to tell if a given market is competitive, although it may be helpful for initial analysis to assume its competitive nature. An example of this difficulty can be shown with the simple observation that, in a given market, all sellers

---

[15] *Id.* at 1296. *See also* DRIESEN, ENVIRONMENTAL LAW.

are offering similar goods and services for the same basic price. Some people will argue that this shows monopoly power or that it indicates a lack of competition. The problem is that different cultural-interpretive devices can be employed to reach conflicting conclusions.

In a competitive market, the market or equilibrium price is set by supply and demand functions for the whole market. If you are one of many suppliers renting out apartments, and your units are like hundreds of others already on the market, then your price will basically flow from the market such that in a competitive market prices tend to be similar for similar services. Only to the extent that you can be cheaper than others (an unusual cost saving such as very low-cost labor or access to special technology and patents), or distinguish your product from the perceived quality of others can you adjust the price. Thus, the observation that all sellers are selling the same basic products for the same basic price and on the same general terms may be evidence of the economist's perfectly competitive market. On the contrary, it may be evidence of monopoly power, or hegemonic market power. Large developer/landlords may control the rental market and have the power to limit supplies and fix rental terms. In such a case consumers have little or no choice. Thus, as discussed in chapter 2, basic economic assumptions are contestable from a cultural–interpretive viewpoint, and as legal actors we need to be aware of the implications of such disagreements.

Questions of competition also extend beyond these general considerations. Competition and market definition are central to the law related to antitrust and regulated industries. It is also important in addressing various tariff and anti-dumping legislation in dealing with international trade. Competition and the degree to which it is present in a given market is also important in cases such as *Honorable* discussed in chapter 2.[16] In that case it was an important factor in determining if the defendant had discriminated against the plaintiffs. Similarly, the presence of a highly competitive market is often the basis for suggesting that government regulation is unnecessary. It is argued to be unnecessary because consumers are adequately protected by competition and the desire of sellers to earn their custom.

In the field of law known as intellectual property, for instance, we see legal policy attempting to balance the perceived benefits of competition with the counter-benefits of limited monopoly. In the areas of both copyright law and patent law, for example, we witness a tension between the

---

[16] Honorable v. Easy Life Real Estate Sys., 100 F. Supp.2d at 890.

desire to promote competition in ideas, and the goal of protecting ideas so that the originator can receive an "appropriate" economic return. On the one hand, free-flowing ideas and the promotion of creative work is good and valuable. Extensive dissemination and easy accessibility make ideas and related inventions readily available for further refinement and adjustment. The foundation for further creativity is easily available to everyone.

On the other hand, ideas and inventions can take years to develop. They require labor and investment and they reflect individual and group achievements. Consequently, there is a feeling that economic incentives are needed to induce an on-going and self-interested pursuit of invention and creativity. To this end copyright and patent law provide various protections and forms of monopoly power over the works that they address. Thus, copyright and patent law provide examples of legal regimes that use a limitation on competition in the "short run" as a means of advancing additional investment and the hoped-for benefit of future competition.

In copyright, patent law, and various areas of trade and market regulation we witness a complexity in the way in which law attempts to deal with a concept such as market competition. And, in socio-legal discourse we can understand that the concept of competition offers a useful framework for directing and limiting the patterns of legal argument.

Preferences

People form preferences that help them make choices.[17] Understanding preferences is important because many areas of law relate to establishing and identifying preferences. For example, contract law involves the private ordering of preferences, and land use and regulatory law involve public ordering of preferences. These *preferences* are formed as a result of many variables, including experience. Accounting for these preferences and making choices involves a process of interpretation. The actor must interpret incoming information and market signals and translate them into action. Consequently, the cultural–interpretive process, described in earlier chapters, is important for understanding the way in which law, markets, and culture interact.

---

[17] *See e.g.* Dau-Schmidt, *Relaxing Traditional Economic Assumptions*; Dau-Schmidt, *Legal Prohibitions*; Dau-Schmidt, *Economics and Sociology*; Dau-Schmidt, *An Economic Analysis of the Criminal Law*.

Some people argue that preferences are formed *exogenously*, which means that these preferences reflect an independent variable. In a sense it implies that market actors are not influenced by the transactions in which they participate. In contrast, others think that certain preferences are dependent variables such that these preferences are informed by our experiences, and thus by the transactions we participate in. This means that preferences are informed *endogenously*.

To better understand this debate, consider your time in high school, or undergraduate school. Participating in those experiences, exchanges, and relationships influenced you because you are a human being rather than a detached and isolated robotic machine. To the extent that you were affected by your experiences, your preferences expressed an endogenous element. As real people, we are not detached from the relationships we experience; we are influenced by them. Consequently, when we examine law and public policy we must be aware of the types of experiences and exchange relationships that are confronted by differently situated individuals. We must consider how this will impact the way in which law and legal institutions operate.

In as much as preferences reflect experience, it is difficult to compare preferences between people. Economists say that it is difficult to make *interpersonal utility comparisons*. Despite this difficulty we can still use reason and logic to make some general policy choices with respect to questions of fairness and resource allocation as between differently situated individuals or groups.

Finally, there is some concern over how we identify competing preferences in society. This is the question of *hidden versus revealed preferences*. Some economists argue that taking surveys or trying to measure preferences indirectly is too arbitrary and inexact. They argue that we should make law and public policy based on revealed preferences, as in "putting your money where your mouth is," or "putting your money on the table." In other words, we should be driven by what people actually do with their money. In this scenario, money functions as a proxy for social preferences. The economist advises, for example, that we should not simply ask people how much they value a clean environment. Instead, we should observe how much they are willing to spend for "green" products and for environmental conservation. Based on actual spending habits of individuals, economists will map revealed preferences. The problem with this view is that not everyone has the same ability to "cast votes" with money because money is not distributed evenly. Therefore, not everyone will be able to express the extent of their preferences. Looking only at revealed preferences in dollar terms favors the preferences of those with wealth. This means that lower-income people will have less input in setting social preferences, and a legal system that favors a preference-setting mechanism linked to dollars perpetuates the conventionalized power relationships of prior distributions. Thus, controlling the way in which reference is made to preferences can facilitate favorable distributive outcomes.

Valuation

Whenever we think about cost and benefit analysis and about computing damages we need to think about valuation. Valuation goes beyond our previous discussion of accounting and economic profits. Valuation is important in many exchanges including the structuring of a contract or mortgage, the levy of a tax, or the payment of damages, among others. This requires us to think about ways in which we can calculate or approximate value in easily translatable market terms.

One measure of value is market price. This is a price that a ready buyer and seller will pay in a voluntary exchange. This is a good measure of value for things that are easily traded, have a well-functioning formal market, have good liquidity, are basically fungible, and for circumstances in which private self-interest is readily convergent with public interest. If there is a breach of a contract to deliver a barrel of oil, for instance, we can look at oil price indexes published in numerous papers to calculate the value of the barrel. One barrel of a given grade of oil is basically fungible with that of another such barrel.

Market price is not very useful if we have a unique good, a specially manufactured good, a good in which there is no ready market, or a situation in which private interest diverges substantially from the public interest. In these situations, we have to take other factors into account and look for "benchmarks" of value.

Some common ways of assessing market value include: *comparable sales*; *cost of replacement*; and *income flow analysis*. The *comparable sales* method involves looking at recent sales of a similar item as a way to approximate value. The difficulty involves assessing similarity, and identifying the appropriate market to reference for sales: local, regional, state, national, or international, for instance. A further complication can involve the terms of various sales. For example, should a cash sale at $20,000 be treated the same as a sale at $20,000 paid over three years at a particular rate of interest? This involves a concern for the *time value of money*. The time value of money simply holds that a dollar today is worth more than getting a dollar next month. We would also need to adjust for such things as the likelihood of actually getting the future payment.

So if we want to compare the value of the cash now or later we need to find the *discounted present value* of the delayed payment.[18] For example the discounted present value of $1,000 using a 10 percent discount rate is $148.64 for 20 years, $8.52 for 50 years, and $.07 for 100 years. Thus, a $1,000 benefit to the environment recognized over 100 years is worth only about 7 cents in terms of a cost and benefit analysis. As a consequence, one can see that arguments over the proper discount rate and the time horizon for benefits become central to the calculation of value in a cost and benefit framework. It should also be easy to see that environmental regulations can be easily undermined using a cost and benefit analysis with an appropriate discount rate and time horizon. If present costs on an industry to comply with a new regulatory proposal are high, and the benefits are highly discounted over a long period of time, there will be little justification for the regulation. Consequently, it is often just as important to win the battle over discount rates and time horizons as it is to win the battle over regulation in the first instance.

The *cost of replacement* method is a useful device when there is not a strong market for resale or the item is unique. Here, one calculates the cost of replacing the item, such as in determining what it would cost to replace a damaged portion of a cathedral.

The *income flow analysis* approach involves determining the value of an item by the cash flow that it entitles the owner to access or control. This might be used to value a shopping mall, an office building, or a book publishing contract.

Each of these methods – comparable sales, replacement cost, and income flow – can result in a different determination of value, so one must think about the appropriate method for any given legal situation. Moreover, one must be careful in selecting or identifying the frame, reference, and representation choices that can lead to very different market value determinations.

Valuation problems become acute when the items in question are very difficult to measure in dollar terms. An example involves the environment. How do we value the Grand Canyon or Glacier Bay, Alaska? When we have an oil spill in an environmentally sensitive bay, how do we determine the loss, how do we assess damages? When we make environmental policy

---

[18] Lewin, *Toward a New Ecological Law & Economics*.

based on a cost and benefit analysis, how do we value the benefits of a cleaner bay as related to the costs of imposing certain regulations?

Two methods used to translate these intangible aspects into market value involve *contingent and hedonic valuation* methods. *Contingent valuation* methods employ social science survey methods to ask people how much they value certain aspects of the environment, or how much they would be willing to pay for certain outcomes. The survey results are then used as a planning guide. Naturally, one must have a good understanding of survey techniques to understand or challenge such results.

Hedonic valuation involves an indirect approximation of value. To use our oil spill in the bay example, we would try to get at value by adding up related or indirect values. For instance, we might assess the loss of fishing revenue from the bay and the related loss in canning activity. To this we could add the estimated loss in tourist dollars as people avoid the bay while the oil spill is in place. We could also add in the cost of clean-up efforts. By adding up these various indirect but related values we can estimate the value of the bay as an economic enterprise. It is difficult to imagine, however, that these indirect measures can also fully account for esthetic and other types of value, but it does provide a starting point for organizing our legal reasoning.

Hedonic and contingent valuation methods raise normative questions with respect to the ability and desirability of quantifying certain values.[19] They imply a desire to commodify everything when perhaps there are some resources or certain relationships that should not be commodified. Perhaps some elements of the human experience should remain outside the bounds of economic quantification and calculation. On the other hand, if we put these methods into proper perspective, they do give us another avenue for thinking about additional ways in which people experience or relate to law, markets, and culture. Hedonic damages force us to think about indirect relationships that we might not otherwise take into account, and contingent valuation methods give us survey data that is free from the economic desire to have all preferences revealed through a willingness and ability to pay. If we address each method in terms of mapping additional cultural–interpretive meanings, rather than as determining a clear mathematical calculus, we can learn something useful.

We can understand the relationship between these various ways of calculating value by making reference to the idea of *fair market value*.

---

[19] For a discussion of hedonic damages in the tort area see McClurg, *It's a Wonderful Life.*

Often the law requires that parties to a dispute calculate a purchase price or a compensation claim with reference to fair market value. The specifics of such a determination can be ambiguous since there are multiple methods for calculating value and because different market assumptions (such as discount rates) will result in different conclusions. In a sense, therefore, we can understand the idea of fair market value as a particular instance of Peirce's three-step mapping process discussed earlier in the book. This involves mapping the various ways in which alternative valuation methods and assumptions inform our thinking about value in a particular case. From this mapping process, sets of plausibly good alternatives emerge and arguments must be offered for the justification of any given choice. Thus, the legal system recognizes that there are sets of plausibly good answers to the valuation question. Therefore, fair market value is not so much an exact or unique calculation as it is an ability to justify the fairness of the process by which a conclusion is reached.

We also deal with valuation questions when we do a *cost and benefit analysis*. For instance, if we want to propose new regulations to control the discharge of pollutants into the water or air, we may want to think about the cost that will be imposed by each of a variety of methods to achieve a stated goal. We may also want to compare the estimated costs against the anticipated gains or benefits. In standard law and economic terms, we may want to argue that the benefits do or do not justify the costs. It should be clear from the above discussion that any cost and benefit analysis is contingent upon the assumptions and methods used to derive the calculation. As legal actors we want to be aware of these contingencies and prepared to respond to these cost and benefit arguments in a variety of ways.

It is worth noting, as an example, that in doing *cost and benefit analysis* the US Department of Transportation (DOT) and the Federal Aviation Administration (FAA) use a figure of $3 million as the value of a human life.[20] When they do a cost and benefit analysis of a proposed safety regulation, they compare the cost of the regulation to its expected benefits. This means that they try to calculate the cost of industry compliance and regulatory supervision, and then they compare that to the expected decrease in fatalities. Thus, if a new safety regulation is expected to save three lives, it is worth spending up to $9 million to achieve that goal. Naturally, we should see the ambiguity in determining the costs and benefits. We have a variety of assumptions and methods to contend with as well as problems

---

[20] 61 F.R. 38992-01, 39007 (1996) (14 C.F.R. 440).

of determining the extent to which we include various transaction costs and secondary or tertiary effects.

Risk and return

Doing a cost and benefit analysis, and valuing or pricing an exchange to obtain a favorable return involves an assessment of *risk*. For every market choice there is a relationship between risk and return. Lawyers are often engaged to manage risk in a transaction or exchange. It is important, therefore, to have a basic understanding of the nature of risk, its relationship to price, and the concepts of *asymmetrical information* and *adverse selection*.[21]

Risk and return relate to each other in opposite directions. Thus, the more risk a seller takes on in a contract the higher will be the price, and likewise the more risk assigned to the buyer in a contract the lower will be the price. This is easy to understand with a simple example involving investing of personal savings. When one puts money into a Federally insured savings account at the local bank the rate of return is much lower than the rate that can be earned from investing that money in a high risk and uninsured investment. The trade off is that the bank can attract savers with low interest rate returns since the savers have no real risk of loss. With the uninsured investment the saver/investor must be offered more interest return because there is more risk that the investment will have a loss. If a person is *risk averse* he or she will generally prefer more certainty of outcome with smaller returns to high risk and the potential of greater returns. In a contract setting we can see that a seller that sells goods "as is" shifts all of the risk of defect to the buyer, and as such should be able to sell at a lower price than a seller that provides extensive warranty protection to the buyer. Sometimes price may look the same between these situations but one must look closely since price can be adjusted indirectly by changing other terms of responsibility under a contract. In the tort area a risk averse person takes more care (a cost) and in the criminal area the risk averse person spends more to avoid being a victim.

There are two broad categories of risk to address. These are *temporal risk* and *transactional risk*. Temporal risk arises from problems related to information and time. Generally, as parties are involved in exchange they make certain decisions based on information about the past, present, and

---

[21] *See generally,* MALLOY & SMITH, REAL ESTATE TRANSACTIONS 24–34.

future. In a transaction to acquire real estate, for instance, a buyer is concerned about the value of the property she is buying. The value will be affected by a number of matters but one key concern involves environmental contamination. To address this concern, she may have tests done on the property and will examine the history of the use of the property for evidence of possible environmental problems. Despite her efforts, the information on past use may be incomplete, incorrect, or inconclusive. Likewise, the conclusion as to its present status may be incorrect. Finally, her expectations about future value may prove wrong when a new testing technology becomes available and shows a trace presence of a hazardous chemical. All of these potential concerns impose risk on the exchange based on the problems of information and time. Other types of temporal risk might involve unexpected changes in the future rates of interest or inflation that upset investment expectations, or erroneous information about past or current ownership or title to property that defeats a buyer's claim.

Transactional risk involves risk or uncertainty as to the transaction itself. This type of risk has several key subcategories. These include investor or ownership risk, marketplace risk, credit risk, and transfer risk.

Investor or ownership risk is the risk associated with being an owner or having control over a right or resource. For instance, as the owner of real property I have certain liability risks associated with potential injuries that may occur to people who come on to my property. I also have the risk that my claim to ownership or control may be defeated. This may result when a previously unsuspected claimant demonstrates that he or she has a better claim to the property. This type of risk is also known as *entrepreneurial risk*. As an investor or owner in a business venture, one may find that he or she is liable for environmental contamination problems, breach of contract claims, or for injuries caused to or by other people involved in the venture.

Marketplace risk involves risk associated with the fact that the market is dynamic. Rates of interest, inflation, and employment all change and changes in these factors, along with others, may dramatically impact on the value of an exchange. Consider a mortgage lender that makes a fixed rate home mortgage loan at 10 percent interest for thirty years only to have markets drive interest rates up to 15 percent within the first year of the loan. Likewise, consider the investor that buys into a promising "dot.com" company, only to have that company go bankrupt three months later when a rival company's new technology makes their product obsolete. The bottom line is that markets are dynamic and every exchange includes an element of risk associated with the unpredictable nature of market activity.

Credit risk is composed of two primary components. These are the *ability* and the *willingness to pay*. In every credit transaction a determination must be made that the person extended the credit will have the ability to pay when due and that he or she will be willing to pay. These are two different questions and risks because some people may be able to pay but unwilling to pay. They may want to dispute the obligation or simply like to delay with the hope of getting the creditor to settle for a lesser sum. Likewise, some people may truly want to pay but due to unexpected changes in their circumstances may be unable to pay when the money is due. Importantly, one must remember that credit transactions involve more than loans. They involve any contract or other arrangement in which the exchange is not simultaneous – when one party performs first and then must count on the willingness and ability of the other side to perform at the agreed-upon time, and on the agreed-upon terms.

Transfer risk focuses on the mechanics of exchange. Consider a real estate transaction, for example. Transfer risk in the real estate transaction simply recognizes the risk of having errors in the documents of exchange, or failing to record or file documents that need to be recorded or filed. It points out the risk of getting things done in accordance with the plan for proceeding. Mistakes happen, and the risk of these mistakes involves transfer or exchange risk.

The law can address some elements of risk by making information more accessible – by protecting rights in the gathering and generation of information so as to create incentives for more and better information. Law can provide mechanisms for enforcement and for damages to reduce the incentive and risk of certain types of breaches or changes in conduct. Law can also provide for insurance mechanisms such as liability insurance, travel insurance, credit card fraud insurance, health insurance, bank deposit insurance, flood insurance, title insurance, mortgage insurance, and home-owner's insurance.

Two related concepts that often get discussed when dealing with risk are issues of *asymmetrical information* and *adverse selection*. These concepts are generally considered opposite sides of the same coin. The idea behind asymmetrical information is that the information available between the parties to an exchange is often very different. The automobile manufacturer, for example, has access to and better knowledge of information relating to the design safety of a given vehicle than does the car-buying consumer or the plaintiff injured by a car that explodes on impact.

Consumer warranty and disclosure legislation attempts to deal with these types of problems. Similarly, strict liability in tort and presumptions of liability against a manufacturer also attempt to adjust for such exchange disparities.

The adverse selection problem deals with a similar imbalance in information. Here, the focus is on the difficulty of selecting when some information may be withheld, misrepresented, or difficult (costly) to uncover. An example might be in the employment area. The employer seeks to hire the hardest-working and potentially most productive employees. In making this selection the employer has less information than the potential employee has about her actual work and productivity skills and values. The employer uses some proxy indicators in trying to assess these qualities and interviews the job candidate. The problem of adverse selection is one of recognizing that even with careful review a bad or inappropriate selection may be made.

It is important to note that not all risk can be eliminated, even though some risk can be reduced by obtaining good information and doing investigative work. The risk that can not be eliminated needs to be allocated to a given party to the exchange so that insurance can be purchased and so that price can be adjusted to reflect the allocation of risk. Ideally, the parties and the law should allocate the risk to the party best able to control or reduce the risk, because this will result in dealing with the risk in the least-cost manner. More importantly, an analysis of exchange should include consideration of risk and the allocation of that risk as between the parties, and as between private or public mechanisms for reducing these risks. In addition, risk must be assessed in terms of variables related to such characteristics as race, gender, age, class, education level, income, and geographic location, among others. We need to understand the way in which risk reveals itself in terms of the experience of differently situated people and groups.

The case of *Int'l Union, United Auto., Aerospace and Agric. Implement Workers of America UAW* v. *Johnson Controls, Inc.* provides a good example of the problem of attempting to deal with risks that affect different groups of people in different ways.[22] This case involved a challenge to a policy by Johnson Controls (a battery manufacturer) that barred all women from working in an area of its factories where they would be exposed to potentially dangerous levels of lead, unless the women could produce

[22] Int'l Union, United Auto., Aerospace and Agric. Implement Workers of America, UAW v. Johnson Controls, Inc., 499 U.S. 187 (1991).

medical documentation of their infertility. Men did not have to produce documentation of this sort and were not barred from this type of work. Johnson Controls was concerned about the potential liability related to the exposure of fertile women to lead.[23] They were concerned that a pregnant woman might end up with a child born with birth defects as a result of lead exposure. The Court held that Johnson Controls failed to establish an adequate basis for the difference in treatment between male and female workers and found the policy to be discriminatory under applicable Federal statutory law.[24]

From the point of view of understanding law in a market context the case is interesting because of the problems it raises for dealing with potentially different risks in different populations. If we were to think about the mapping of this dispute we could start by looking at the exchange in terms of the immediate parties. As between Johnson Controls and its workers, the work environment was within required safety standards but the nature of the work still left a potential risk from lead exposure that could not be eliminated. The workers could be given disclosure information and be required to sign a disclosure acknowledgment and consent form. They might also be paid a wage premium as added compensation for their risk from exposure to lead. In this mapping we can deal with the problems of information, disclosure, market power, and consent as between the adult parties to the exchange.

We have a different set of issues, however, if we map this exchange to include the fetus as a third party to the exchange. The unborn child raises a problem for a company that has a legitimate concern with respect to potential harm to a fetus. When born, the fetus may have its own cause of action for harm caused as a result of risk exposure. It is unclear that a mother should be permitted to waive the rights of her child by simply executing her own consent form. This could leave an employer open to liability on two counts. It might be subject to a lawsuit for treating female employees in a manner that differs from that of male employees, and at the same time it might be liable for birth defects if fertile women were allowed to work in these environments.

This type of policy must also be considered from the perspective of female workers. Women employees, under such a policy, are eliminated from access to good-paying jobs and from an important participatory role in the marketplace. This is particularly troublesome when the pregnancy itself is uncertain (the policy is directed at too broad a group classification)

[23] *Id.* at 191.   [24] *Id.* at 211.

and does not interfere with the ability of a woman to perform her work. The Court concluded that Federal law had already struck a balance on this matter and that balance was in favor of requiring equal treatment between men and women.[25] In reaching its conclusion the Court also addressed two potential defenses available to Johnson Controls. These involved the business necessity rule, and the showing of the infertility requirement to be a Bona Fide Occupational Qualification under applicable Federal law. Johnson Controls was held to have been unsuccessful in making out either of these potential defenses.[26]

The point of this example is that it demonstrates a basic problem that legal institutions are forced to address. Legal institutions must mediate tensions and disputes over resources (jobs and job opportunities) that arise in a market context. In a society based on a capitalist form of economic organization, it is important to have equal access to the market. Thus, the very nature of the dispute in this case hinges upon an understanding of market forces and on access to market power. Furthermore, the successful lawyer in a situation such as this has to understand the nature of risk and its consequences. She must also understand market concepts at a level sufficient to effectively develop and advance a theory of the case that accounts for both legal and economic implications. Being ill-prepared to understand the market context and the references to risk in these and other types of disputes will leave her at a disadvantage in developing sound and useful legal strategies.

Transactional misbehavior

Transactional misbehavior involves "cheating" on a cooperative exchange.[27] In this sense it is related to the discussion concerning the prisoner's dilemma in chapter 2. The basic idea is that it sometimes makes economic sense (it is economically rational) to cheat on a deal or attempt to change a deal after the fact. For example, I may go to the bank to borrow money and "represent" myself as a very conservative and cautious borrower deserving of a low interest rate on a loan. I may provide the bank with a plan for using the money in a very low-risk approach to starting a new business or buying some land. The bank may agree to a low rate of interest and extend me $700,000 of credit. Once I have the money, I may have an incentive to change the deal so as to extract more value from

---

[25] *Id.* at 197.   [26] *Id.* at 206.
[27] MALLOY & SMITH, REAL ESTATE TRANSACTIONS 17–21.

the exchange. I might do this by using the money for a much more risky investment than the one I described to the bank. The riskier investment has the potential for a bigger return to me (more risk and more return) and I feel lucky so I misdirect the money. I get more value out of this conduct because it would have cost a lot more in terms of the interest rate charge to borrow money for the riskier investment I actually made. Thus, I unilaterally change the terms of the deal by, in a sense, cheating on my obligation under the original deal. From the bank's point of view, it is a problem of adverse selection. Perhaps the bank should have done more information-gathering before making the loan. The bank also needs to think about how it can monitor or police its loans better to reduce the risk of transactional misbehavior. Perhaps it needs to control the money more closely rather than simply disbursing it to me all at once. Maybe it needs better accounting requirements or other controls. The point is that many transactions may involve this sort of predictable misbehavior and the exchange must account for it up front.

This type of problem becomes an even higher risk when one party's expectations drop after a deal is entered into. For example, in the above situation I may have very good intentions to invest that $700,000 just as I had represented it to the bank, but market changes or other problems put me into a severe cash flow problem. Under the pressure of potential financial collapse, I take action that hurts the bank. This is a very real problem and it must be accounted for up front. As circumstances change, the dynamics of an exchange also change and this may trigger incentives for behavior that must be anticipated.

Rent seeking and opportunistic behavior

People look for opportunities to capture and create value from exchange.[28] They look for opportunities to improve their position and to earn special returns where and when possible. *Opportunistic behavior* is behavior that evidences a move or action to seek out better returns from exchange. This is related to *rent seeking behavior*. A *rent is* a special return that one gets over and above the normal market return that would prevail if a right, a talent, or resource were fungible. A gifted musician or athlete, for instance, may earn a very high salary because of unique skills that give them a rent return above the normal market rate. Likewise, I may earn a special return

[28] *Id.* at 21–24.

on property that serves as the only access to prime fishing spots along a given river.

In more specific terms, an *economic rent* is a payment amount in excess of one's next-best alternative. Thus, if I earn $100,000 per year in my present employment and my next-best employment opportunity would pay me $95,000, I earn an economic rent of $5,000. An older notion of economic rent (attributed to Ricardo) would compare my current pay not to my next-best alternative, but to the minimal pay it would take to induce me to take the employment. Thus, if I would be willing to work for $30,000 and I am currently paid $100,000 I would have an economic rent of $70,000. The idea of economic rent in either form can be relevant to figuring damages because it makes reference to the value of lost opportunities.

One basic idea behind rent seeking behavior and its relationship to legal reasoning is that the law itself creates value and opportunities for rent seeking and opportunistic behavior. In a sense, law is a commodity and certain laws can be used to provide special returns or rents. For example, laws restricting the number of plumbers, hairdressers, or surgeons all act to reduce competition and permit members of the trade or profession to earn higher returns than if there were no restrictions or barriers to entry or exit. This encourages people to seek licensing and permit restrictions that will reduce access and raise the cost of entry. To paraphrase a popular American Express credit card commercial, "membership has its privileges, and its rents."

In a similar way, tax laws create special opportunities for particular types of investments, and understanding this provides incentive for people to lobby Congress for special tax treatment. Zoning laws also create value differences between properties, and rent seeking behavior might involve investing money in an effort to influence a zoning change that results in raising the value of your property. In yet other situations, this type of behavior may result in businesses moving away from America to foreign jurisdictions where there are fewer labor, environmental, and safety regulations that all add costs to the production process. In this way, one can earn a special return over competitors that have not yet relocated and who are confronted with different legal infrastructure and costs.

Whenever we deal with law and legal policy we need to think about the implications for exchange. We need to think about the ripple effects of the law or policy with respect to rent seeking and opportunistic behavior that may raise its own problems or multiply the original problem. We must also have these ideas in mind when we think about the political process, the dynamics of public choice, and the influence of special interests on the law making process.

Coase's Theorem

Activities by consumers and producers often result in *externalities*. An externality is an adverse (or beneficial) side effect of consumption or production, for which no payment is required (or no payment is received). The emission of pollution as a by-product of a manufacturing facility is an example of an externality. This type of externality can have a negative impact on others. If the neighborhoods surrounding the factory are entitled to clean air and water, the factory owner will have to negotiate with area residents in order to be allowed to pollute. Similarly if the factory has a right to cause a certain amount of pollution, residents of the neighborhood will have to negotiate with the factory owner in order to obtain cleaner air and water. The question arises, therefore, as to the best way to allocate entitlements and resources between the factory and the residents of the neighborhood. The Coase Theorem provides a useful framework for addressing this question.

According to Ronald Coase, society can allocate resources and entitlements efficiently even when there are externalities.[29] In order for this to be accomplished, however, the cost of negotiating must be nominal. The costs of negotiating are known as *transaction costs* and include such things as the costs of identifying the parties with whom one has to bargain, the costs of getting together with them, the costs of the bargaining process itself, and the costs of enforcing any bargain reached.

Coase's Theorem is best illustrated with an example (see figure 5.3). A classic example involves a polluting factory discharging waste into the environment. To explore this idea better, let us consider a situation where a factory discharges waste into a nearby river causing injury to six homeowners living downstream. In this situation we can assume, as is typically the case, that several options are available for solving this externality problem. Let us assume that the outcome options available to our community

---

[29] *See generally* Coase, *The Problem of Social Cost;* COASE, THE FIRM, THE MARKET, AND THE LAW; Swygert & Yanes, *A Primer on the Coase Theorem;* Hoffman & Spitzer, *The Coase Theorem;* Nutter, *The Coase Theorem on Social Cost;* Hovenkamp, *Marginal Utility and the Coase Theorem;* Daly, *The Coase Theorem;* Cordato, *Time Passage and the Economics of Coming to the Nuisance;* Eastman, *How Coasean Bargaining Entails a Prisoners" Dilemma;* Schlag, *The Problem of Transaction Costs;* COOTER & ULEN, LAW AND ECONOMICS 82–87; MALLOY, LAW AND MARKET ECONOMY (2000) 90–99, 103–04.

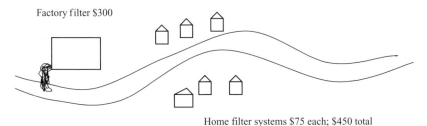

Figure 5.3

include: (1) allowing the factory to discharge but requiring the payment of damages to the downstream home owners; (2) requiring the factory to install a filter system at the point of discharge to eliminate the waste before it enters the river; or (3) requiring the downstream homeowners to install personal home filters in each home so that water intake from the river will be cleaned at the point of entry into the home environment. Assume further that there is a price differential between the above three outcomes such that the filter at the factory point of discharge is the lowest-cost alternative at $300. This is followed by the aggregate cost of an at-home filter system that each home owner would have to purchase at $75 each for a total of $450, and then by the amount of damages that must either be paid by the factory to the homeowners or absorbed by each of them if no filter system is used, assume $100 of damages for each household and a total cost of $600.

The Coase Theorem holds that in a world of zero transaction costs, the efficient (wealth-maximizing) choice alternative will be selected without regard to the legal rule. That is, it makes no difference if (1) the law permits the factory, as a land owner with riparian rights, to discharge by-products into the river, or (2) the law protects the rights of all home owners to have clean water. Whether the legal rule grants the factory a right to discharge (pollute) or it grants the home owners a right to clean water, the Coase Theorem suggests that the most efficient outcome will be selected from the three options identified above. As long as all parties are aware of the three options (as would be the case in perfect competition) and there are little or no costs of transacting, the lowest-cost alternative, the filter for the factory, will be purchased without regard for the legal rule. Under the first rule, permitting the factory to pollute, the filter for the factory will be purchased by the collective action of the home owners and under the second rule, providing for a legal right to clean water, the filter will be purchased by the factory.

The explanation for this is that under the first rule the factory has a right to discharge – that is, it has certain property or use rights in the river – some form of riparian rights, let us say. Thus, the legal burden to provide clean water falls upon the home owners and they must correct the dirty water problem. Assuming no transaction costs, perfect information, and economically rational actors they will buy a filter for the factory (as a gift) because it is the cheapest way for them to solve their problem. The $300 filter for the factory costs each of them $50 as compared to the $75 for a personal home filter and $100 of damages for each. Similarly, if the rule is reversed and the home owners have a right to clean water, making the factory legally responsible for the purity of the water, the factory will assess the situation and purchase a filter for the point of discharge because it is the most economically efficient way to act within the contextual constraints of the assumptions. Buying a $300 filter to install at the factory is cheaper than buying a $75 filter for each of the six home owners ($450 total cost), and it is cheaper than paying each home owner $100 in damages ($600 total cost).

When there are no transaction costs we get the same efficient outcome regardless of the legal rule. Under either rule, the filter is purchased for the factory and the problem is addressed using the least-cost and most efficient method. Even though we get the same outcome we must be careful in how we frame our legal analysis. When the rule requires clean water discharge (the factory is responsible) the factory pays for corrective action. The alternative rule places the cost of corrective action on the home owners. Thus, even though we get the same outcome, we observe a distributive impact with respect to who pays.

The Coase Theorem acknowledges that the real world is not cost-free. There are transaction costs. The importance of the zero transaction costs assumption is to provide an idealized reference point for further dis-cussion of the implications of transaction costs. Thus, Coase goes on to suggest that transaction costs can change this outcome and cause the par-ties involved to make a less than socially optimal choice. If, for instance, the homeowners confront significant transaction costs in getting orga-nized and acting collectively to deal with the pollution problem, they may opt to purchase their own personal filter system when the legal rule grants the factory a right to discharge pollutants. To understand this let us assume that the cost of getting good information about the problem and the available corrective options, together with the difficulty of organizing all the home owners and enforcing a contribution or collective agreement between them is high – let us assume transaction costs of $40 per household. With transaction costs of this amount, home owners might end up selecting the option of buying their own home filter system rather than working collectively to purchase a single filter system for the factory. The high transaction costs mean that they will not act collectively but will consider the individual options that they confront. Given this frame of reference the cost of the filter for the factory would be $50 plus $40 per household or a total of $90 each. This makes the factory filter more expensive than the $75 personal home filter system.

Given transaction costs, the personal home filter system erroneously appears to the home owners as the best-choice outcome, but this is not the most economically efficient outcome, as can be seen by anyone capable of understanding all of the trade offs and distanced from the problem of transaction costs. The factory filter costs $300 or $50 per household, but the purchase of the individual units costs a total of $450, or $75 each. Because an inefficient choice is made, society wastes valuable resources. That is, as a community, the group spends more money than needed to correct the dirty water problem. It spends $450 rather than $300 and this means that $150 that could have been available for other activities is wasted. This is an inefficient outcome.

In our situation, with $40 of transaction costs per household, the socially efficient outcome, the least-cost alternative, will be selected only if the legal rule places liability on the factory by granting the home owners a right to clean water. Under a clean water rule the factory is legally responsible and since it does not need to coordinate with any other parties its transaction costs are substantially lower than those of the home owners. Thus, the factory will purchase the $300 filter for the point of discharge rather than pay $600 in damages or $450 to provide each home owner with a personal home filter system. Consequently, the legal rule does make a difference when there are transaction costs. Transaction costs can result in inefficient choices. This results in the wasting of scarce resources and in causing a divergence between self-interest and public interest. It means that people pursuing their own self-interest will make choices which are efficient as to them but which are inefficient for society.

Now consider a situation involving something called the *wealth effect*. If the legal rule places the burden on the home owners, and they happen to be poor, they may lack the resources to address the problem. They may be living at a subsistence level in their community and lack the resources to keep their homes in full repair. In our example, for instance, these poor home owners may lack the discretionary income to contribute $50 each to a group purchase of a factory filter, and to spend $75 to purchase an individual filter for each of their homes. If the legal rule places the burden on such home owners they will not be able to take corrective action. The wealth effect will cause them to take a course of action that requires no out-of-pocket payments. They will each suffer $100 of damages. This is the least desirable outcome because we have people suffering $600 worth of damages that could be prevented by spending only $300 on a filter for the factory or by spending a total of $450 on individual home filters. The wealth effect informs us of the need to examine the identity of the parties to be affected by the choice in legal rule, and to address the fairness as well as efficiency of that rule.

Placing the burden on the factory also has its complications. If the legal rule places the burden on the factory owner it might be argued that the factory owner could easily absorb the cost, or that it could easily pass the costs on to its customers. The ability to pass on costs, however, depends on the competitive nature of the market. It should also be noted that its customers may, or may not, be the beneficiaries of the clean water. Thus, to the extent customers pay, they may be a different interest group than the people living in the downstream households. Furthermore, customers may be located in different jurisdictions than either the factory or the home owners. In other words, there may be transboundary jurisdiction issues, with different legal regimes operating. The factory could be in one state or country, the households downstream across the jurisdictional boundary, and the customers scattered across global markets. All of this means that political trading may also play a role in these distribution matters, and as a result it may become difficult or impossible to determine the real efficiency value of any given choice.

This analysis of the Coase Theorem further suggests that in order to reduce the inefficient use of scarce resources the law should attempt to clearly define private property rights and work to reduce transaction costs. It implies a course of legislative action if *experts* are better able, than countless individuals, to identify and overcome the choice and cost structure of alternative approaches. Naturally, if an expert can understand the relevant choices better than other non-experts he can overcome the problem of high transaction costs for each of the households. He can do this by delivering legislation, under our above assumptions, that adopts a legal rule in favor of home owners and provides for a right to clean water. This rule promotes the efficient outcome by placing responsibility for clean water on the factory. The factory then makes the efficient choice and purchases the point of discharge filter. *Assuming* that his cost and choice assumptions/constraints are correct, the expert can use law to move us in the direction of economic efficiency. This is an important caveat. We have assumed knowledge of costs and damages in a way that might not be so clear in the real world. We can use different references for figuring costs and some damages may not be quantifiable. Thus, there is room for manipulation within the framework. Given that his valuation choices are open to debate, the expert can work to frame the debate in terms of high transaction costs and establish an economic justification for legislative action. In the alternative, he or his antagonists might work to frame the debate in terms of low transaction costs and establish an economic justification for non-intervention.

The choice of legal rule also raises implications that go beyond questions of distributional impact and the role of legislative expertise. The rule, itself, changes the cultural-interpretive frame of reference for exchange. Rule choice, in other words, affects the meaning and value formation process. Consider our polluting factory example. We have two rules to consider. The factory is given a right to discharge or the home owners are given an entitlement to clean water. This is a simple dualistic choice. If we pick a rule that protects the home owners' right to clean water we impose a duty on the factory, and given transaction costs we can see that factory liability is the efficient rule.

This approach, of placing the cost of corrective action on the producer, is one that represents the framing of the vast majority of environmental regulations in the United States. One problem with this type of framing is that it denies the explicit role of the consumer in activities that cause environmental degradation. It tends to obscure the relationship between production and consumption. Thus, consumers fail to fully comprehend that their demand for goods and services at low prices drives and influences production and producer action. Likewise, they seldom seem to make the connection between their environmental concerns and the fact that many American consumers simply want to pay the lowest possible prices for the products and services that they demand. For example, if a television set or a pair of running shoes will cost less when produced by child labor under conditions that require little regard for the environment, American consumers have generally shown that they will buy it. Feeling no direct responsibility for production, the American consumer guiltlessly complains about environmental degradation while all the time fueling the competitive pressure for businesses to cut corners and seek lower-cost methods of production. For the consumer it's the best of both worlds, high levels of consumption without responsibility.

One reason for this misunderstanding is that the selection of the legal rule raises implications for the meaning and value formation process. The interpretive reference for most rules on environmental regulation imposes legal duties and responsibilities on producers, and because of dualistic thinking this is translated into the idea that consumers must therefore be innocent. I suggest that if rule choices made consumers responsible, or if consumers had to pay an explicit environmental tax on everything that they consumed, meanings and values would be different. Consequently, the choice of the legal rule, even under conditions of zero transaction costs, makes a difference. It makes a difference not only in terms of distributional impact but also in terms of the interpretive framework and meanings given to particular exchange relationships.

Other interpretive issues are also raised by the Coase Theorem. Our Coase Theorem example, for instance, demonstrates thinking within a reactive framework and this type of thinking restricts the process of choice. In our example we were presented with three alternative methods for correcting the dirty water problem. Each method is known and each is given a price (factory filter $300, home filter $75 \times 6 = 450, and damages of $100 \times 6 = 600). Anyone that has the relevant information can easily calculate the most efficient way to allocate resources, and can, thus, readily select the socially optimal course of action. This example illustrates thinking within the status quo, within the context of identifiable constraints and options. Efficiency analysis, in traditional law and economics, takes this form. It is reactive in that it tells us how to make the best use of the resources we already know that we have, but it says little about the conditions under which new options might be facilitated and discovered. It also promotes a sense of certainty to the analysis of the problem because we can use simple math to calculate an efficient result. The numbers used in these calculations, however, are often "fuzzy" and based on debatable assumptions. This means that the calculus of efficient outcomes can be influenced by or manipulated with minor variations in assumed costs and benefits.

We might also ask why the Coase Theorem typically addresses problems such as pollution from within the language of *externality*. Why are these effects framed as external or foreign to the activity of the factory? Why aren't the third-party consequences of a manufacturing process considered to be *internal* effects of the profit seeking venture within the factory? How might this framing change our thinking?

There is yet another implication of the Coase Theorem when it is used as a frame for socio-legal analysis. This implication takes us back to the idea of zero transaction costs and to the role of experts. Under an assumption of zero transaction costs an implication arises that the judgment of every individual is in some sense equal. There are no information problems (perfect information), no barriers to market entry or exit, and no problems related to prior distributions. There is free and frictionless mobility of goods, services, and resources, and people act with complete rationality. Personal experience provides no advantage or disadvantage in the exchange process. Race, gender, age, education, culture, and other factors make no difference. In such a fictive world there would be no reason to give primacy to any particular individual's judgment, and choice would involve a simple factual calculation. On the other hand, the implication changes once we acknowledge the presence of transaction costs, externalities, and spillover effects as part of the real world.

Life in a world of greater than zero transaction costs, however, is life in a world of personal and subjective experiences that make a difference in the networks and patterns of exchange. There is imperfect information, there are barriers to entry and exit, there are problems of distributional and historical consequence, there is less than free and frictionless mobility of goods, services, and resources, and emotion, instinct, and other forces sometimes deform and distort the assumptional meaning of rationality. Transaction costs burden the networks of exchange.

In such a world issues of access and mobility, for instance, may vary significantly by such factors as race, gender, ethnicity, religion, education level, geography, age, family composition, and other variables. In a world of transaction costs these factors are important because different experiences mean that different fragments of knowledge are dispersed in an uncoordinated manner over countless individuals. Tapping into these knowledge fragments is important to the idea of market efficiency. Thus, efforts at reducing transaction costs, promoting diversity, affirmative action, inclusion, and equality can all be helpful in advancing the flow of information and knowledge.

A further implication of a world of positive transaction costs is that some people, "experts," may be deemed better situated than others to shape the decision making process. This is easy to imagine. It is like the difference between making a decision about which road to take to work when you see the road from behind the wheel of your car vs. from the position of a helicopter pilot surveying the traffic patterns from above. Driving on the highway, in your car alongside hundreds of other drivers, gives you a very different basis for decision making than that of the helicopter pilot who is able to see a multi-vehicle accident a mile up the road from your current location.

Likewise, your ability to exercise some control over the speed and direction of your car is very different from the position of the person who rides the bus and submits to the judgment of a bus driver. Each of the people in this example, the pilot, the car driver, and the bus commuter, have access to different information and have different experiences upon which to base expectations and make choices. In some sense, the pilot in our example is positioned like our fictional expert in the water pollution problem as confronted by our factory and six households in the earlier example. Somewhat removed from the immediate situation on the ground, the pilot can more clearly appreciate the options available and select a more efficient course of action for traffic flow than the drivers and commuters below. Furthermore, with an eye toward facilitating the overall flow of traffic, for the benefit of the public at large, she can make choices that are seemingly superior to those of the less informed people on the ground. She can appreciate the lack of unity between the public interest and the individual driver's perception of self-interest in this situation.

Therefore, in a world of transaction costs, "experts" would seemingly be given more authority than non-experts, and inequality between exchange participants increases as some are cloaked in expertise and others are not. It thus becomes important to consider the basis upon which one becomes an expert. What factors, in our example, place one person in the pilot seat while others are drivers and commuters on the ground below, and what elements of the human experience go unappreciated as a result of our expert's privileged position? These are questions of relational exchange – questions of law and market economy rather than economic efficiency.

Thus the Coase Theorem is important to legal argument. It is clear that an ability to shape and frame the legal rule, and the identification and value of transaction costs can be instrumental in successfully advancing a given position or outcome.

Now let us consider an application of Coase in a standard legal setting. We can better understand the application of the Coase Theorem to legal reasoning when we examine its application in two specific areas – nuisance law and takings law. The first area, involving nuisance, arises when one person's use of property causes an externality that unreasonably interferes with someone else's use of property (private nuisance), or when the negative externality presents a threat to the public health, safety, welfare, and morals (a public nuisance). An example of a nuisance application is provided in the next section of this chapter (pp. 192–4). The key idea, however, is that Coase gives us a way of organizing legal reasoning and argument based on references to externalities and transaction costs – for example, it organizes the argument for placing the entitlement with a given party to facilitate an efficient outcome when there are transactions costs. We will explore this when we discuss the ideas of Pareto and Kaldor–Hicks efficiency in connection with a cement factory imposing externalities on nearby households.

As to takings law, the Coase Theorem helps us understand and explain the *essential nexus and rough proportionality* tests developed by the United States Supreme Court in the *Nollan* and *Dolan* cases.[30] These tests are used as part of the analysis for determining if a regulatory taking of private property has occurred. If it has occurred the 5th Amendment to the United States Constitution requires the payment of just compensation to the property owner.

As background, it should be noted that the Constitution permits the government to take private property for a public purpose upon payment of just compensation. There are two ways in which a taking of private property occurs. First, the taking can be by a physical invasion, as when Malloy's property is taken for construction of a public highway. Such a taking is permitted without Malloy's consent but requires payment to Malloy of just compensation.

The second category of takings involves government regulation restricting the property owner's ability to enjoy the full characteristics of ownership. This can result from imposition of zoning, land use, and environmental regulations. In the regulatory context, the government does not physically invade the property of Malloy, as in the case of building the public highway. To the contrary, Malloy is left with control over his property but is prohibited from making certain uses of it. For example, Malloy may be prevented from building anything other than a one-story single-family residence on his property, or he may be prevented from changing the exterior of an historical building on his property. Other types of regulation may require Malloy to take certain affirmative actions and spend certain sums of money on his property. For instance, if Malloy is operating a commercial facility near a residential area he may be required to construct noise buffers along the perimeter of his property, or he may need to undertake the construction of highway and traffic improvements abutting his property. In these regulatory settings the question arises as to when the regulation becomes so burdensome that it should be considered

---

[30] Nollan, 483 U.S. 825 (1987); Dolan v. City of Tigard, 512 U.S. 374 (1994). The nexus and rough proportionality tests developed in these cases continue to play a significant role in takings law analysis.

a taking of Malloy's private property for which just compensation is due. In the *Lucas* case, the United States Supreme Court provided the guidance of a *per se* rule establishing that a regulation resulting in a 100% loss of economic value to private property is a taking requiring just compensation.[31] Short of this *per se* rule, however, regulatory takings law involves a relatively complex set of inquires and arguments.

Part of the complex analysis of a regulatory takings situation involves the two tests mentioned earlier – the nexus and rough proportionality tests. These tests can be readily understood with reference to the Coase Theorem. To start with, one must recall that the takings clause of the Constitution is premised upon the idea that no individual should be forced to carry an inordinate share of the cost of a public project. Consequently, the United States Supreme Court has required that the regulation of private property meet certain standards, including the need to establish an essential nexus between the goal and object of the regulation, and that the cost imposed by the regulation be roughly proportional to the property owner's responsibility. With reference to Coase, one can show an essential nexus if one demonstrates that a regulation is directed at the control or abatement of an externality caused by the property owner's current or potential use of the property. As to the rough proportionality test, one can show this by demonstrating that the cost imposed on the property owner by the regulation is closely related to the cost of the externality being regulated – such that the cost of the externality is essentially internalized by the property owner. Generally, to the extent that a regulation relates to and internalizes the cost of an externality it is not going to be a taking for which compensation is required. (Remember, of course, that there is no protected right to conduct a nuisance on your property.)

To provide an example, let us consider the earlier situation of the factory discharging pollutants into the river and causing $600 of damages to the households located downstream. Assume that nothing has been done to abate this problem and the town has passed a new land use and zoning code. The new code is designed to enhance land uses along the river and to enhance water quality. About a year after enacting the new land use and zoning code the factory owner applies for a permit to expand its building to include more office and manufacturing space. This will not add to the current discharge problem. The plans call for building in an area currently used for parking. The factory owner plans to relocate parking space to an area behind the present facility – between the factory building and the

---

[31] Lucas v. South Carolina Coastal Councal, 505 U.S. 1003 (1992).

river. The parking lot will be paved and will cause run-off of rain water and melting snow into the river. Citing the new land use and zoning code the town approves the expansion plan for the factory but with three regulatory requirements. These requirements are set out below:

(1) The factory owner must install a water discharge filter on its facility.
(2) The factory owner can not put any part of the proposed parking space within 200 feet of the river and must leave this space as green space. This requirement is based on engineering studies indicating that factory filter systems are enhanced in effectiveness when there is adequate soil and surface absorption of rain and snow run-off. The 200 feet set back from the river banks is within the standard guidelines used by other towns. This requirement will cause the factory owner to relocate 10% of the proposed parking to a front or side lot area at a cost of an additional $100.
(3) The factory owner must build a nature path along its property and within the designated green space. It must also pay for the cost of building two footbridges over the river, to be located in a public park near the factory. The path will connect to a path at the adjoining public park, and the bridges, while not on the factory owner's property, will also enhance public enjoyment of the river.

Now assume that the factory owner objects to these regulatory requirements and asserts that an unlawful taking has occurred. Using the Coase analysis we can explore the way in which concepts from Coase help in addressing the essential nexus and rough proportionality tests.

First we can identify the externality related to the factory owner's use of his property. This involves the discharge into the river that causes damages to the households. The first two regulatory requirements relate directly to this externality. They both focus on the reduction in the consequences of the negative externality on the home owners. For this reason they should pass the essential nexus test. The third requirement, however, seems to have no direct connection to the control or elimination of the externality and it should therefore fail this test. Even if the green space can be shown as benefiting the abatement of the discharge, there is no reason to believe that the land in question must be open to the public rather than held as private property with a traditional right to exclude others. There seems to be no nexus between correcting the discharge problem and permitting the public to access the property. Likewise, the bridges may in fact enhance the enjoyment of the river to the public but there is no nexus between building such bridges and correcting the externality. In general, the public should not be able to fund public projects at forced private expense just because a property owner happens to be seeking to make a lawful use of his property, even if a building permit and zoning approval are required. Therefore, the third requirement should fail the nexus test – should be considered an unlawful regulatory taking.

As to rough proportionality we need to consider the cost imposed by the externality – $600 of damages to the downstream households. With reference to the cost imposed by the externality the factory is regulated in a way that imposes a burden of $400 ($300 for the factory filter, and $100 to adjust the proposed parking spaces). Such a regulatory burden of $400 seems reasonable (roughly proportionate) to the $600 cost of the externality. In fact, it addresses the problem and internalizes the cost at $400 which is $200 less than the factory owner paying damages, and $50 less than the $450 it would cost for the factory owner to purchase home water filters for each of the six households. Consequently, the first two regulatory requirements seem to meet both tests. Therefore they should not be an unlawful taking for which compensation is due.

Keep in mind that this is a simplified example of a takings problem, and the discussion is limited to two key tests for a regulatory taking. It should, however, provide useful guidance for thinking about this important way of using references to the Coase Theorem in legal reasoning.

Pareto and Kaldor–Hicks efficiency

Traditional law and economics is constantly concerned with efficiency, or in other words with acting with a minimum of expense, effort, and waste. Efficiency involves getting the most value for the cost. Value is measured in monetary terms, and efficiency calculations require cost and benefit analysis. There are two types of efficiency that are frequently used in economics applied to law. These two types of efficiency are *Pareto efficiency* and *Kaldor–Hicks efficiency*. With respect to Pareto efficiency, reference is often made to the concepts of *Pareto superiority* or *Pareto optimality*.

A change in the status quo is considered to be Pareto superior if it makes at least one person better off without making anyone else worse off. A point is considered to be a Pareto optimum if no more Pareto superior points are available. That is, a *Pareto optimum* occurs where it is impossible to make any individual better off without making someone else worse off. Pareto optimums are also said to be Pareto efficient. The classic example of a *Pareto efficient* exchange is a voluntary market exchange where, by definition (in the absence of fraud, duress, or the like), both parties are made better off, in their own estimation, by virtue of the exchange. They each valued the other thing more than that which they were originally holding, otherwise they would not have made the exchange. In this situation it is easy to see that references to imperfect information or high transaction costs may prevent otherwise efficient exchange conclusions.

The focus on voluntary exchange favors what some people refer to as a *property rule*.[32] A voluntary exchange rule is considered a property rule because our legal tradition creates a very strong presumption in favor of protecting an individual's rights in property. Generally, a property rule promotes the idea of self-interested exchange and assumes that the pursuit of self-interest advances the public interest. This approach (of non-interference and no regulation) makes sense if the exchange can be framed as having low transaction costs and the market demonstrates characteristics that seem to be reasonably related to our perfect competition model discussed in chapter 2. If the transaction is framed as having high transaction costs or other types of problems then we may want the law or legal rules to "force" a particular exchange or outcome. We would want this if we could use law to reduce or avoid transaction costs or if law could be used to reach a more efficient outcome.

When we consider a "forced" exchange or a social measure of efficiency, we generally make reference to another concept of efficiency. Two British economists, Nicholas Kaldor and John R. Hicks, came up with a different measure of efficiency now referred to by reference to their last names. The Kaldor–Hicks theory is not concerned with whether or not a reallocation of resources will make certain individuals worse off, but rather with whether or not society's aggregate utility has been maximized. According to the Kaldor–Hicks theory, a reallocation of resources is efficient if those who gain from it obtain enough to fully compensate those who lose from it, although there is no requirement that actual compensation occur. This type of efficiency permits redistribution when calculations can be made to reference the appropriate outcome.

In other words, an exchange is considered to be Kaldor–Hicks efficient as long as the increased benefit to one party (the winner) more than offsets the decrease in utility (or cost) to the other party (the loser). In such a situation, society is better off because there is more total utility as a result of the exchange than there was before the exchange. Such a move is, therefore, justified under a Kaldor–Hicks efficiency analysis even if not justified under a Pareto analysis.

---

[32] *See generally,* Ghosh, *Property Rules, Liability Rules, and Termination Rights.*

Sometimes the Kaldor–Hicks test is associated with the term, *liability rule*.[33] A liability rule is distinguished from treating something as a property rule because the law gives it a weaker presumption of protection relative to the tension between private/self-interest and the public interest. When a right is protected by a liability rule it is subject to a Kaldor–Hicks efficiency analysis and can be subject to a forced exchange if social utility can be enhanced.

The Kaldor–Hicks test is also sometimes referred to as a *hypothetical efficiency* standard. This idea is of particular importance when using legal reasoning to think about transactions that are not consensual or voluntary. Injuries in tort law or coerced exchanges under the criminal law involve classic examples of non-voluntary exchanges. Taking of private property for a public purpose also involves a non-voluntary transfer. In all of these types of exchange relationships it is difficult to think in terms of Pareto efficiency because there is no voluntary consent and it is generally unlikely that someone wants to be injured by a tort or a crime. As to the taking of private property it is clear that withholding consent implies a non-Pareto efficient exchange. In these non-voluntary exchange situations we can use a Kaldor–Hicks test to position an argument for the best social response to these transactions. We can use it to think about what rules and institutional mechanisms might best advance social welfare.

As an example of how one might use Kaldor–Hicks as a hypothetical efficiency test, consider a simple example. Let us say that Margaret is on the way to a football game when she is knocked over by the crowd and hits her head on the hard pavement, thus cutting her head and being rendered unconscious. Robin, a medical doctor, is nearby and comes over to provide aid. In providing some basic and immediate treatment, Robin was able to prevent Margaret from having complications from delay which would have been much more traumatic and costly. After taking care of Margaret, therefore, Robin sends her a bill for $100 that is a reasonable amount for the aid actually rendered. Should Margaret have to pay this bill, after all she did not agree to the fee? Here, we can ask a hypothetical question, if Margaret had been conscious and able to negotiate this exchange for care, would she have been likely to do so on the terms in question? Assuming Margaret is a rational and self-interested actor she should have agreed to pay the reasonable price for emergency medical treatment as it was appropriate to the situation and it prevented the onset of much more traumatic and costly medical consequences. Since a reasonable person would have struck such a deal we can assume that Margaret would have

[33] *Id.*

agreed to the deal as well. Furthermore, the deal seems socially desirable because we want to encourage doctors to provide aid, and we all benefit from resolving medical problems in a way that reduces the overall trauma and cost of an injury. Thus, social welfare is maximized by a rule that requires a reasonable fee to be paid for the rendering of appropriate aid to a stranger in need.

We can also use this concept to discuss the rights of strangers to commit trespass and to take shelter from a storm. A stranger can dock her boat on my property or take shelter in my vacation home when an emergency necessitates such action. This can be done without obtaining the owner's permission. Even though the stranger acts out of necessity and without the private property owner's consent, we look at the inability of the parties to negotiate a deal *ex ante*, and weigh the social benefits of the rule against the costs. Generally, the law takes the position of allowing strangers to take shelter and holds them liable only for damages caused thereby.

Likewise, in land use and environmental law one can understand the idea of a regulation being in the public interest such that the government is permitted to prevent a given use even though the use restriction results in a substantial loss to the property owner. In such cases, one way of understanding the idea behind takings clause analysis is that compensation is generally owed for such a coerced exchange. This follows from the logic of the Kaldor–Hicks efficiency test as related to a liability rule rather than a property rule because the non-consensual action is permitted but compensation is required.[34]

We can also explore this concept in relation to the paradigmatic frame of Coase. Let us consider the case of *Boomer* v. *Atlantic Cement Co.*[35] The *Boomer* case involved a private nuisance dispute between adjoining land owners. Atlantic Cement operated a facility that discharged pollutants into the ambient air. These discharges affected the property of surrounding land owners. In response to the discharge, the surrounding land owners brought a law suit to close down the facility (to enjoin its continued operation). The court examined the situation and found that advancing technology might mitigate the discharge in the future but that the operation of the facility would nonetheless continue to result in adverse consequences for the surrounding property owners. Framing the analysis

---

[34] Of course compensation might not be required if the regulation merely functioned to internalize externality costs on the regulated property owner. There are many other factors that go into takings law jurisprudence. *See generally*, DANA & THOMAS, PROPERTY (a basic primer on takings law).

[35] Boomer v. Atlantic Cement Co., 257 N.E.2d 870 (N.Y. 1970).

in terms of the immediate parties to the dispute, the court determined that enjoining the operation of the facility would cost Atlantic Cement in excess of $45 million whereas the cost of the negative externality to the nearby property owners was less than $1 million. Thus, a $1 million benefit (pollution abatement) would be achieved at a cost of $45 million. Consequently, the court identified the entitlement in favor of Atlantic Cement and then refused to enjoin the operation of the facility. It did, however, award money damages to the surrounding property owners as compensation for their losses.

We can see that this fact pattern is very similar to the Coase example discussed earlier in this chapter. Elaborating upon this fact pattern can bring some additional issues to light. First, the discharge of the pollution should be understood as a negative externality because it imposes a cost on the surrounding property owners. This is a cost of operating the facility but prior to the law suit, the cost was not internalized by Atlantic Cement. In the absence of paying this cost Atlantic Cement was indirectly obtaining a free equitable servitude over the surrounding property. That is, the surrounding property was burdened with the discharge that was a necessary by-product of operating the facility. A right to burden other property, to acquire an equitable servitude, is valuable. And in this case, the surrounding property owners were unable to exercise their right to exclude. Assuming that the facility came to the location after the current property owners, the discharge resulted in the constructive acquisition of a valuable property right without compensation.[36]

In this case, if the court chose to protect the property rights of the surrounding land owners with a *property rule*, it would have enjoined the operation of the facility (an injunction effectuates the purpose of a property rule). Instead of using a property rule the court chose to use a *liability rule* and permitted the continued operation of the facility with compensation paid to the losers. Thus, the court can be understood as seeking to promote the overall social welfare by using a liability rule to express a result that is Kaldor–Hicks efficient.

In the above consideration of *Boomer*, the Coase frame is considered with respect to two alternative references, a property rule and a liability rule. Each *reference* is initially framed in terms of the immediate parties to the suit. There is, however, another way to evaluate

---

[36] If the facility was there first, it might be said that the cost of the surrounding property already reflected the value of the negative servitude in that it would have been acquired at a discounted price.

this exchange. An alternative approach might include a cost and benefit analysis of the employment and tax-base impact of the facility to the local community. Closing the facility may cost local jobs and it may hurt the local treasury. Thus, the facility may have positive externalities that exceed its negative externalities, although the people receiving the benefits may not be the same individuals as those enduring the costs. Consideration of the factors at play in a broader framing of the exchange could weigh heavily on a court's implicit, if not express, choice of a referencing rule. And, this is likely even if the court formally limits its express framing of the exchange to the immediate parties to the suit.

Another way to understand the distinction between a liability rule and a property rule is with reference to two types of interests in real property – the real covenant and the equitable servitude. Both of these interests are considered to be property entitlements. Traditionally, however, real covenants were protected by contract remedies. This means that a breach of a real covenant permitted a remedy for damages. Thus, the real covenant is a property entitlement protected by a liability rule. On the other hand, property remedies, such as injunctive relief, have traditionally been used to protect the equitable servitude. Thus, the equitable servitude is a property entitlement protected by a property rule.

We can also observe the property rule and liability rule distinction in the takings law area. Generally, a taking of private property by the government involves the protection of the private property entitlement with a liability rule. The government can take the property, under appropriate circumstances, but it must provide just compensation. In contrast, a private property entitlement that is encroached upon by a private party is typically subject to a property rule protection. Thus, when Gina owns lot "*A*" and Giovanni, the adjoining property owner of lot "*B*," erects a fence that encroaches on to Gina's property she can have the fence removed (assuming the elements of adverse possession have not been met).

Public choice and Arrow's Impossibility Theorem

An important and related concept for an understanding of law in a market context is *Arrow's Impossibility Theorem*.[37] The Theorem gives us

---

[37] *See generally* BUCHANAN & TULLOCK, CALCULUS OF CONSENT; OLSON, LOGIC OF COLLECTIVE ACTION; Macey, *Promoting Public Regarding Institutions*; Easterbrook, *Some Tasks in Understanding Law*; FARBER & FRICKEY, LAW AND PUBLIC CHOICE; Farber and Frickey, *The Jurisprudence of Public Choice*; Farber and Frickey,

important insight into the *public choice* process and into the process of legislative decision making.[38] This is important if one is concerned with trying to legislatively implement laws that promote particular notions of economic efficiency.

Decision making in the public sector can occur in a number of different ways. Elected government officials may base their decisions on what they think a majority of the people want, on what they think the people should want, or on what they think is most likely to get them reelected. Kenneth Arrow did research (Arrow's Impossibility Theorem), showing that there is no general rule which can rank social states that is based only on the way that these states are ranked by individual members of society. The research illustrates the difficulty government officials face when they seek to make decisions based on what the majority of their constituents want.

To begin with communities often times turn to the political process to address collective problems, problems that might be deemed difficult for individuals to resolve on their own or beyond the proper consideration of individual self-interest. Problems such as water pollution might best be addressed by experts or by public bodies capable of considering a multiplicity of perspectives and points of reference. When decision making and regulation emerges from the process of collective action it is often analyzed under the guise of public choice theory. Public choice theory, like the Coase Theorem, raises interesting issues for our understanding of the relationship between law, markets, and culture.

If we reconsider the water pollution problem used in our earlier discussion of the Coase Theorem we can better appreciate the issues raised by public choice theory. In our illustrative fact pattern we saw how transaction costs might prevent the individual households from making the most efficient choice. As a consequence of transaction costs we saw that home owners would select the individual home water filter systems rather than the cheaper system installed at the factory. This decision resulted in spending $450 rather than $300 to correct the problem. The difference of $150 represents the inefficient use of scarce resources – resources that could have been used to provide other goods and services. The significance of this observation is that the choice of the legal rule does make a difference in terms of the efficiency of the outcome. In a situation where

---

Legislative Intent and Public Choice; Tohlison, *Public Choice and Legislation*; MALLOY, LAW AND ECONOMICS 42–45; MALLOY, LAW AND MARKET ECONOMY 99–105.

[38] *Id. See also* BRIGHAM, CONSTITUTION OF INTERESTS (discussing the way in which we organize ourselves from the perspective of a political scientist).

households confront substantial transaction costs, an expert might be able to see beyond this problem and work to achieve the socially efficient outcome by legislating a legal rule that granted home owners a legal right to clean water. This legal rule, as we saw, placed the burden for clean water on the factory owner and promoted the efficient outcome. This raises an important question. How are we to interpret the meaning of legislation? Does a particular legal rule reflect an expert determination that overcomes transaction costs to provide a more efficient use of valuable scarce resources? Does the rule, therefore, reflect a public interest or purpose as well as an economically efficient choice? On the other hand, might the rule merely reflect the pressure and influence of special interest groups without regard for efficiency? Maybe the chosen rule reflects rent seeking behavior rather than an assessment of the public good. Perhaps some labor unions and environmentalists joined forces with our six households in order to get a legal rule that simply placed the cost of corrective action on the factory owner, and no one ever considered transaction costs or efficiency. Perhaps many people exercised rational ignorance and failed to inform the legislature of their opinions on the matter. Likewise, the legal rule might simply be the product of incentives and disincentives within the internal structure of the legislative body – a product of horse trading and deal making done somewhat independently of any real deliberative consideration of the underlying issues in the specific situation at hand.

Since understanding law in a market context involves an interpretive process, the nature of public choice is important. The best place to begin an analysis of this framing device is with Arrow's Impossibility Theorem. Arrow's Theorem informs us that it is impossible to satisfy all of the conditions necessary for public decision making to reflect the preferences of the individuals comprising the society, and that public decisions may or may not be taken as attempts to promote the socially efficient rule. The Theorem maintains that four conditions would need to be met in order for social choices to reflect democratic decision making. These four conditions are: (1) social choice must be transitive (if x is preferred to y and y is preferred z, z can not be preferred to x); (2) social choices must not respond in an opposite direction to changes in individual choice (the fact that some people come to hold a certain preference can not result in society rejecting that preference if society would otherwise have chosen it); (3) social choice must not be controlled by anyone inside or outside of the group; and (4) the social preference between two alternative choices must depend only on people's feelings with respect to those alternatives and not with reference to any other alternative.

A simple example of the voting process reveals further insight. For ease of understanding let us continue with our polluting factory example as set up in the earlier section of this chapter. Suppose a given legislative body is considering legislation with respect to the legal rule to govern the issue of water quality as between our factory owner and our six households living downstream from the factory. To keep the example simple assume that there are only three legislators (*A, B, C*) and three legislative proposals (1, 2, 3) to consider. Furthermore, assume that by good fortune we know the revealed preferences of each legislator in terms of how they rank each of the possible rule options.

The options involve legislative proposals that reflect three alternative approaches described as:

(1) Dirty Water Rule ("Dirty"): this rule protects the rights of all owners of land abutting a navigable waterway and entitles them to discharge waste into the stream. Thus, there is no liability on the factory for a discharge.

(2) Clean Water Rule ("Clean"): this rule protects the right of all residents to draw clean and safe water from all streams and rivers. Thus, polluters are liable for degradation of water quality.

(3) Contract Rule ("Contract"): this rule leaves the matter to the individual owners of land abutting and using navigable waters and provides for them to freely contract with each other as to liability. This is basically a "hands-off" approach that appeals to those who would rather see the absence of a clean water rule, and who prefer less government intrusion into the marketplace. Leaving the matter to individual contracting means that transaction costs will be a factor in reaching a final outcome, assuming one believes that transaction costs are significant enough to be of concern.

The revealed preferences of legislators as to each of these rules is reflected in table 5.1.

Assume that for ease of discussion and voting the group has selected a voting procedure mandating that only two alternatives can be considered at a time. The alternative receiving the most votes is than considered relative to the third or remaining option in order to determine the final rule adopted. Following this simple procedure we can see what happens. If the legislators vote between Dirty water and Clean water, Dirty will win (two of the three rank the Dirty water rule higher than the Clean water rule). Then as between the Dirty water rule and the Contract rule, the Contract rule will win and be adopted by the group (two of them

Table 5.1

| | Legislator | | |
Rank	A	B	C
1st	Dirty	Clean	Contract
2nd	Clean	Contract	Dirty
3rd	Contract	Dirty	Clean

prefer the Contract rule to the Dirty water rule). If they vote first on Dirty water versus Contract, Contract will win and then compared with the Clean water rule, the final outcome will be the Clean water rule. If they vote first on Contract versus Clean water, Clean water will win and then compared to Dirty water, Dirty water will be the final rule. Given three different voting patterns we observe three different rule outcomes. In the first the Contract rule, in the second the Clean water rule, and in the third the Dirty water rule. Consequently, even under these assumptions we see that the outcome reflects authoritative influence over the voting process rather than a clear commitment to a particular "efficient" outcome. Such a situation directs attention toward an investigation of voter preferences so that one might strategically work to influence the order of the vote, and thereby impact the ultimate rule adopted.

From the point of view of law and market economy, the above example illustrates an important concept. It informs us of the difficulty in assessing the extent to which a legislative rule has anything to do with efficiency, or with a deliberate attempt to advance a particular public interest. This is true even though legislative intervention may have been prompted by an assertion of numerous transaction costs that prevented the affected parties from achieving the most efficient outcome. Like the broader marketplace of which the legislative body is merely a smaller representation, collective decision making involves dynamic and complex variables. Neither the legislative outcome nor the legislative process can be fully governed by the deterministic constraints of efficiency.

The process of public choice raises yet additional considerations. For instance, to the extent that legislative bodies represent the public, they operate within the guise of agency. As "agents" for others we need to consider the degree to which the agents either can or do represent their principals. As a collective and representative body, the legislative group is a symbol or sign of the public-at-large, but like any sign, it can represent the public only in some respects and not in all respects. Thus, to understand the meaning of legislation, cloaked in the legitimacy of *public* interest, we must investigate the nature of the public that is represented by the legislative group. We must consider access, influence, and other factors as related to a variety of criteria such as gender, race, age, education, income, and geographic location, among others.

Furthermore, to the extent that the legislative group performs the role of expert, as in my Coase example of the helicopter pilot, we must again be concerned with how one attains this privileged position. Similarly, we must consider the extent to which our figurative pilot can know and appreciate the points of view of those who are positioned in dramatically different cultural–interpretive communities. This consideration takes on added importance when we remember that life, in a world of positive transaction costs, results in the dispersion of fragmented and subjective experiences and information – therefore, race, gender, age, education, class, culture, and other characteristics are significant.

In addition, we must appreciate the power of framing the outcome of legislative action. Public choice theory indicates that an outcome may have more to do with the power to control the rule making process than with deliberate consideration of efficiency or anything else. Importantly, because the outcome is framed as the result of a democratic process it is made to appear (is represented) to the public as fair, neutral, and broadly representative. On careful review we may find that a rule choice is not so democratic and that interpretation and application of the rule requires re-framing to achieve a suitable and alternative objective.

Using the framing device of public choice we may undercut the idea that a particular legislative rule advances a public interest. We may be able to show that the rule is the product of a "deal" struck in favor of identifiable special interests. This may permit us to shift from a discourse concerning legislative history and move to one based on the economics of upholding a particular deal. It may also facilitate the use of patterns of legal argument that justify replacing the rule or restricting its application.

Efficient breach

The idea of the efficient breach is that under certain conditions the law should encourage people to breach their contracts. The breach is justified in situations of Kaldor–Hicks efficiency where non-performance leaves the breaching party with an economic gain that exceeds the economic loss to the losing party against whom they committed the breach. A classic example of a fact pattern that illustrates the doctrine of efficient breach is found in the case of *Peevyhouse* v. *Garland Coal & Mining Co.*, decided by the Supreme Court of Oklahoma in 1962.[39] In that case Willie and Lucille Peevyhouse, as owners of a farm containing coal deposits, leased the property to Garland for a five-year period for purposes of "stripmining" the coal from the land.

The stripmining process involved removing the coal by digging large pits into the surface of the land as opposed to coal mining methods that involve digging underground mine shafts. The stripmining process leaves the surface of the land dramatically scarred and disfigured. In an effort to assure themselves that the surface of the land would not permanently remain in this exhausted state the lease agreement between the parties required Garland to reclaim the land. The reclamation provision required restorative effort to return the land to a more natural and pre-mining state or condition. Garland operated under the lease and extracted the coal deposits. At the end of the lease term, however, it refused to restore and reclaim the land. Garland justified its breach of the agreement by presenting evidence that restoration work would cost $29,000 while expert testimony indicated that the value of the land would increase by only $300. In other words, the gains to Garland from non-performance readily exceeded the loss in value to Peevyhouse. Thus, Garland argued that it would be a waste of social resources to spend $29,000 to achieve a $300 gain and therefore it should be allowed to breach the agreement. The court agreed, but it required Garland to pay Peevyhouse $300 as damages representing the loss in value to the land from failure to reclaim it. This result is perfectly consistent with the idea of an efficient breach because the winners win more than the losers lose (it is Kaldor–Hicks efficient). Therefore, the breach also results in greater social value. Note that it also works to heavily discount environmental values associated with reclaiming the land. In other words, the breach is efficient primarily because of the low value assigned to the reclamation of the land.

Efficient breach theory seeks to address the situation of new market opportunities emerging after a contract has been entered. The idea is that society should encourage a breach when it makes economic sense to do so – when the new economic opportunity offers a sufficient return capable of compensating the losing party while making the breaching party better off, even after compensating the loser.

---

[39] Peevyhouse v. Garland Coal & Mining Co., 382 P.2d 109 (S. Ct. Okla., 1962). This example is also discussed in MALLOY, LAW AND MARKET ECONOMY 144–46.

Let us consider another fact pattern to further illustrate this concept. Assume that Robin owns a factory that manufactures imaging screens used in a variety of expensive computer games, called "game screens." These screens require special technology to manufacture. Robin's company is one of ten major suppliers in the market. Of the ten companies, Robin is the only operator that currently has the ability to readily adjust his manufacturing line to make special filter imaging screens used to view images of the contents inside of boxes, suitcases, and other containers. He gets occasional orders for these screens that he sells to airports and other facilities. He calls these his "filter screens." A few of his competitors could also make these screens but they do not currently have the same ability as Robin to make quick changes in the line production process between products.

On August 1, Robin contracts with Dan to supply Dan with 100,000 screens to be used for computer games. The contract calls for Robin to commence production of the screens on September 25 and to run continuous production for six weeks to complete the order for 100,000 units. Under Robin's normal operating procedure he will need three days prior to September 25 to set up and retool his production line to complete the order placed by Dan. At the end of the six-week production run, he will then need three days to retool his production line for the next order. Under the contract, Dan pays $20 per screen and Robin earns a net profit of $5 on each screen. This means that the contract pays $2,000,000 and on that contract Robin makes $500,000.

On September 14, before any work takes place on the contract between Robin and Dan, Maggie approaches Robin. Maggie seeks to contract with Robin to produce 100,000 of the special imaging screens or filter screens. Maggie will pay $50 per screen and Robin will earn a net payment of $15 per screen on the deal. This contract would pay $5,000,000 and would provide Robin with $1,500,000 in profit. Production can be done over the same time frame as the one for the contract with Dan.

If Robin breaches the contract he has with Dan, Dan will be able to cover his needs by going to Janet. Janet can do his order within the same basic time frame but will charge $25 per game screen. In addition, Dan will have incidental and administrative expenses of $100,000.

In analyzing this fact pattern we can identify a classic situation for efficient breach. If Robin breaches the contract with Dan, Dan can cover production by shifting to Janet. This will cost Dan $100,000 in administrative expenses plus the fact that the screens from Janet are $5 more per screen than under the contract with Robin. Thus, shifting to Janet for production of the screens will cost Dan an additional $500,000 for the screens and $100,000 in administrative expenses for a total of $600,000. Robin will need to make enough from the new deal to compensate Dan and still come out ahead as a result of the newly emerging market opportunity with Maggie. On the new contract with Maggie, Robin earns a profit of $1.5 million. This means that Robin can pay Dan $600,000 and still have $900,000 accounting profit from the new deal. The $900,000 is $400,000 more than Robin would have made under the original contract with Dan. Consequently, Robin makes an economic profit of $400,000 and it is efficient, in a wealth-maximizing sense, to encourage Robin to breach the contract with Dan.

Even if a breach is thought of as efficient, the efficiency of the breach does not necessarily inform us about which party should get the added economic rewards arising from the newly emerging opportunity. For example, consider the above described situation between Robin and Dan. In that situation Robin is the owner of the factory and he contracts to supply Dan with 100,000 game screens. When the opportunity arises to make more money by supplying filter screens to Maggie, Robin gets the benefit of the extra money because the background legal rules favor him with an entitlement as owner of the means of production. There is, however, no necessary reason to presume that the economic benefits should go to Robin. Perhaps the economic benefits should go to Dan, or maybe they should be shared with the workers at the factory. The point is, that even in recognizing an efficient breach, we learn little with respect to how to allocate the alleged social benefits of the breach.

For example, we can ask if it would make a difference in the outcome of our above example if the background legal rule gave the entitlement to Dan rather than Robin. Assume that we have a background legal rule that recognizes in Dan, as a contract buyer, a right to the productive output (capacity) of the facility over the six-week production period required to meet the terms of the agreement between the parties. Now we can ask, with reference to our earlier discussion of Coase, whether the choice of legal rule makes a difference in the outcome.

If the law protects an entitlement in Dan rather than Robin we should observe the same basic outcome as when the law protected an entitlement in Robin. (In the absence of transaction costs the choice of rule should not affect the outcome.) In this new situation Maggie comes along and wants to find someone to produce the higher-value filter screens. She learns that Dan has the "rights" to the productive capacity of the factory for the next six weeks. In order to get access to this capacity she understands that the law requires her to negotiate with Dan. Maggie goes to Dan and offers to buy out his legal right to the productive capacity of the factory so that she can make the imaging screens. Maggie is willing to pay Dan an amount equal to buying the screens at $50 each. This means that Maggie will take over the use of the factory to produce imaging screens at a cost of $35 each, and she will pay Dan a fee equal to $15 per unit to induce him to sell her the right to use the factory. Dan should, assuming he is rational, agree to do the deal with Maggie and have his game screens produced at Janet's factory. This will cost Dan $100,000 in administrative expenses, plus an additional $500,000 for the production of his game screens. Thus, Dan will have $600,000 of additional expenses but he will earn a profit of $1.5 million on the deal with Maggie. Even after he accounts for the added expenses he makes $900,000 on the deal. The difference in this situation is that Dan, rather than Robin, gets to pocket the economic benefits of the new opportunity presented by Maggie's order. Thus, the choice of the legal rule does not affect the efficient outcome but it does have a distributive consequence. Moreover, given that the newly arising opportunity is so much more profitable than the original deal, there is a rational economic incentive for either Robin or Dan to do the new deal even if they are required to pay some amount of money, say $100,000, to the factory workers. The added profits would more than cover such costs.

In thinking about the efficient breach situation, one should also be reminded of the prisoner's dilemma. If one thinks of the prisoner's dilemma in terms of the risk of cheating on a cooperative deal, one can see that the desire to pursue an efficient breach will be tempered by the nature of the primary exchange. If the primary exchange is a one-time transaction rather than a repeat transaction (a long-term or on-going business relationship) a seller such as Robin will be more likely to breach. On the other hand, if the particular contract is one of a series of on-going transactions between the parties, Robin will be less likely to make the opportunistic move to breach. In other words, the value of reputation between contracting parties may off-set some of the anticipated gain of an efficient breach where the relationship is on-going.

Conclusion

This chapter presented many terms and concepts that are important to understanding law in a market context. It is important to understand that these concepts are used to define and clarify legal problems. They help us focus attention on particular facts and issues to be addressed by legal analysis and the formation of public policy. They operate as interpretive devices and provide a variety of opportunities for influencing the meanings and values of exchange. With so many fluid and dynamic concepts and terms to select from, economics presents a useful framework for promoting a multiplicity of interests and outcomes. It is important, therefore, to learn how and when to use these concepts in developing patterns of legal argument that will advance the interest of a given client or constituent.

While this chapter is no substitute for a longer and more detailed study, it should provide a solid foundation for improving one's ability to make more careful and insightful analysis of law and public policy.

Problems

(1) Gina and Giovanni go into business with their cousins Heather and Kelly and decide that they will open the G&G Pizza shop and Deli. After the first six months, they find that revenue is very good and they have many customers who want to have home delivery service. As a result the G&G Pizza shop starts a delivery service. In the first few months they determine that delivery is a major money maker but they identify different levels of profit for different neighborhoods in which they deliver. In particular they have had some serious problems with a four-block area in and around the City Office Building just north of downtown. In this area they have had ten pizza delivery personnel robbed, have been stuck with fifteen bad checks, have had twelve pizza orders denied upon delivery (crank orders), and have had three car windshields busted on delivery vehicles; all in a two-month period. As a result, delivery drivers do not want to enter this area and G&G makes a business decision to abandon service in this high-cost area. It will continue to deliver to other nearby areas where problems have been few and profits have been high.

In reaction to the cut in service people living in the four-block area near the City Office Building object that this is unfair and discriminatory service. They complain to the local press and to city officials.

City officials want you to tell them how to handle this policy question. Does it make any difference who lives in this four-block area (race, ethnicity, income, etc.)? Does it make a difference if G&G show that they deliver to other areas of the city that include a variety of middle-income minority and low-income white neighborhoods? Does it make any difference if other pizza places do or do not deliver to the area in question? Does it matter if other pizza places are located within the four-block area and are available for on-sight or pick-up and take-out service? What factors should be considered and why?

(2) Jannel is a recent law graduate who graduated in the top quarter of her class. She is hired by the largest law firm in her mid-sized city along with four other top law graduates. Jannel has some physical constraints that affect the way she works. Under the Americans with Disabilities Act (ADA) Jannel needs a reader to assist her in her research and she has been allowed twice as much time to complete assignments, course examinations, and the Bar Examination. The firm understands this and agrees to hire Jannel and is willing to make reasonable accommodations for her.

The firm has set the starting salary for new associates at $70,000. This is what it will pay the other four people it hired. The firm will hire a reader for Jannel at a cost of $15,000. In addition, the firm has calculated the salary of new people based on billing them out at $100/hour. Since Jannel needs extra time to complete the work, the firm figures she will either have to be billed out at a lower rate of $60/hour or at the same rate but with an internal reduction in the allocated hours to achieve the same effect, and to fairly bill the client for the work done. Taking all of this into account, the firm agrees to pay Jannel a salary of $42,000 (60 percent of $70,000) less $15,000 as the cost of a reader. Thus, Jannel is offered $27,000.

Jannel says that this is unfair and is discrimination. The firm says that the arrangement is the only thing that is fair otherwise the firm will be unfair to the other associates, the clients, or to the partners that would all have to subsidize Jannel. The managing partner for the firm says "fairness is being paid for what you add to the bottom line . . . after you work here for a few years you may prove that you add more value than can be reflected in hours billed, but at the outset what else would be fair?"

Discuss the justification and rational for the position of the firm. Prepare a market- and law-based response for Jannel. What possible framing and referencing devices can one use? How is the cost of a reasonable accommodation to be born? Should it be covered by Jannel, by the partners, the other associates, passed on to clients, subsidized by taxpayer payments, or by some other means?

(3) Quicky car rental has rental offices in 130 locations across New England and the Mid-Atlantic states. It has average rental rates that are the cheapest of any competitors in its markets. Quicky does this by keeping costs and risks down. Quicky says it deals with all kinds of people every day and it does not have time to assess the risk of renting to any particular customer. It keeps costs down by charging different prices to customers

with a higher risk profile. That is, it charges rental rates that vary with the profile of the customer. Customers that fit a profile of lower income, higher credit risk, etc. pay a higher rate but those with a low risk profile pay a lower rate. Quicky says its profiles are based on Federal Government census data. An examination of its profile format indicates that a person who pays for the rental on a "high profile" gold or platinum credit card will get a better rate then someone with a standard or easy access card that requires less income. The rate also varies by zip code of the home address of the customer based on census tract data related to average-income level in the zip code area. Another key indicator is linked to crime rates, education levels, home ownership rates, and housing values all linked to zip code. Using readily available computer software, Quicky generates customer profiles based solely on the above data and prices its rentals differently based on the different profiles, with higher rental rates for the higher-risk profiles. In practice, this has lowered Quicky's costs, making it the lowest-cost rental provider in terms of credit risk, accidents, and damages to vehicles.

Based on customer complaints the several State Attorney offices in the region investigate Quicky. A report is issued showing that the Quicky pricing practices reveal a pattern of racial discrimination. Based on racial correlations, Quicky provides the best rate to Asian businessmen, then to whites and the highest rates to African-Americans and Latinos. Quicky denies any racial motive or activity and says that its rates are simply based on sound business judgment related to the profile information outlined above. It also notes that it made sure that nothing concerning race was selected for use in profile data. Moreover, Quicky points out that a number of its customers are African-American and Latino professionals with high income and great credit backgrounds. These customers get the same low-rates as all other customers with the same low-risk profiles. Furthermore, Quicky charges white customers with low income and high credit risk the same high rates it charges others with the same or similar profiles. Quicky can even show that in absolute numbers it has more white customers who are low income and high risk, and they are paying the higher rates. It is true, however, that of those customers that are African-American and Latino there is a disproportionately higher percentage paying a higher rate, on average, than the white and Asian customers. Quicky asserts that this merely reflects income distribution in the broader American society and that it should not be punished for such factors.

Explain the fairness, or lack of fairness, of the policy being used by Quicky. Offer a response to Quicky and explain the reasons for prohibiting or permitting its current practices. What factors should Quicky be able to take into account? Can Quicky simply refuse to offer rentals to certain areas of a city, either to people from the area or to people who seek to rent them for use within the areas?

(4) Special Product Chemical Company (SPCC) is a small firm that employs four research chemists. SPCC specializes in the production of highly toxic and nuclear products used in certain advanced industrial manufacturing processes. The work environment is highly regulated at SPCC, and the company exceeds all of the government's minimum health and safety standards applicable to all phases of its operations. Even so, the research facility presents potential harms to health that cannot be readily eliminated. Over the recent years a number of employees have complained about the health risk of their work at SPCC and at other similar companies. At the present time a legislative committee is looking into the situation to address ways of protecting workers in these situations.

The primary workers being affected are highly educated professional chemists with PhD degrees working in the research laboratories. While the current risks cannot be fully eliminated using current technology, special high-risk health insurance can be provided to cover the risk and make certain that any future need for health care is affordable to the injured party. So far, the Committee has gathered some limited information. It determined that the expected injury or damage to an individual would be $1,000 per year. It also found that the risk of insuring against this injury would cost SPCC $400 per year for all four of its employees under a group policy, and cost $150 per year per employee if purchased individually.

Considering only the SPCC situation, the Committee is getting ready to implement one of two possible legal rules.

Rule 1: Workers are entitled to a safe work environment and companies shall be liable for all known health risks associated with a given work environment.

Rule 2: Companies are liable to employees only for job-related health risks when they fail to comply with minimum health and safety standards established by the government.

(a) SPCC asserts that nothing needs to be done because the employees already receive compensation for the added risk associated with their job. Explain the basis for such an assertion and comment on its merit.

(b) Setting aside any concern for transaction costs, comment on the implications of the Committee passing rule 1 and, in the alternative, rule 2.

(c) Assume that there are transaction costs of $70 for each employee associated with negotiating and enforcing any cooperative action on their part. Comment on the implications of the Committee passing rule 1 and, in the alternative, rule 2.

(d) Assume that the people affected by the health risk are not highly paid professionals but are low-paid and part-time cleaning staff. Comment on the potential wealth effect problem in this situation.

(5) RPM Construction Company enters into an agreement to build two homes, each on 5 acre lots. The lots abut an old and unsightly landfill. It is agreed that RPM will construct a landscape barrier of earth and brick along the back of the lots to screen out the sight of the landfill. The barrier will rise to a height of 9 feet and will contain grass, trees, and shrub plantings, and otherwise blend into the yard of each home. Each of the homes with lots is contracted for sale at $180,000. After several months of work, the homes are built and all of the work is complete except for the construction of the barriers. RPM calculates that it will cost $52,000 to build the barrier walls in the manner contracted. On a pro-rata basis, that amounts to $26,000 per home. It also learns, from having three separate appraisals done, that the barrier will enhance the value of each lot by only $3,000 relative to its value with no barrier. RPM decides not to build the barrier and writes a check to each lot owner for $3,000. The lot owners sue RPM to get what they bargained for but RPM says it should not have to do the work because it would be a waste of scarce social resources.

(a) Offer a defense of RPM's position. Prepare a response defending the homeowners' right to performance.

(b) Should it make a difference if RPM refuses to do the work because it claims that a secretary made a mistake in not adding $26,000 to the contract for each lot price? (The amount was on the work papers but was left off the contract by accident, and RPM failed to notice this when the contracts were signed.)

(c) Should it make a difference if the original contract allocated $10,000 to barrier construction in each contract, but price increases and unforeseen excavation problems caused the cost to rise to the $52,000 amount?

(6) Analyze this problem involving an effort to reduce pollution. Assume our example of the factory discharging pollution into the river and having a negative impact on our households located down stream. (Example from Coase Theorem in this chapter, p. 177) Now assume that there are two factories located upstream from our households, instead of

one, and each discharges waste into the river. Factory "*A*" discharges 200 tons of toxins and factory "*B*" discharges 150 tons. After careful investigation and study, the government implements a new regulation to reduce the level of toxins in the river to a safe level. The regulation is designed to reduce the total level of toxins in the river by 100 tons. In its initial regulatory allocation, it requires each factory to reduce its discharge by 50 tons of toxins. In accordance with this, it issues "*A*" with a permit to discharge 150 tons, and "*B*" with a permit to discharge 100 tons.

"*A*" is a newer factory with better technology and greater economies of scale. It is able to reduce and control its toxic discharge at a cost of $100 per ton. "*B*" is an older factory with much higher costs. It will cost "*B*" $400 per ton to reduce and control its output.

Explain and analyze the consequences of the original permit-based allocations in a situation where no private trading is permitted between the parties. Then compare this to a situation where private trading in permits and toxin reduction is allowed. If trading is allowed, what is the bargaining range for pricing an exchange between "*A*" and "*B*"? Identify relevant considerations and potential issues that result from these approaches.

(7) Triangle Development Co. is undertaking a major expansion of a mall that it owns and operates in Townsville. The mall expansion is known as Four-Twenty Center. The project is enormous and will cost upwards of $2 billion to complete. Townsville is working with Triangle to support the project. The project will increase the size of the current mall by five times. This will result in greatly increased traffic congestion, and increased noise from the number of vehicles attracted to the location.

There are two residential neighborhoods within close proximity to the mall expansion, one on the northeast side of the expansion and one on the northwest side of the expansion. Home owners in each of these neighborhoods complain about the expansion project and its impact on their quality of life. The Greenwood neighborhood to the northeast is an upscale neighborhood of about 300 single-family homes, each in the $400,000 price range. People here are professionals with one- or two-income earners, with an average of three new cars in the driveway, and well-maintained homes and lawns. The Old Mills neighborhood in the northwest is a lower-income area of about 100 homes, each in the $60,000 price range. People here are either unemployed and living on government support programs or are working at jobs paying minimal and substandard wages. Homes in Old Mills are often times left in ill repair for lack of resources to repair and upkeep them.

Townsville and Triangle have figured out how to expand road capacity to keep congestion to a minimum but the noise problem is more complicated. Widening roads, for instance, can reduce congestion but it does not reduce the noise. Two approaches to noise reduction have been identified, each with similar effect. In the absence of a noise abatement (reduction) system it is determined that each resident in either neighborhood will experience damages in the amount of $100 per home. Thus, the total social damages are $40,000 ($100 × 400 homes). Two ways of avoiding the harmful impact of the noise involve the building of a 10 feet-high buffer fence along the property line of the new Four-Twenty Center in the area of the two residential neighborhoods at a total cost of $24,000, and in the alternative having each home install special noise-reduction insulation at a cost of $80 per home.

The neighborhood residents argue that they have a right (entitlement) to be free of the excessive noise intrusion that will result from the mall expansion. Triangle argues that it has a right (entitlement) to develop its mall in a way that makes the best use of its property. It explains that the mall and everything planned for the expansion are in compliance with all building and zoning code regulations. Therefore, Triangle feels that it need not have to pay damages of $40,000 nor should it have to spend $24,000 on a buffer fence.

In examining the dispute between the parties, the city of Townsville has hired an independent expert to do a number of studies and to confirm the above cost estimates. This expert has also estimated that coordination and cooperation logistics for the residents will be costly and time-consuming. The expert figures that the residents will have costs of $25 per home if they work to coordinate their efforts and act collectively in response to the situation.

Should Triangle be required to build a buffer fence?

(a) Analyze this situation in the absence of transaction costs.
(b) Analyze this situation giving consideration to transaction costs.
(c) Identify any other factors that should be considered.

(8) Big Town undertakes to build a new baseball stadium for its local baseball team, the Flyers. Big Town enters into a lease with the Flyers providing the team with exclusive use of the stadium for a ten-year period. The Flyers agree to pay $10,000 per year for the life of the lease. The team will make money from ticket sales and concessions. A short time after entering into the lease agreement with the Flyers a local soccer team, the Dogs, starts to negotiate with Big Town to use the new stadium to play

soccer matches on days when the Flyers are not making use of it. The Dogs also agree to pay $10,000 per year for a lease of ten years.

Big Town figures out that having the Dogs share the facility with the Flyers will result in getting more use out of the publicly funded stadium and will result in $10,000 of additional yearly lease revenue. The downside is that the Flyers will lose about $1,000 per year in team revenue from ticket sales as some people shift attendance to soccer games and away from baseball. Big Town will probably be sued by the Flyers if they break the exclusive lease arrangement.

(a) Provide a market rationale for Big Town to breach the exclusive deal it made with the Flyers. Why or why not protect the Flyers' lease rights with a liability rule rather than a property rule?
(b) Address the various considerations for Big Town to account for when deciding about the breach of the exclusive lease arrangement with the Flyers.
(c) Assuming that you can justify a breach of the exclusive lease arrangement with the Flyers, does it necessarily follow that Big Town rather than the Flyers should get the $10,000 in lease payment to be paid by the Dogs?

6

The not-for-profit exchange context

Most books on traditional law and economics or on an economic analysis of law fail to discuss the role and nature of the not-for-profit economy.[1] I include a chapter on this topic because non-profit organizations and associations account for a large part of the economy in countries such as the United States, and because issues related to the exchange function of non-profits pertain to non-governmental organizations, or NGOs, that are becoming increasingly important in global exchange situations.[2] In addition, many people experience the intersection of law, markets, and culture through the operation and mediation of non-profit organizations. This is important because experience influences cultural-interpretive perspective. Therefore, the book presents a brief overview of the non-profit marketplace in an effort to provide a more complete "map" of the networks and patterns of human exchange.

To begin with, the economy of the United States can be analyzed in terms of three major market sectors or segments. These include the private sector, the public sector, and the not-for-profit or non-profit sector. Each of these sectors is important to the overall economy and to the process of social and market exchange. The non-profit sector accounts for hundreds of billions of dollars in economic activity each year, and non-profit organizations employ hundreds of thousands of people. Probably every person reading this book has had important dealings with

---

[1] This chapter is based on a number of lectures that I gave on the basic connection between the private marketplace and the market for non-profit activities. Helpful sources that I used as background for these lectures include: NON-PROFIT ORGANIZATIONS IN A MARKET ECONOMY (Hammack & Young, eds.); REEDER, IN PURSUIT OF PRINCIPLE AND PROFIT; NON-PROFITS & GOVERNMENT (Boris & Steuerle, eds.); TO PROFIT OR NOT TO PROFIT (Weisbrod, ed.); Brody, *Agents Without Principals*; Brody, *Institutional Dissonance In the Non-profit Sector.*

[2] For a good discussion on NGOs and how they are both similar and different from regular non-profits *see* LEWIS, MANAGEMENT OF NON-GOVERNMENTAL DEVELOPMENT ORGANIZATIONS; NGO MANAGEMENT (Edwards & Fowler, eds.).

non-profit organizations in his or her lifetime, and it is interesting to find such a large number of people and organizations committed to not making a profit in a society deeply committed to the pursuit of wealth. Despite or perhaps because of this, very few treatments on the relationship between law and economics undertake to provide a basic discussion of the non-profit economy and the non-profit market sector.

Therefore, this chapter sets out to identify the non-profit organization, to explain the general functions of the non-profit sector relative to the other two sectors of the economy, and to explore the major concepts to be considered in the process of legal reasoning and the formation of public policy when dealing with non-profit organizations.

The non-profit organization

Although we seldom think of it, non-profit organizations have a pervasive presence in the economy and in each of our lives. These organizations are involved in a vast array of activities and operate to provide numerous goods and services to a large cross-section of our population. Popular non-profit organizations that come readily to mind include the Red Cross, the United Way, the Salvation Army, and Catholic Charities, but the list of organizations and the nature of their activities are much more varied than can be represented by this group. Non-profits include: unions (e.g. United Steel Workers, and United Auto Workers); trade associations (e.g. the National Manufacturers Association, and the National Homebuilders Association); professional associations (e.g. the American Bar Association, and the American Institute of Certified Public Accountants); churches and religious groups; colleges, universities, and private schools; many hospitals and healthcare providers; fraternities, sororities, and fraternal orders; volunteer fire departments; sporting associations and clubs; museums; orchestras; historical societies; the Urban League; the NAACP; the Jewish Community Centers; housing facilities for the elderly and disabled; libraries; environmental groups like the Sierra Club and National Geographic; Alcoholics Anonymous; the Ford Foundation; the Boy Scouts; the Girl Scouts; all home owner associations and condominium boards: the list could go on for pages. The point is that non-profit organizations play an active and significant role in the economy and in our lives, yet; for the most part we remain relatively unaware of their unique role.

In the United States all non-profit organizations are governed by state law. They are incorporated as not-for-profit corporations under state law and enjoy the legal status provided for under that law. Non-profits typically enjoy an exemption from the regular payment of state and local property taxes, and from state and local sales taxes, but this is governed in particular by state law. The key characteristic of a non-profit organization is that it can not make a distribution to stockholders. It is not so much that these entities can not make money, but that any money earned over expenses must basically be kept as retained earnings. This means that the money must be put back into the mission of the organization. These organizations, even though they are non-profits, must be conscious of costs so that they stay within their budgets and many of them do make money and have a strong positive cash flow. Incidentally, many of them pay very good salaries and wages to the people they employ, even though they typically rely on volunteers for part of their workforce.

Many people mistakenly believe that these organizations are controlled by or are chartered under Federal law. At the Federal level, the US Department of the Treasury makes decisions concerning the special tax treatment available to non-profit organizations under Federal law.[3] If an organization qualifies under the Federal tax laws it will have a special tax status. This usually means that anyone making a contribution to the organization can do so and get a Federal tax break. This provides an incentive for people to make a contribution toward funding non-profit groups. If a non-profit loses its status as an organization in good standing under state law, it will lose the basis for recognition for special Federal tax treatment, but the decision to grant favorable Federal tax treatment is a separate matter from that of proper state incorporation.

One can reasonably ask why it is that we provide special local, state, and Federal tax benefits to non-profits as opposed to private or for-profit organizations. As will be discussed later, many people believe it is important to do so because non-profits tend to supply *public goods*, the provision of which is usually under-provided in the private market. Furthermore, non-profits generally seek to promote values that are difficult to measure in economic terms. The non-profit framework, therefore, raises some important cultural-interpretive issues. The focus on values, and the rejection of a pure profit motive, are two very important points of divergence from the conventionalized norms expressed in our private market narratives.

---

[3] For an innovative and detailed discussion of an example of how tax law and policy work in connection with race, see a trilogy of articles by David A. Brennen: Brennen, *The Power of the Treasury*; Brennen, *Tax Expenditures*; Brennen, *Charities and the Constitution*.

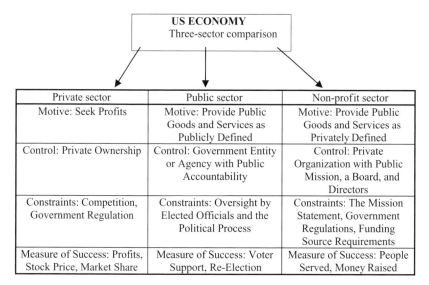

Private sector	Public sector	Non-profit sector
Motive: Seek Profits	Motive: Provide Public Goods and Services as Publicly Defined	Motive: Provide Public Goods and Services as Privately Defined
Control: Private Ownership	Control: Government Entity or Agency with Public Accountability	Control: Private Organization with Public Mission, a Board, and Directors
Constraints: Competition, Government Regulation	Constraints: Oversight by Elected Officials and the Political Process	Constraints: The Mission Statement, Government Regulations, Funding Source Requirements
Measure of Success: Profits, Stock Price, Market Share	Measure of Success: Voter Support, Re-Election	Measure of Success: People Served, Money Raised

Figure 6.1

The three-sector economy

In reviewing and discussing the elements presented in this chapter, it is important to remember that the non-profit sector is a third way of framing, referencing, and representing exchange relationships. The non-profit organization accounts for costs and economic reality but operates outside of the self-interested profit motive. It operates on the basis of a criterion other than wealth-maximization. This is important because the non-profit sector of the economy reveals the error of thinking in simple binary terms. Markets and human relationships are complex. We do not live in a simple and oppositional world of private vs. public, or market vs. government. We live in a dynamic web of interrelated networks and patterns of exchange. These networks and patterns take many shapes and forms, and even the most basic model of market organization should account for the unique role and function of the non-profit organization or association.

The US economy can best be examined in terms of three key sectors: the private sector, the public sector, and the non-profit sector. We can easily compare and contrast the basic elements of each sector by discussing each sector's organization in terms of organizational motive, control, constraints, and measures of success. The overview framework for this discussion is presented in figure 6.1.

Private sector

The private sector is composed of private businesses and organizations that operate with the purpose or motive of making a profit. In this sense, they are privately organized to pursue a private interest. These businesses are trying to serve a market demand by providing goods and services to consumers in return for wealth. They must make an economic profit to cover their expenses, and they must also have a favorable position as to economic profits; otherwise, the private parties would be better off earning income by pursuing alternative market opportunities.

The entities in this sector of the economy are privately owned and controlled. This means that they are generally closely held entities or business associations in which the principals are the owners and managers, or else they are entities such as large corporations in which the owners are the stockholders. When management and ownership are split, as in the typical corporation, the managers generally act as agents and have a duty to the owners. A private sector entity can have a number of control dynamics related to tensions or differing interests between owners (equity investors), management, and labor. Each of these groups will see themselves as stakeholders in the enterprise even though the object of the business is to make the most profit for the owners. Competing interests within the firm may sometimes prevent the firm itself from acting in the same way that might be presumed for a single individual under traditional microeconomic assumptions. The private sector business usually views the people it services as customers or consumers.

The primary constraint on private business is the marketplace. Competition, to the extent that it exists, forces the company to remain innovative and attentive to both consumer demands and the profit objectives of the owners. If the enterprise fails in either respect, it will go out of business from a lack of sales, a lack of investment capital, or both. In today's economy the private market is also subject to extensive regulation by government. These regulations constrain the private entity and shape the contours of its market activities.

The private sector entity has several ways of measuring its success. This is important because the organization, like all others, must have a basis for making a variety of decisions such as whether to take on new activities or to depart from a current activity. Generally, success in this sector is measured by profits earned, by reference to market share, and by favorable stock prices. All of these indicators provide feedback for decision making along standard economic lines.

Public sector

The public sector of the economy involves government at all levels: local, state, and federal. These entities are funded with tax revenue and have a purpose or motive of serving the public interest. They provide public goods and services to people based on a publicly defined definition of the public interest. This means that the political process establishes the agenda for public entities and agencies.

As public entities, these organizations are part of the government and are, theoretically, publicly owned and operated in the sense that government works for the people. The administrators and public officials operating these entities operate as agents for the public, but as with all government activities, it is difficult to say exactly whom they really represent – which special interests influence the direction and magnitude of public action. Problems of public choice and rational ignorance abound.

Constraints for these entities come from oversight by elected officials and the political process. Generally, meetings and records are accessible to the public. These entities operate within a budget but they do not face the pricing system of the marketplace. This means that there is little competitive pressure and the tendency is to seek and receive funding based on the cost of operations even though cost-based funding is highly controlled by the entity itself. For these reasons, many public entities are accused of being inefficient and unresponsive. These entities usually think of the people they serve as constituents.

Public entities can generally measure their success in terms of voter support, election results, and political contributions. For many entities, the key to success is simply to keep a low profile, avoid public controversy, and maintain or increase a budget appropriation.

Non-profit sector

The non-profit sector is made up of organizations seeking to promote the public interest and the production of public goods and services. The difference between the non-profit and the public entity is that the definition of the public interest is determined privately. Private individuals define the public interest and the public goods and services they seek to provide within the mission of the non-profit entity. Thus, the public interest may be given a very specific religious definition or it may be concerned with a very narrow or single issue.

Control of the non-profit organization is generally split between its board members and its directors. As a corporate entity, it has a board of directors and the board members are responsible for setting policy and providing oversight. Day-to-day operations are managed by the executive director of the entity. In practice, the executive director has a great deal of influence over the information available to the board and over policy choices. In addition to the board members and the executive director, there may be associate directors, managers, staff, contract workers, and volunteers. There are no owners in a non-profit entity, only assorted stakeholders. The people served by the organization are typically thought of as clients.

The non-profit entity is constrained by several factors; first is its mission statement. Every non-profit has a mission that sets out the purpose for which it is organized and operated. This is its corporate purpose. For example, consider a group of people that get together to provide short-term emergency shelter for battered women. Given this mission statement, the entity should not be operating a grade school, a daycare center, or a soup kitchen. A second constraint involves government regulation. A third comes from the requirements dictated by funding sources. For instance, in our example of the shelter for battered women, the entity might receive a $100,000 per year operating grant from the county to assist in providing this service. The county government funding will impose requirements about how the money is used and reported. It will also prohibit the organization from denying access to the shelter based on religion, race, ethnicity, and other constitutionally protected grounds. Thus, even if the shelter were operated by Jewish Family Services, the government funding source could constrain its operations. Similarly, if a private donor gives money to a non-profit it may restrict the use of the gift. A donor to a college or university may require that the money only be used for construction of a new library, for instance. There are some competitive pressures on most non-profit entities. Many compete with each other for business, funding, and donors. Because many of the goods and services they provide are duplicates of public entity provisions, the non-profits generally need to be more efficient and lower cost than the public entities.

Despite the fact that many non-profits have budgets substantially composed of public funds, there is little feeling by the public that these entities have to be as open and responsible to taxpayers as public entities. Religious groups like Catholic Charities and the Salvation Army provide a vast assortment of services to the public that are funded by taxpayer dollars, and yet most people do not feel that these entities are public. Many essential public services funded by the government are contracted out to non-profit groups. These services include everything from basic health-care to provisioning for the poor, the elderly, children, the disabled, the mentally and physically ill, and the homeless. Government often uses these entities because they contract to deliver the goods and services at a lower cost than the public entity. There is also a feeling that the presence of an organizational mission, rather than the pursuit of profit and self-interest, makes these entities more responsible than private businesses. Related issues include the fact that most non-profits have lower costs, in part because they do not have to deal with unionized workers and because they have volunteers. This raises some complaints from labor groups. Similarly, private businesses complain that they can provide some ser-vices more efficiently than either the public or non-profit entity and that the non-profit has an unfair advantage because of its special tax treatment.

The non-profit entity typically measures its success with reference to the promotion of its mission. It looks at the number of clients served and is more interested in its mission than in its profit margin. It can also look to the amount of funds raised, donations pledged or collected, and the value of contracts or grants received. Like the public entity, it has no easy market reference points for signaling what kinds of market activities to continue, start, or terminate. Unlike the public entity, it must cover all of its expenses and have a positive cash flow or it will go out of business.

Additional market considerations for the non-profit entity

A great deal of the activity of a non-profit entity relates to the delivery of public goods and services. This means that many public goods issues are confronted by these organizations. There are the key problems of dealing with *free riders* and with the issues of *nonexcludability*. Also, as with other organizations, there are *coordination* problems, *asymmetrical information* problems, and agency problems. Coordination problems are more difficult than in the private entity because it is harder to measure and compare performance between different activities in the organization. A private company can compare different activities, services, or products by looking at the bottom-line contribution of the activity to profit margin or by ability to meet target market share numbers. In the non-profit orga-nization, this is more difficult because the mission is the key benchmark of success and this goal may not be as readily compared in dollar terms as between different types of activities. Success in the non-profit organi-zation is more of a normative judgment than it is for the private entity because there are fewer external market indicators available. Failure is easier to measure than success. Running out of money and shutting down is always a concern so non-profits must pay attention to the cost effective delivery of the goods and services that they provide.

Agency problems arise for the non-profit organization because it attempts to act for a public purpose, and this means acting on behalf of the interest of another. In providing adoption services, childcare, education, or healthcare, for instance, the non-profit organization tries to do what it believes is in the best interest of the clients being served. As with the activities of a public entity, this involves making choices for another person and this conflicts with an important general assumption of competitive markets. It conflicts with the idea that the individual is best able to make her own decision about resource allocations. The entire idea behind the perfectly competitive paradigm is that no one is in any better position to make a decision than anyone else, so the individual under those key assumptions should be allowed to make the decisions on her own. Competitive market assumptions would favor giving cash or vouchers directly to the clients and letting them decide how to spend it. By giving it to the non-profit organization, the organization expresses its preferences in actions designed to promote the best interest of the client.

Even though non-profits deal extensively with public goods, some types of public goods can be excludable. This is the case with many types of non-profit associations. A union is able to obtain benefits for its members, for example. Likewise, the American Medical Association and the American Bar Association work to obtain special benefits for members and these benefits are generally not available to non-members.

Why support non-profits?

Some people ask the reason for giving subsidies to non-profits. They want to know why our legal system encourages non-profit organizations and activities. If these organizations serve a public purpose and produce public goods, why not have the government produce these goods and services? Presumably, government programs should reflect public policy better than privately directed organizations, and public entities seem more accountable to the public. Private non-profit organizations can keep a great deal of their financial records private and, as in the case of a private university, clients do not even get the full protection of the constitutional right to free speech. These organizations have religious and other agendas and perhaps they should not get direct (cash, grants, contracts) or even indirect (tax-related) subsidies. The response to these and other concerns usually includes three key factors:

(1) Non-profit organizations are generally more efficient and cost effective than the government in providing some goods and services. Their fee or rate for services is lower. In part, this is due to paying lower wages, having less reliance on union workers and union work rules, and the availability of volunteers and donations. There is also some competitive pressure as various non-profits compete for providing similar goods and services to the same clients. Some of these organizations also have better access to certain clients in specific neighborhoods, and some clients feel more comfortable getting service from a local church or community group than from a government office.

(2) Non-profit organizations are considered to be public spirited, trustworthy and socially responsible because they are not motivated by a desire to maximize profit. They are motivated by a mission to benefit the public and as long as they can cover expenses, they will try to do what is best for the client even if it is more costly than some alternative course of action.

(3) Non-profit organizations are useful because they help produce public goods that are under-produced in the private sector. The inability to exclude and to prevent free riders makes some goods less profitable in the private sector. Similarly, mixed goods like education and healthcare provide mixed benefits. Some of the benefit is direct as to the person receiving the education or care, and some of the benefit is indirect as to the public that enjoys a healthier and more informed electorate and workforce. These mixed goods are under-produced because neither the individual nor the public captures the full benefit and it is, therefore, difficult to determine the proper investment value. Related to this idea is the feeling that non-profits help to extract a willingness by some people to pay more for the provision of public goods and services than they are otherwise willing to pay in taxes to the government. This is because tax payments can not be targeted by the taxpayer. They go into general revenue funds or are payments for specific benefits which the taxpayer has no option to reject, such as social security taxes. The feeling is that many people will voluntarily give up more of their income if they feel that they have some say over the purpose for which it is used. Thus, if a non-profit serves a public need, it helps to function as an indirect way to raise more revenue for the provision of public goods and services.

Demands on public services

One concern about non-profit organizations is that they use public services but they do not pay local property taxes to cover the cost of those services. In some cities, as much as 50 percent or more of all the property within the city is exempt from property tax because it is owned by non-profit organizations. Religious organizations and schools (colleges and universities) often account for the biggest property tax exemptions. If one thinks about a major university, it is easy to see how police and fire services are important to the university community; likewise snow removal in northern climates. These services are expensive and some people feel that the costs should be internalized by the organization rather than subsidized by other taxpayers.

In many cases, large organizations, such as a university, enter into special arrangements with local government. They may agree that the university will operate its own police and fire services to be paid for out of student tuition or fees. They might also agree to have the university acquire certain adjoining streets or lease them so that it becomes responsible for snow removal and repair. They sometimes agree to an arrangement for the university to make a large annual cash payment to the local government as a fee "in lieu of taxes." These arrangements are political and practical. They promote good relationships between the community, the government, and the non-profit organization.

Cross-over activities

Today many non-profit organizations engage in cross-over activities by producing goods and services that compete with private sector providers. In other words, many non-profits now engage in a certain amount of activity that is not centered on public goods and services. Most organizations claim that this is important because they need additional sources of revenue to fund their public mission. Most non-profit organizations deliver goods and services that are very labor-intensive. This makes them relatively expensive. There are also limits to the ability to attract volunteers and donations. As a percentage of income, the rate at which Americans give to non-profits has remained relatively constant for many years, in single digits. There is only so much room for growth in this area.

In looking to produce more revenue, many non-profits have found that they can be successful in the private sector. The Save The Children organization, for instance, sells rather expensive ties, and private non-profit universities run very profitable bookstores and operate profitable food services and housing facilities. Ties, bookstore items, meals, and housing are all readily provided for in the private sector and they do not suffer from any of the market problems associated with public goods. This may make good economic sense for the non-profit organization but many private entities claim that it is unfair competition because of the direct and indirect tax breaks that non-profits enjoy. The private entities argue that it is difficult to compete when the competition has lower costs as a result of government approved subsidies. Likewise, they argue that there are some unfair practices that make it difficult for a private company to compete with a non-profit organization. An example might be a situation where a university requires all students in their first and second year of college to live in university owned housing. This requirement effectively eliminates private housing groups from competing to serve these students.

In response to claims of unfairness, many non-profit supporters assert that there is still plenty of room for everyone in the market and they say this is evidenced by all of the competing providers. For instance, shops and private housing still flourish in areas that surround the typical university even when the university competes as a non-profit offering similar goods and services. More importantly, the claim can be made that the cross-over subsidy is not bad because profits in the private sector area get pushed back into the furtherance of the non-profit organization's mission. The cross-subsidy, therefore, helps to provide additional public goods that are otherwise the subject of under-investment.

Non-government organizations (NGOs)

On the international scene, there is more and more talk about the role of non-governmental organizations or NGOs. These NGOs operate like a not-for-profit organization. The basic concepts that have been addressed in this chapter can help you understand and deal with these organizations. They act as entities with a public mission yet with independence from the government under which they are legally structured. They provide goods and services to clients and constituents, and they serve as vehicles for accepting and using international funds for domestic purposes. This is useful because there are a number of situations in which direct aid to a particular government may be politically impossible. In such a situation, the NGO permits the delivery of funding, goods, and services by indirect means. The NGO also permits a form of participation in international organizations that do not permit governments as members.

Conclusion

Non-profit organizations play an important role in the economy. They function to provide public goods and services, and they complement the private and public sectors. While these organizations do not pursue a profit motive, success in their mission requires them to operate profitably. In so doing non-profit organizations raise a number of important policy issues. Understanding these issues and the way in which people experience exchange with the non-profit sector is useful to understanding law in a market context.

Problems

(1) The State of California operates a very extensive and expensive prison system. In an attempt to cut costs and become more efficient, the State legislature decides that the prison system should be privatized. Having made this initial decision, legislative debate gets bogged down in a heated discussion of how best to run the prisons if they are not to be operated by the government. All agree that prison operations should be contracted out to a qualified operator with the lowest contract bid. The main line of discussion here concerns the question of collecting bids from not-for-profit entities or from private, for-profit enterprises. Offer your advice on the positive and negative aspects of going with either type of organization.

(2) The County Department of Social Services has $2 million to allocate to a counseling program for teenage girls. The counseling is to cover matters of hygiene, sexuality, birth control, sexually transmitted diseases, and pregnancy alternatives. The local Planned Parenthood office puts in to receive $1 million; Catholic Charities puts in for $500,000; and Teenage Birth Prevention, Inc. puts in for $1 million. Catholic Charities runs a number of teenage intervention and counseling programs, and in some respects it has an overlapping mission with some of the counseling that is available at Planned Parenthood. Unlike Planned Parenthood, however, Catholic Charities is not allowed, by its mission statement, to advise clients to obtain abortions nor can it direct women to abortion clinics or devices. Teenage Birth Prevention, Inc. also overlaps in many ways with the counseling services of both of the other two groups, but unlike either of them it is a for-profit corporation. It also operates three abortion clinics

in the county and has exclusive distribution rights to a new, high-cost but effective birth and disease control drug that only recently became available in the United States. The drug has shown some severe negative side effects in a small percentage of users taking the drug over the past two years in Europe.

How would you evaluate the legal and economic considerations involved in the allocation of county tax-resource dollars to each of these entities?

(3) Identify a non-profit organization (or NGO) in which you have an interest. Prepare a short paper in which you explore the decision making process and the functioning of a non-profit organization as it operates within a market economy. Look at a particular organization by reviewing materials published about it, or by going to the Internet, or by interviewing a manager. Consider the economic justifications offered for the existence of the organization. Also consider the economic impact of the organization in terms of jobs and the production of goods and services. Where and how does it get its money? Start with reference to the issues discussed in this chapter but also be sure to integrate concepts, terms, and ideas from earlier chapters. In an effort to assist you in organizing your thoughts for the paper, a suggestive list of questions is provided that should be among those that are addressed in your paper.

(1) What is the identity and organizational structure of the non-profit you are examining?

(2) Who are the various stakeholders or stakeholder groups for this organization, and how might their interests be different?

(3) Who sets the organizational mission, how do they set it, and how does the mission serve the public interest? Who are the clients or customers of the organization?

(4) Who runs the organization on a day-to-day or programmatic basis, and what is the accountability of these people, and to whom are they accountable?

(5) Does the mission complement, overlap, or extend a public or private program already in place?

(6) Does the mission respond to a perceived failure in the private market sector?

(7) Does non-profit status provide an "unfair" competitive advantage to such organizations with respect to the potential for private responses? Would privatization be helpful, workable, or preferred to either public or non-profit provision of the goods or services?

(8) How does the organization measure its success? What role or func-
     tion do profits or revenue margins play in this measure? How are
     costs determined and allocated?
(9) How does the organization raise capital for major projects and pro-
     grams?
(10) How much of the organizational budget comes from private dona-
     tions vs. direct or indirect public sources as in contracts or grants
     from local, state, or federal government entities?
(11) What role, if any, do competition and profit play in the functioning
     and decision making process of the organization? For instance, how
     does the organization decide to start a new program, end an existing
     program, or acquire a new operation/affiliate entity?
(12) To what extent does the organization, in making use of public funds,
     remain accountable to the public? If the organization uses taxpayer-
     related money, is it, or should it be, as fully and openly accountable
     as a government agency? Does the typical citizen think of it this way?
(13) What economic justification supports the need for special non-profit
     status for the entity? From a law and market economy perspective,
     can it be justified?

7

Parting thoughts

Understanding law in a market context

Understanding law in a market context is different from engaging in an economic analysis of law. It involves a consideration of the way in which people *experience* the intersection of law, markets, and culture. And it recognizes that this experience varies with a number of characteristics such as race, gender, class, age, and geographic location, among others. Moreover, this experience is understood by way of a process of interpretation – a process that situates the individual within a cultural-interpretive community.

For this reason, the book presents a framework for understanding the interpretive process and the ways in which interpretive institutions facilitate wealth formation and (re)distribution. Likewise, it focuses on the way in which law functions to mediate the tension between culture and the market to provide a framework for understanding the borrowing and incorporation of market concepts into law. The book also introduces a number of important economic terms and concepts that are frequently used in legal analysis. It is important to appreciate the way in which these terms and concepts can be selected, substituted, and re-characterized to advance alternative lines of legal argument. There are multiple market frames, references, and representations to choose from – thus, the creative lawyer should be able to advance market-based arguments for a variety of competing socio-legal outcomes.[1]

In addressing these ideas attention is focused on the community context of law and market exchange. This point is important, and in this regard it should be noted that law in a market context does not give primacy to the economic idea of *methodological individualism*.[2] Instead, it

---

[1] To consider an earlier illustration of this point, return to chapter 3 and the examples concerning "sexual favors" and "car sales."

[2] See MALLOY, LAW AND MARKET ECONOMY 57–70 (discussing the problem of methodological individualism).

examines the process of human exchange by positioning the individual within a deliberative community.[3] Rather than fixating on an atomistic calculus of individual choice, it seeks to understand the human practice of exchange. Consequently, it involves the study of decision making based on the relationship between an individual and her points of community reference.[4] As Roberta Kevelson explains it:

> although Freedom is the key term, or value, from which semiotic method derives its basic principles, Peirce is not concerned with the notion of "free individuals" but rather with freedom of individuals in community. The Peircean method of methods is an overt rejection of Cartesian principles of inquiry, and therefore it rejects implicitly the notion of the individual as a referential model, or sign. It supports, instead, the kind of model which represents communal or dialogic inquiry.[5]

In this context, the exchange process is one of relational substitution, and it is an experience in which individuals simultaneously leave their imprint on, and are imprinted by the drama in which they participate:[6]

---

[3] *Id.*

[4] PHILOSOPHICAL WRITINGS OF PEIRCE (Buchler, ed.), at xiv. Science requires a community of inquirers to work continuously toward agreement, *id.* But Peirce is not anti-individual – the individual is understandable only as a relate, in relation to community, *id.*

[5] KEVELSON, CHARLES S. PEIRCE'S METHOD OF METHODS 11. Peirce tells us that meaning arises only within community. It emerges from a dialogue in which the individual is not the key referential sign. *See* KEVELSON, PEIRCE, SCIENCE, SIGNS 1, 28, 60, 88–90; KEVELSON, PEIRCE'S ESTHETICS OF FREEDOM 140. Meaning comes from the interaction of individuals within community. KEVELSON, LAW AS A SYSTEM OF SIGNS 147, 208. *See also* HAUSMAN, CHARLES S. PEIRCE'S EVOLUTIONARY PHILOSOPHY 60–66 (explaining the anti-Cartesian basis of Peirce's pragmatism).

[6] In this context, it is important to remember that the rational allocative "individual" of traditional law and economics is, itself, merely an idea or sign and the idea of "individual" stands in reference to a real person but it is not the person to which it refers. Real people are affected by the environments in which they participate. The idea of the individual, therefore, like that of "person," "alien," "family member," or "refugee," is continually evolving within the market context and is given coherence by its reference to a real person and also by reference to a particular legal framework. When we forget the distinction between the idea of the individual and the real person to whom it refers, we collapse an essential element of their semiotic relationship and fall prey to the constraints of habitually blinding conventionalism that can deny us the possibility of envisioning further substitutional interpretation or change. *See* KEVELSON, PEIRCE, SCIENCE, SIGNS 165–78; Peirce said that man not only uses signs but that he himself is a sign. APEL, CHARLES S. PEIRCE at xxii. *See also* MERRELL, PEIRCE SIGNS AND MEANING 52–68.

The upshot is that there is no pure, absolutely autonomous "I" or self. No sign-or-self- is an island, an entity unto itself and absolutely autonomous. We, all signs, are thoroughly socialized. The "I" addresses itself to its otherness, its social other as well as the other of physical "reality," both of which are "out there" in contrast to the self's own inner "other." Part of that social otherness is that which is emerging and that into which the "I" is merging: the "I" is incessantly flowing into the otherness of which it is a *part of* and at the same time *apart from*. For, to repeat Peirce's words, "a person is not absolutely an individual," and at the same time, a person's "circle of society is a sort of loosely compacted person."[7]

Therefore, a problem with methodological individualism, as a foundation for economics applied to law, is that it artificially abstracts exchange from the community reference points that make it understandable – capable of interpretation.

Community-based referencing is of evident importance in a number of areas of law. For instance, in tort law we think not only in terms of injury or loss to an individual involved in an accident, we also think of the pain, suffering, and loss to those people closely connected to the victim or the event. We likewise judge the degree of one's negligence not by an isolated review of conduct, but with reference to a community standard and an expectation of reasonable care. Similarly, in contract law we interpret the terms of an agreement with reference to industry standards, course of dealing, and reasonable commercial expectations. And, with respect to property law we know that a piece of real property is not priced or valued by an isolated consideration of its own intrinsic qualities but with reference to the qualities of other surrounding properties and uses. The value of any given property can be affected by its location – near a peaceful ocean beach or next to a toxic waste dump, in a high-crime area, or in a quiet suburban neighborhood.

Law in a market context embraces the cultural and community context in which market action takes place. It does not isolate the individual from her cultural context any more than an appraiser of real estate would ignore the environment surrounding a particular piece of property. As Chief Judge Breitel explained in connection to real estate:

> It is recognized that the "value" of property is not a concrete or tangible attribute but an abstraction derived from the economic uses to which the property may be put . . . It would be . . . simplistic to ignore modern recognition of the principle

---

[7] MERRELL, PEIRCE, SIGNS AND MEANING 61. *See also* Malloy, *Letters from the Longhouse* (concerning how one imprints and is imprinted by an environment).

that no property has value except as the community contributes to that value. The obverse of this principle is, . . . no property is an economic island, free from contributing to the welfare of the whole of which it is but a dependent part.[8]

Judge Breitel's words have application beyond the area of property law. His words speak, metaphorically, to the basic nature of human existence more generally. It is, therefore, insufficient to think exclusively or even primarily in terms of an imaginary individual exercising rational and scientific decision making on an island detached from the rest of humanity. People, even more so than property, are situated in and affected by their communities.

In focusing on a process of exchange, rather than a calculus of choice, law in a market context involves a community perspective on legal reasoning and analysis. It also embraces a fundamental role in the marketplace for judicial, legislative, and administrative institutions. These institutions do not stand in opposition to the market; they function as the mediating and conventionalizing infrastructure that facilitates the market. These institutions permit individuals to transcend the frames and references of individualized and competing cultural-interpretive boundaries. They do this by creating a space and a place for cultural-interpretive exchange, and by recognizing the need to think of law in relation to both markets and culture. This kind of thinking acknowledges the relationship between economics and the law, while appreciating the lack of universality in the *experiencing* of law in a market context.

Moreover, as discussed previously in this book, the community context of law and market exchange does not make this approach completely subjective, indeterminate, or purely self-referencing. To the contrary, law in a market context involves an understanding of *objectivity* in legal reasoning. In this context, objectivity involves an expression of a recognizable and authoritative pattern of legal argument that is capable of being interpreted by other legal actors as reasonably independent of personal feelings, opinions and prejudice. This is possible when the expression has a cultural-interpretive (semiotic) relationship to both the real (experiential) world and to our understanding of that world. Objectivity, as such, is a "semiotic sign" expressed in the triadic relationship among firstness, involving the fundamental *qualities* of the experiential world; secondness, involving the frames, references, and representations used to interpret the

---

[8] Fred F. French Investing Co. v. City of New York, 39 N.Y.2d 587, 350 N.E. 2d 381 (Ct. of Appeals N.Y., 1976), *appeal dismissed*, 429 U.S. 990 (1976).

world; and thirdness, involving the arguments and conclusions drawn from the relationship between firstness and secondness.

Consequently, objectivity involves three levels of analysis. First, it accounts for the fundamental qualities of the real world such as the way in which people experience scarcity, externalities, transaction costs, and a variety of other constraints that are usefully expressed in market terms. Thus, market concepts are important for persuasive legal reasoning. Second, it relates the recognition of these fundamental qualities to a reasoned identification and selection of cultural-interpretive frames, references, and representations. Thus, one needs to examine the meanings of these qualities in terms of a variety of recognizable patterns of legal argument. These recognizable patterns of legal argument are not self-defining, they are the product of cultural-interpretive communities. Third, it uses abductive logic and speculative rhetoric to justify a conclusion or call to action in terms of the chosen frames, references, and representations used in the argument.

Such an approach to objectivity is not unfamiliar. We observe it in disciplines other than law. For example, consider the theory of evolution. The theory of evolution is objective in the sense that it is grounded in experiential evidence such as fossils. And the theory frames and explains certain elements of the qualitative evidence in terms of recognizable and authoritative patterns of argument. This does not mean that the theory of evolution is objective in all respects. Some parts of the theory of evolution may have a higher degree of "objectivity" than others. For example, fossil evidence tells us of the existence of dinosaurs but knowing exactly what they looked like, how they behaved, and why they became extinct is less clear. In this sense objectivity co-exists with the simultaneous presence of subjectivity and indeterminacy. The fact that some elements of evolutionary theory are more speculative than others does not make the idea of objectivity inapplicable. This is because objectivity arises from the ability to link experiential evidence to cultural-interpretive patterns of argument that are not fully self-defining. This is what makes it possible for others to accept the argument as something other than the author's personal feelings, opinions, and prejudice.

In the final analysis, therefore, understanding law in a market context does not involve a rejection of market theory or of objectivity. Instead, it suggests that important insights can be gained from using the humanities to explore the relationship among law, markets and culture, and from recognizing both the subjective and objective nature of law in a market context. Furthermore, it recognizes that economics and the social sciences are already an accepted part of meaningful (authoritative) legal discourse. It acknowledges that law is not an autonomous discipline and, therefore, lawyers must be fully conversant in such things as basic market terms and concepts.

Consequently, the patterns of legal argument have been made more complex in recent years – particularly because legal actors have recognized the importance of market concepts and the social sciences in legal reasoning. This means that the rationales and justifications we offer in support of legal conclusions and social action must now be informed by interdisciplinary work. In the end, however, we must come to realize that this added complexity has not changed our fundamental role as lawyers. Law has not been replaced by the social sciences, and law has not become a legal science. Applying market concepts to legal reasoning is useful but it offers us no simple answers, only new ways of understanding the underlying qualities and constraints of our exchange relationships. Ultimately, we have no economic calculus that relieves us from the challenge and opportunity of doing justice – we have no escape from engaging in a normative discourse concerning the ethical and esthetic values of the law.

Conclusion

This book offers a basis for rethinking the relationship between law, markets, and culture, and it explains that this relationship is community-based. In this context, economic terms and concepts help us to understand the social process of exchange. And, because market thinking has risen to a place of authoritative prominence in socio-legal discourse, the book explains how to begin to use these ideas strategically, as tools for legal reasoning and public policy making.

Problems

(1) Now that you have completed the book go back to "An outline of basic tools" at the end of chapter 3. After reviewing this outline, revisit some of the problems at the end of each of the earlier chapters. See if you can refine and improve on your initial approach to these problems.

(2) Drug Tech Ltd. is a pharmaceutical company based in Britain. Over the past ten years it has been engaged in a research project involving a team of scientists in both Canada and the United Kingdom. The project has cost the company about half a billion US dollars but has recently proven successful. Drug Tech has produced a new drug called drug "X." Drug X,

in trial testing, has proven to be an effective cure for HIV. Drug Tech has obtained patent protection for drug X and has complied with all international agreements relating to patents so that the patent is recognized and protected globally.

Drug Tech sets the price of a unit of X at $100 per dose. This price is selected to give Drug Tech the best return on its long and expensive research and development process. It also provides a return for the risk of the venture, as many drug development programs never result in a useful product. The typical patient in need of drug X will require a dose once every week for one–two years. The actual cost of producing a generic version of drug X, now that it has been discovered, is about $6 per dose.

The development of drug X is hailed as a major break-through in science and as a great achievement in the fight against the spread of HIV and Aids. In developed countries the government and various private health insurance companies undertake to pay for a high percentage of the cost of Drug X treatments for qualified patients. At the same time, drug X is too expensive for large-scale use in many poor and developing countries.

Zandue is a very poor country with a major public health problem. Some 30 percent of the population have HIV or Aids. There is no way that Zandue can afford to address its public health problem by using drug X because the cost is too high. After careful consideration, the government of Zandue decides to open a small pharmaceutical company to produce a generic version of drug X to be called "Generic X." This drug will be for use within Zandue, although it is realistic to believe that some of the drug will find its way into other markets. This plan is approved even though Zandue has signed several international agreements on patent law and patent protection. Zandue acknowledges that the production and distribution of Generic X will violate the patent law protection of Drug Tech to drug X.

In response to complaints by Drug Tech, and by the governments of various countries with substantial patent activity, Zandue explains that public health concerns outweigh the private property rights of Drug Tech. Thus, Zandue Drug Company begins the manufacture of Generic X and distributes it within the country at a cost of $7 per dose. This provides the government with a nominal profit on each dose. In addition, it is announced that the courts of Zandue will refuse to protect the Drug Tech patent, and that Zandue will not respond to any foreign law suits as Generic X is manufactured by a company under the authority of the sovereign government of Zandue.

(a) Develop arguments for and against the action taken by Zandue. Pay close attention to private and public tensions and try to apply a number of the tools outlined at the end of chapter 3.

(b) How, if at all, would your arguments change if Zandue expanded its production of Generic X and began exporting its product to Europe, North America, Australia, and Japan. The Zandue export price is $25 per dose, thus this activity provides an important source of revenue to the Zandue government. At the same time, as a lower-price alternative to drug X, Zandue makes the product available to many more people in these other countries. In some of these importing countries private health insurance programs cover only a small percentage of the people in need of the drug. In other countries, availability is limited under public health care coverage by using rationing to contain costs. In all cases, it is clear that Generic X infringes upon the patent and property rights of Drug Tech Limited.

(c) In the alternative, consider the issues and arguments that might be raised if the product in question is not a drug that is useful to control HIV and Aids. What if the developing world demands affordable access to advanced computer technology, military technology (particularly that which can be used for defensive purposes), water purification systems, or other products and technologies which are useful but very expensive? Do the arguments change with the product or technology in question, and if so why?

SOURCES

All footnotes in the book are prepared as short-form citations of the identified sources in this section. All source citations have been prepared with reference to *The Bluebook: A Uniform System of Citation* (17th ed., 2000).

Books

Adams, Henry C., *Relation of the State to Industrial Action and Economics and Jurisprudence* (Joseph Dorfman, ed., Augustus M. Kelley, 1954)

Allen, Tom, *The Right to Property in Commonwealth Constitutions* (Cambridge, 2000)

Apel, Karl-Otto, *Charles S. Peirce: From Pragmatism to Pragmaticism* (Prometheus, 1995)

Arrow, Kenneth J., *Social Choice and Individual Value* (1931, 2d ed., Yale, 1970)

Auyang, Sunny Y., *Foundations of Complex-Systems Theories in Economics, Evolutionary Biology, and Statistical Physics* (Cambridge, 1998)

Ayres, Clarence E., *The Theory of Economic Progress* (Schocken, 1944)

Barnes, David W. & Stout Lynn A., *Law and Economics* (West, 1992)

Becker, Gary S., *Accounting for Tastes* (Harvard, 1996)

Becker, Gary S., *The Economic Approach to Human Behavior* (Chicago, 1976)

Becker, Gary S., *The Economics of Discrimination* (2d ed., Chicago, 1971)

Becker, Gary S., *Economic Theory* (McGraw-Hill, 1971)

Becker, Gary S., *The Economics of Life* (McGraw-Hill, 1996)

Becker, Gary S., *Human Capital: A Theoretical and Empirical Analysis with Special Reference to Education* (3d ed., Chicago, 1993)

Becker, Gary S. & Murphy, Kevin M., *Social Economics: Market Behavior in a Social Environment* (1st ed., Belknap, 2000)

Bell, Derrick, *And We Are Not Saved: The Elusive Quest for Racial Justice* (Basic Books, 1989)

Berger, *Arthor Asa, Signs in Contemporary Culture* (Sheffield Publishing Co., 1984, reissued 1989)

Bix, Brian, *Jurisprudence: Theory and Context* (Carolina Academic Press, 2000)

Bix, Brian, *Law, Language and Legal Determinacy* (Clarendon, 1996)

Blaug, Mark, *The Methodology of Economics* (Cambridge, 1980)

Briggs, John & Peat, F. David, *Turbulent Mirror: An Illustrated Guide to Chaos Theory and the Science of Wholeness* (HarperCollins, 1989)

Brigham, John, *The Constitution of Interests: Beyond the Politics of Rights* (New York University, 1996)

Brown, Dee, *Bury, My Heart at Wounded Knee: An Indian History of the American West* (Henry Holt & Co., 1970)

Buchanan, James & Tullock, Gordon, *The Calculus of Consent: Legal Foundations of Constitutional Democracy* (Michigan, 1962, Ann Arbor Paperbacks, 1965)

Calabresi, Guido, *A Common Law for the Age of Statutes* (Harvard, 1982)

Calabresi, Guido, *Cost of Accidents: A Legal and Economic Analysis* (Yale, 1970)

Calabresi, Guido, *Ideals, Beliefs, Attitudes, and the Law: Private Law Perspectives on a Public Law Problem* (Syracuse, 1985)

Chamallas, Martha, *Introduction to Feminist Legal Theory* (Aspen, 1999)

Chancellor, Edward, *Devil Take the Hindmost, A History of Financial Speculation* (Plume, 1999, paperback, 2000)

Chatwin, Bruce, *The Songlines* (Penguin, 1987)

Chinese Women Traversing Diaspora: Memoirs, Essays, and Poetry (Sharon K. Hom, ed., Garland, 1999)

Coase, Ronald H., *The Firm, the Market, and the Law* (Chicago, 1988)

Colapietro, Vincent M., *Peirce's Approach to the Self: A Semiotic Perspective on Human Subjectivity* (State University of New York, 1989)

Commons, John R., *Institutional Economics: Its Place in Political Economy* (Transaction, 1934)

Cooter, Robert & Ulen, Thomas, *Law and Economics* (3d ed., Addison-Wesley, 2000)

Dana, David A. & Merrill, Thomas W., *Property: Takings* (Foundation Press, 2002)

Deely, John, *Basics of Semiotics* (Indiana, 1990)

DeSoto, Hernando, *The Mystery of Capital: Why Capitalism Triumphs in the West and Fails Everywhere Else* (Basic Books, 2000)

Driesen, David, *Economic Dynamics of Environmental Law* (MIT, 2003)

Dwyer, John P. & Menell, Peter S., *Property Law and Policy: A Comparative Institutional Perspective* (Foundation, 1998)

Eco, Umberto, *Foucault's Pendulum* (Ballantine, 1989)

Eco, Umberto, *The Limits of Interpretation* (Indiana, 1990)

Eco, Umberto, *Misreadings* (Harvest, 1993)

Eco, Umberto, *The Name of the Rose* (Harvest, 1983)

Eco, Umberto, *The Open Work* (Anna Cancogni, trans., Harvard, 1989)

Eco, Umberto, *The Search for the Perfect Language* (Blackwell, 1995)

Eco, Umberto, *Semiotics and the Philosophy of Language* (Indiana, 1984)

Eco, Umberto, *Theory of Semiotics* (Indiana, 1976)

Elster, Jon, *The Cement of Society: A Survey of Social Order* (Cambridge, 1989)

Epstein, Richard A., *Simple Rules for a Complex World* (Harvard, 1995)

The Essential Peirce Vol. 1 (Nathan Houser & Christian Kloesel, eds., Indiana, 1992)

The Essential Peirce Vol. 2 (The Peirce Edition Project, eds., Indiana, 1998)

Farber, Daniel A. & Frickey, Philip P., *Law and Public Choice* (Chicago, 1991)

Ferber, Marianne A. & Nelson, Julie A., eds., *Beyond Economic Man: Feminist Theory and Economics* (Chicago, 1993)

Friedman, Milton, *Essays in Positive Economics* (Chicago, 1953)

Gagnier, Regina, *The Insatiability of Human Wants: Economics and Aesthetics in Market Society* (Chicago, 2000)

Geuss, Raymond, *Public Goods, Private Goods* (Princeton, 2001)

Ghez, Gilbert R. & Becker, Gary S., *Allocation of Time and Goods over the Life Cycle* (National Bureau of Economic Research, 1975)

Gleick, James, *Chaos: Making a New Science* (Penguin, 1987)

Goodrich, Peter, *Reading the Law: A Critical Introduction to Legal Method and Techniques* (Blackwell, 1986)

Gordon, Ian H., *Competitor Targeting: Winning the Battle for Market and Customer Share* (John Wiley, 2001)

Greene, Brian, *The Elegant Universe: Superstrings, Hidden Dimensions, and the Quest for the Ultimate Theory* (Vintage, 1999)

Hardin, Garret & Garling, Scipio, *The Immigration Dilemma: Avoiding the Tragedy of the Commons* (The Social Contract Press, 1995)

Hausman, Carl R., *Charles S. Peirce's Evolutionary Philosophy* (Cambridge, 1993)

Hayakawa, S. I. & Hayakawa, A. R., *Language in Thought and Action* (5th ed., Harcourt Brace, 1990)

Hayek, Friedrich A., *The Constitution of Liberty* (Chicago, 1960)

Hayek, Friedrich A., *Law, Legislation, and Liberty* (Vol. 1, *Rules and Order*, Chicago, 1973) (Vol. 2, *The Mirage of Social Justice*, Chicago, 1976) (Vol. 3, *The Political Order of a Free People*, Chicago, 1979)

Hayman, Robert, Levit, Nancy, & Delgado, Richard, *Jurisprudence – Classical and Contemporary: From Natural Law to Postmodernism* (West 2d, ed., 2002)

Head, John G., *Public Goods and Public Welfare* (Duke, 1974)

Higginbotham, A. Leon, Jr., *In the Matter of Color: Race & the American Legal Process: The Colonial Period* (Oxford, 1978, paperback, 1980)

Hodge, Robert & Kress, Gunther, *Social Semiotics* (Cornell, 1988)

Hookway, Christopher, *Peirce: The Arguments of the Philosophers* (Routledge, 1992)

Judgment Under Uncertainty: Heuristics and Biases (Kahnieman, Slovic, and Tversky, eds., Cambridge, 1982)

Kauffman, Stuart, *At Home in the Universe: The Search for the Laws of Self-Organization* (Oxford, 1995)

Kay, Neil M., *Patterns in Corporate Evolution* (Oxford, 1997)

Kevelson, Roberta, *Charles S. Peirce's Method of Methods* (John Benjamins, 1987)

Kevelson, Roberta, *The Law as a System of Signs* (Plenum, 1988)

Kevelson, Roberta, *Peirce, Science, Signs* (Lang, 1996)

Kevelson, Roberta, *Peirce's Esthetics of Freedom: Possibility, Complexity, and Emergent Value* (Lang, 1993)

Kirzner, Israel M., *Discovery and the Capitalist Process* (Chicago, 1985)

Kirzner, Israel M., *The Meaning of Market Process: Essays in the Development of Modern Austrian Economics* (Routledge, 1992)

Kukathas, Chandran, *Hayek and Modern Liberalism* (Clarendon, 1989)

Landa, Janet Tai, *Trust, Ethnicity and Identity: Beyond the New Institutional Economics of Ethnic Trading Networks, Contract Law, and Gift-Exchange* (Michigan, 1994)

Law and Economics: The International Library of Critical Writings in Economics (Richard A. Posner & Francesco Parisi, eds., Edward Elgar, 1997)

Law and Economics: New and Critical Perspectives (Robin Paul Malloy & Christopher K. Braun, eds., Lang, 1995)

Lewis, David, *The Management of Non-Governmental Development Organizations: An Introduction* (Routledge, 2001)

Liszka, James Jakob, *A General Introduction to the Semeiotic of Charles Sanders Peirce* (Indiana, 1996)

Locke, John, *Second Treatise on Government* (3d ed., Prometheus Books, 1986)

Malloy, Robin Paul, *Law and Economics: A Comparative Approach to Theory and Practice* (West, 1990)

Malloy, Robin Paul, *Law and Market Economy: Reinterpreting the Values of Law and Economics* (Cambridge, 2000)

Malloy, Robin Paul, *Planning for Serfdom: Legal Economic Discourse and Downtown Development* (Penn., 1991)

Malloy, Robin Paul & Smith James C., *Real Estate Transactions: Problems, Cases, and Materials* (2d ed., Aspen, 2002)

Matthiessen, Peter, *In the Spirit of Crazy Horse* (Penguin, 1992)

McCloskey, Deidre N., *If You're so Smart: The Narrative of Economic Expertise* (Chicago, 1990)

McCloskey, Deidre N., *The Rhetoric of Economics* (Wisconsin, 1998) (1st ed., 1985)

Menand, Louis, *The Metaphysical Club: A Story of Ideas in America* (Farrar, Straus & Giroux, 2001)

Mercuro, Nicholas & Medema, Steven G., *Economics and the Law: From Posner to Post-Modernism* (Princeton, 1997)

Merrell, Floyd, *Peirce, Signs, and Meaning* (Toronto, 1997)

Merrell, Floyd, *Semiosis in the Postmodern Age* (Purdue, 1995)

Merryman, John Henry, *The Civil Law Tradition: An Introduction to the Legal Systems of Western Europe and Latin America* (2d ed., Stanford, 1985)

Milovanovic, Dragan, *An Introduction to the Sociology of Law* (Criminal Justice Press, 2003)

Minda, Gary, *Postmodern Legal Movements: Law and Jurisprudence at Century's End* (New York University, 1995)

Morrison, Toni, *Racing Justice, Engendering Power: Essays on Anita Hill, Clarence Thomas, and the Construction of Social Reality* (Pantheon, 1992)

Mueller, Dennis C., *Public Choice II* (Cambridge, 1989)

NGO Management (Michael Edwards & Alan Fowler, eds., Earthscan, 2002)

Non-profit Organizations in a Market Economy: Understanding New Roles, Issues, and Trends (Hammack and Young, eds., Jossey-Bass, 1993)

Non-profits & Government: Collaboration and Conflict (Elizabeth T. Boris & C. Eugene Steuerle, eds., Urban Institute, 1998)

Nooteboom, Bart, *Learning and Innovation in Organizations and Economies* (Oxford, 2000)

North, Douglass C., *Institutions, Institutional Change and Economic Performance* (Cambridge, 1990)

Noth, Winfried, *Handbook on Semiotics* (Indiana, 1995)

Olson, Mancur, *The Logic of Collective Action: Public Goods and the Theory of Groups* (Harvard, 1965)

Patterson, Dennis, *Law & Truth* (Oxford, 1996)

Paul, Ellen Frankel, *Equity and Gender: The Comparable Worth Debate* (Transaction, 1989)

Philosophical Writings of Peirce (Justus Buchler, ed., Dover, 1955)

Posner, Richard A., *Economic Analysis of Law* (5th ed., Aspen, 1998) (1st ed., 1972)

Posner, Richard A., *Economic Structure of the Law* (Francesco Parisi, ed., Edward Elgar, 2000)

Posner, Richard A., *The Economics of Justice* (Harvard, 1981)

Posner, Richard A., *Economics of Private Law* (Francesco Parisi, ed., Edward Elgar, 2001)

Posner, Richard A., *Economics of Public Law* (Francesco Parisi, ed., Edward Elgar, 2001)

Posner, Richard A., *Frontiers of Legal Theory* (Harvard, 2001)

Posner, Richard A., *The Problematics of Moral and Legal Theory* (Belknap, 1999)

Posner, Richard A., *Problems of Jurisprudence* (Harvard, 1990)

Posner, Richard A., *Sex and Reason* (Harvard, 1992)

Potter Vincent G., S. J., *Charles S. Peirce on Norms & Ideals* (Fordham, 1997)

Public Goods and Market Failures: A Critical Examination (Tyler Cowen, ed., Transaction, 1992)

Race, Rights, and Reparation: Law of Japanese American Internment (Erik K. Yamamoto, Margaret Chon, Carol Izumi, Frank H. Wu, & Jerry Kung, eds., Aspen 2001)

Rawls, John, *A Theory of Justice* (Harvard, 1971)

Reasoning and the Logic of Things: Charles Sanders Peirce (Kenneth Laine Ketner, ed., Harvard, 1992)

Reeder, Alan, *In Pursuit of Principle and Profit: Business Success Through Social Responsibility* (Putnam, 1994)

Representation: Cultural Representations and Signifying Practices (Stuart Hall, ed., Sage, 1997)

Rosen, Harvey S., *Public Finance* (McGraw-Hill/Irwin, 2002)

Rosenbaum, David I., *Market Dominance* (Praeger, 1998)

Samuels, Warren J., *Law and Economics: An Institutionalist Perspective* (Martinus Nijhoff, 1981)

Schumpeter, Joseph A., *Capitalism, Socialism, and Democracy* (Harper Torchbooks, 1975 ed.)

Scoles, Robert, *Semiotics and Interpretation* (Yale, 1982)

Self-Interest: An Anthology of Philosophical Perspectives (Kelly Rogers, ed., Routledge, 1997)

Sen, Amartya, *Development as Freedom* (Knopf, 1999)

Shand, Alexander H., *The Capitalist Alternative: An Introduction to Neo-Austrian Economics* (New York University, 1984)

Sheriff, John K., *Charles Peirce's Guess at the Riddle: Grounds for Human Significance* (Indiana, 1994)

The Sign of Three (Umberto Eco and Thomas Sebeok, eds., Indiana, 1983)

Singer, Seph William, *Introduction to Property* (Aspen 2001)

Smith, Adam, *An Inquiry into the Nature and Causes of the Wealth of Nations* (Edwin Cannon, ed., Modern Library, 1976)

Smith, Adam, *Essays on Philosophical Subjects* (Liberty, 1980)

Smith, Adam, *Lectures on Jurisprudence* (R. L. Meek, D. D. Raphael, & L. G. Stein, eds., The Glasgow Edition, Liberty, 1978)

Smith, Adam, *Lectures on Rhetoric and Belles Lettres* (J. C. Bryce, ed., Liberty, 1983)

Smith Adam, *The Theory of Moral Sentiments* (E. G. West, ed., Regnery, 1969)

Solo, Robert A., *Economic Organizations and Social Systems* (Michigan, 1967)

Sprankling, John G., *Understanding Property Law* (Lexis, 2000)

Strobel, Lee Patrick, *Reckless Homicide? Ford's Pinto Trial* (And Books, 1980)

Sunstein, Cass R., *Behavioral Law & Economics* (Cambridge, 2000)

Sunstein, Cass R., *Feminism & Political Theory* (Cass R. Sunstein, ed., Chicago, 1990)

Swanson Timothy M., *The Economics of Environmental Degradation: Tragedy for the Commons?* (Edward Elgar, 1996)

Throsby, David, *Economics and Culture* (Cambridge, 2001)

To Profit or Not to Profit: The Commercial Transformation of the Non-profit Sector (Burton A. Weisbrod, ed., Cambridge, 1998)

Tynan, Kevin B., *Multi-Channel Marketing: Maximizing Market Share with Integrated Marketing Strategy* (Probus, 1994)

Veblen, Thorstein, *Theory of the Leisure Class* (Penguin, 1899)

Articles and book chapters

Akerlof, George, *The Market for Lemons: Qualitative Uncertainty and the Market Mechanism, in* FOUNDATIONS OF THE ECONOMIC APPROACH TO LAW 239 (Avery W. Katz, ed., Foundation, 1998)

Ayres, Ian & Talley, Eric, *Solomonic Bargaining: Dividing Legal Entitlement to Facilitate Coasean Trade*, 104 YALE L. J. 1027 (1995)

Becker, Gary S., *Crime and Punishment: An Economic Approach*, 76 J. POL. ECON. 169 (1968)

Becker, Gary S., *A Theory of Competition Among Pressure Groups for Political Influence*, 98 Q. J. ECON. 371 (1983)

Bender, Leslie, *An Overview of Feminists Torts Scholarship*, 78 CORNELL L. REV. 575 (1993)

Beveridge, Norwood P., *Does the Corporate Director Have a Duty to Obey the Law?*, 45 DEPAUL L. REV. 729 (1996)

Blair, Margaret M. & Stout, Lynn A., *Trust, Trustworthiness, and the Behavioral Foundations of Corporate Law*, 149 U. PA. L. REV. 1735 (2001)

Brennen, David A., *Charities and the Constitution: Evaluating the Limitation for Charities*, 5 FLA. TAX REV. 779 (2002)

Brennen, David A., *The Power of the Treasury: Racial Discrimination, Public Policy and "Charity" in Contemporary Society*, 33 U.C. DAVIS L.R. 389 (2000)

Brennen, David A., *Tax Expenditures, Social Justice, and Civil Rights: Expanding the Scope of Civil Rights Laws to Tax-Exempt Charities*, 2001 B.Y.U.L. REV. 167 (2001)

Brion, Denis J., *The Ethics of Property: A Semiotic Inquiry Into Ownership*, 12 INT'L J. FOR THE SEMIOTICS OF L. 247 (1999)

Brion, Denis J., *The Pragmatic Genesis of Constitutional Meaning*, 10 INT'L J. FOR THE SEMIOTICS OF L. (1997)

Brion, Denis J., *Rhetoric and the Law of Enterprise*, 42 SYRACUSE L. REV. 117 (1991)

Brody, Evelyn, *Agents Without Principals: The Economic Convergence of the Nonprofit and the For-Profit Organizational Forms*, 40 N.Y.L. SCH. L. REV. 457 (1996)

Brody, Evelyn, *Institutional Dissonance in the Non-profit Sector*, 41 VILL. L. REV. 433 (1996)

Calabresi, Guido, *The Pointlessness of Pareto: Carrying Coase Further*, 100 YALE L.J. 1211 (1991)

Calabresi, Guido & Melamed, Douglas, *Property Rules, Liability Rules, and Inalienability: One View of the Cathedral*, 85 HARV. L. REV. 1089 (1972)

Carbone, June, *The Role of Contract Principles in Determining the Validity of Surrogacy Contracts*, 28 SANTA CLARA L. REV. 581 (1988)

Ciscusi, Kip W., *Corporate Risk Analysis: A Reckless Act?*, 52 STAN. L. REV. 547 (2000)

Coase, Ronald H., *The Problem of Social Cost*, 3 J.L. & ECON. 1 (1960)

Commons, John R., *Law and Economics*, 34 YALE L.J. 371 (1925)

Cordato, Roy E., *Time Passage and the Economics of Coming to the Nuisance: Reassessing the Coasean Perspective*, 20 CAMP. L. REV. 273 (1998)

Daly, George, *The Coase Theorem: Assumptions, Applications, and Ambiguities*, 12 ECON. INQUIRY 203 (1974)

Dau-Schmidt, Kenneth G., *Economics and Sociology: The Prospects for Interdisciplinary Discourse on Law*, 1997 WISC. L. REV. 389

Dau-Schmidt, Kenneth G., *Legal Prohibitions as More than Prices: The Economic Analysis of Preference Shaping Policies in the Law*, in LAW AND ECONOMICS NEW AND CRITICAL PERSPECTIVES (Robin Paul Malloy & Christopher K. Braun, eds., Lang, 1995)

Dau-Schmidt, Kenneth G., *Relaxing Traditional Economic Assumptions and Values: Toward a New Multidisciplinary Discourse on Law*, 42 SYR. L. REV. 181 (1991)

Dau-Schmidt, Kenneth G., *An Economic Analysis of the Criminal Law as a Preference-Shaping Policy*, 1990 DUKE L. J. 1

Debate: Is Law and Economics Moral? (Malloy vs. Posner), 24 VAL. U. L. REV. 147 (1990)

Demsetz, Harold, *Toward a Theory of Property Rights*, 57 AM. ECON. REV. PAPERS & PROCEEDINGS 347 (1967)

Dennis, Jeanne M., *The Lessons of Comparable Worth: A Feminist Vision of Law and Economic Theory*, 4 UCLA WOMEN'S L.J. 1 (1993)

Dewey, John, *Logical Method and Law*, CORNELL L. Q. 17 (1924)

Easterbrook, Frank H., *Some Tasks in Understanding Law Through the Lens of Public Choice*, 12 INT'L. REV. L. & ECON. 284 (1992)

Eastman, Wayne, *How Coasean Bargaining Entails a Prisoner's Dilemma*, 72 NOTRE DAME L. REV. 89 (1996)

Evensky, Jerry, *Setting the Scene: Adam Smith's Moral Philosophy*, in ROBIN PAUL MALLOY & JERRY EVENSKY, ADAM SMITH AND THE PHILOSOPHY OF LAW AND ECONOMICS (Kluwer, 1994) (Paperback, 1995)

Farber, Daniel A. & Frickey, Philip P., *The Jurisprudence of Public Choice*, 65 TEX. L. REV. 873 (1987)

Farber, Daniel A. & Frickey, Philip P., *Legislative Intent and Public Choice*, 74 VA. L. REV. 423 (1988)

Fick, Jeffrey A., *Calif. Jury Rules Ford Explorer "Defective,"* USA TODAY, Feb. 1, 2002, at B1

Frank, Jerome, *What Courts Do In Fact*, 26 ILL. L. R. 645 (1931)

Freeman, Walter J., *A Neurobiological Interpretation of Semiotics: Meaning, Representation and Information*, INFORMATION SCIENCES 124: 93–102 (2000)

Garrison, Marsha, *Law Making for Baby Making: An Interpretive Approach to the Determination of Legal Parentage*, 113 HARV. L. REV. 835 (2000)

Ghosh, Shubha, *Gray Markets in Cyberspace*, 7 J. ITEL. PROP. L. 1 (1999)

Ghosh, Shubha, *The Merits of Ownership; or How I Learned to Stop Worrying and Love Intellectual Property*, 15 HARV. J. L. & TECH 453 (2002)

Ghosh, Shubha, *Property Rules, Liability Rules, and Termination Rights: A Fresh Look at the Employment at Will Debate with Application to Franchising and Family Law*, 75 OR. L. REV. 969 (1996)

Ghosh, Shubha, *Turning Gray Into Green: Some Comments on Napster*, 23 HAST-INGS COMMUNICATIONS/ENTERTAINMENT L. J. 563 (2001)

Gostin, Lawrence O., *Surrogacy From the Perspectives of Economic and Civil Liberties*, 17 J. CONTEMP. HEALTH L. & POL'Y 429 (2001)

Hadfield, Gillian K., *An Expressive Theory of Contract: From Feminist Dilemmas to a Reconceptualization of Rational Choice in Contract Law*, 146 U. PA. L. REV. 1235 (1998)

Hadfield, Gillian K., *The Price of Law: How the Market for Lawyers Distorts the Justice System*, 98 MICH. L. REV. 953 (2000)

Hanson, Jon D. & Kysar, Douglas, *Taking Behavioralism Seriously: The Problem of Market Manipulation*, 74 N.Y.U. L. REV. 630 (1999)

Hardin, Garret, *The Tragedy of the Commons*, 162 SCIENCE 1243 (1968)

Harris, Curtis E. & Alcorn, Stephen P., *To Solve a Deadly Shortage: Economic Incentives for Human Organ Donation*, 16 ISSUES L. & MED. 213 (2001)

Heller, Michael A., *The Tragedy of the Anticommons: Property in the Transition from Marx to Markets*, 111 HARV. L. REV. 621 (1998)

Hoffman, Elizabeth & Spitzer, Mathew L., *The Coase Theorem: Some Experimental Tests*, 25 J. L. & ECON. 73 (1982)

Hom, Sharon & Malloy, Robin Paul, *China's Market Economy: A Semiosis of Cross Boundary Discourse Between Law and Economics and Feminist Jurisprudence*, 45 SYRACUSE L. R. 815 (1994)

Houh, Emily, *Critical Interventions: Toward an Expansive Equality Approach to the Doctrine of Good Faith and Fair Dealing In Contract Law*, 88 CORNELL L. REV. 1025 (2003)

Hovenkamp, Herbert, *Marginal Utility and the Coase Theorem*, 75 CORNELL L. REV. 783 (1990)

Hutchenson, Joseph C., *The Function of the "Hunch" in Judicial Decisions*, 14 CORNELL L. Q. 274 (1929)

Kevelson, Roberta, *Transfer, Transaction, Asymmetry: Junctures Between Law and Economics From the Fish-Eye Lens of Semiotics*, 42 SYRACUSE L. REV. 7 (1991)

Kevelson, Roberta, *Property as Rhetoric*, 4 CARDOZ. ST. L. & LIT. 189 (1992)

Lessig, Lawrence, *The Regulation of Social Meaning*, 62 CHICAGO L. REV. 943 (1995)

Lewin, Jeff L., *Toward a New Ecological Law & Economics*, in LAW AND ECONOMICS: NEW AND CRITICAL PERSPECTIVES 249 (Robin Paul Malloy & Christopher K. Braun, eds., P. Lang, 1995)

Macey, Jonathan R., *Promoting Public Regarding Legislation Through Statutory Interpretation: An Interest Group Model*, 86 COLUM. L. REV. 223 (1986)

Malloy, Robin Paul, *Framing the Market: Representations of Meaning and Value in Law, Markets, and Culture*, 51 BUFF. L. REV. 1 (2003)

Malloy, Robin Paul, *Law and Market Economy: The Triadic Linking of Law, Economics, and Semiotics*, 12 INT'L J. FOR THE SEMIOTICS OF L. 285 (1999)

Malloy, Robin Paul, *Letters from the Longhouse: Law, Economics and Native American Values*, 1992 WISC. L. REV. 1569

Malloy, Robin Paul, *Toward a New Discourse of Law and Economics*, 42 SYRACUSE L. REV. 27 (1991)

McAdams, Richard H., *An Attitudinal Theory of Expressive Law*, 79 OR. L. REV. 339 (2000)

McAdams, Richard H., *A Focal Point Theory of Expressive Law*, 86 VA. L. REV. 1649 (2000)

McAdams, Richard H., *Signaling Discount Rates: Law, Norms, and Economic Methodology*, 110 YALE L.J. 25 (2001)

McClurg, Andrew Jay, *It's a Wonderful Life: The Case for Hedonic Damages in Wrongful Death Cases*, 66 NOTRE DAME L. REV. 57 (1990)

McCluskey, Martha T., *Insurer Moral Hazard in the Workers' Compensation Crisis: Reforming Cost Inflation Not Rate Suppression*, 5 EMPL. RTS. & EMPLOY. POL'Y J. 55 (2001)

Meighan, Katherine Wells, *In a Similar Choice: A Unifying Economic Analysis of Gillian's Amy and Jake*, 2 AM. U. J. GENDER SOC. POL'Y & L. 139 (1994)

Modak-Truan, Mark C., *Pragmatic Justification of the Judicial Hunch*, 35 U. RICH. L. REV. 55 (2001)

Mosely, Philip, *Laying Down the Law: Bruce Chatwin's The Songlines and Australian Aboriginal Concepts of Land*, in III LAW AND SEMIOTICS 267 (Roberta Kevelson, ed., Plenum, 1989)

North, Douglass, *Transaction Costs, Institutions and Economic Performance*, in INTERNATIONAL CENTRE FOR ECONOMIC DEVELOPMENT OCCASIONAL PAPERS NO. 30 (1992)

Nutter, G. Warren, *The Coase Theorem on Social Cost: A Footnote*, 11 J. L. & ECON. 503 (1968)

O'Connor, Marlene, *Promoting Economic Justice in Plant Closings: Exploring the Fiduciary/Contract Law Distinction to Enforce Implicit Agreements*, in PROGRESSIVE CORPORATE LAW (Lawrence Mitchell, ed., Westview Press, 1995)

O'Neil, Terry, *Self-Interest and Concern for Others in the Owner-Managed Firm: A Suggested Approach to Dissolution and Fiduciary Obligation in Close Corporations*, 22 SETON HALL L. REV. 646 (1992)

Posner, Richard A., *Rational Choice, Behavioral Economics, and the Law*, 50 STAN. L. REV. 1551 (1998)

Posner, Richard A., *Utilitarianism, Economics, and Legal Theory*, 8 J. LEGAL STUD. 103 (1979)

Radin, Margaret Jane, *Property and Personhood*, 34 STAN. L. REV. 957 (1982)

Rao, Radhika, *Property, Privacy and the Human Body*, 80 B.U. L. REV. 359 (2000)

Regan, Donald, *The Problem of Social Costs Revisited*, 15 J.L. & ECON. 427 (1972)

Resnik, David B., *DNA Patents and Human Dignity*, 29 J.L. MED. & ETHICS 152 (2001)

Rostain, Tania, *Educating Homo Economicus: Cautionary Notes on the New Behavioral Law and Economics Movement*, 34 LAW & SOC'Y REV. 973 (2000)

Sanger, Carol, *(Baby) M is for the Many Things: Why I Start With Baby M*, 44 ST. LOUIS U. L. J. 1443 (2000)

Schlag, Prerre, *The Problem of Transaction Costs*, 62 CAL. L. REV. 1661 (1989)

Swygert, Michael I. & Yanes, Katherine Earle, *A Primer on the Coase Theorem: Making Law in a World of Zero Transaction Costs*, 11 DEPAUL BUS. L. J. 1 (1998)

Symposium: Law, Economics and Norms, 144 U. PA. L. REV. 1643 (1996)

Tollison, Robert, *Public Choice and Legislation*, 74 VA. L. REV. 339 (1998)

Voris, Bob Van, & Fleischer Matt, *Feeding Frenzy over Firestone*, 9/11/00 NAT'L L.J. A1 (2000)

Ulen, Thomas, *Rational Choice and the Economic Analysis of Law*, LAW AND SOCIAL INQUIRY (Spring, 1994)

White, Barbara Ann, *Feminist Foundations for the Law of Business: One Law and Economics Scholar's Survey and (Re)review*, 10 UCLA WOMEN'S L.J. 39 (1999)

Williams, Joan, *The Rhetoric of Property*, 83 IOWA L. REV. 277 (1998)

Yablon, Charles M., *Justifying the Judge's Hunch: An Essay on Discretion*, 21 HAST. L.J. 231 (1990)

Cases

American Nurses' Ass'n v. Illinois, 783 F.2d 716 (7th Cir. 1986)

Boomer v. Atlantic Cement Co., 257 N.E.2d 870 (N.Y. 1970)

Dolan v. City of Tigard, 512 U.S. 374 (1994)

Dynamics Corp. of Am. v. CTS Corp., 794 F.2d 250 (7th Cir. 1986)

Fred F. French Investing Co. v. City of New York, 39 N.Y.2d 587, 350 N.E.2d 381 (Ct. of Appeals N.Y., 1976), *appeal dismissed*, 429 U.S. 990 (1976)

Frigaliment Importing Co. v. B.N.S. Int'l. Sales Corp., 190 F. Supp. 116 (S.D.N.Y. 1960)

Grimshaw v. Ford Motor Co., 174 Cal. Rptr. 348 (Ct. App. 1981)

Honorable v. Easy Life Real Estate Sys., 100 F. Supp.2d 885 (N.D. Ill. 2000)

In the Matter of Baby M, 109 N.J. 396 (1988)

Int'l Union, United Auto., Aerospace and Agric. Implement Workers of America, UAW v. Johnson Controls, Inc., 499 U.S. 187 (1991)

Keystone Bituminous Coal Ass'n v. DeBenedictis, 480 U.S. 470 (1987)

Lucas v. South Carolina Coastal Council, 505 U.S. 1003 (1992)

Merritt v. Faulkner, 697 F.2d 761 (7th Cir. 1983)

Moore v. Regents of the Univ. of California, 793 P.2d 479 (Cal. 1990)

Nollan v. Calif. Coastal Comm., 483. U.S. 825 (1987)

Peevyhouse v. Garland Coal & Mining Co., 382 P.2d 109 (S. Ct. Okla. 1962)

Penn Central Transp. Co. v. City of New York, 438 U.S. 104 (1978)

Pennsylvania Coal v. Mahon, 260 U.S. 393 (1922)

Raffles v. Wichelhaus, 2H.& C. 906, 159 Eng. Rep. 375 (EX. 1864)

Samperi v. Inlands Wetlands Agency of West Haven, 628 A.2d 1286 (Conn. 1993)

Suntrust Bank v. Houghton Mifflin Co., 268 F.3d 1257 (11th Cir. 2001)

U.S. v. Carroll Towing Co., 159 F.2d 169 (2d Cir. 1947)

Vande Zande v. Wisconsin Dept. of Admin., 44 F.3d 538 (7th Cir. 1995)

Movies

CLASS ACTION, Twentieth Century Fox (1990)

DO THE RIGHT THING, MCA Universal (1989)

OTHER PEOPLE'S MONEY, Warner Bros. (1991)

POCAHONTAS, Walt Disney (1995)

WALL STREET, Twentieth Century Fox (1987)

Miscellaneous

Conversation with Dr. Ivan Velev of Land and Real Estate Initiative (LARI) Group of the World Bank, Washington D.C., April 10, 2001

Proposed Rules Department of Transportation, Fed. Reg. 38992–01, 39007 (July 25, 1996) (to be codified at 14 C.F.R. pt. 440)

INDEX

abductive logic/speculative
    rhetoric, 93, 97, 231
abstractions
    representations, 10
    transferable development rights
        (TDRs), 129
accounting profit
    efficient breach, 202
    opportunity cost, 149–50
    see also economic profit
adverse selection
    discrimination, 134
    risk, 169, 171, 172, 175
agency problems
    law and market economy, 64
    medical treatment, 87, 120
    multi-party transactions, 121
    non-profit entities, 220
    surrogate motherhood, 46
American Nurses' Ass'n v. *Illinois*, 9–10
American Pragmatism, 4
analogy, semiotic devices, 81
anti-commons, 3
Arrow, Kenneth, 195
Arrow's Impossibility Theorem
    economics, 194
    paradigmatic market frame,
        106
    see also public choice
asymmetrical information
    non-profit entities, 219
    risk, 169, 171
asymmetrical positioning, 49
asymmetrical relationships, 49
atomism, 5, 29, 36, 49, 228
Austrian economics, 5

Becker, Gary, S., 2
benchmarks, 165, 219
Boomer v. *Atlantic Cement Co.*, 192–4
Breitel, Chief Judge, 229

Calabresi, Guido, 2
capitalism
    market access, 174
    values, 33
chaos, 94
cheating
    exchange, 130
    prisoner's dilemma, 130, 131, 132,
        174, 203
Chicago School, 91, 92
China, gender perspectives, 23
civil codes (civil law), 58
Coase, Ronald, 2, 177, 202
Coase's Theorem
    case law, 192–3
    economics, 177–85
    externalities, 177, 184, 187, 188–9,
        193
    nuisance, 185
    paradigmatic market frame, 106, 192
    pollution, 177, 192–3
    spillover costs, 106, 184
    takings law, 186, 187
commodification
    corporate culture, 66
    human body, 14, 15, 44
    human reproduction, 45, 48
    property rights, 17, 129
    representations, 108
    valuation, 167
    wealth maximization, 39

common interest, public/private
    interest, 117
commons
    boundaries, 123
    case law, 128
    characteristics, 122
    copyright, 128
    impact fees, 126, 127
    non-excludability, 123
    property rights, 111
    self-interest, 125
    social gains/costs, 125
    tragedy of the commons, 21, 106
communicating *see* interpretive
    institutions
comparable sales, valuation, 165
compensation
    Kaldor–Hicks efficiency, 190
    takings law, 186, 187
competition
    economics, 161–3, 216
    equilibrium, 162
    intellectual property, 162
    meaning and value formation, 39
    perfect *see* perfect competition
    prior distribution, 28
    unfair competition, 223
complementary goods, 155
complex systems
    coordination problems, 118
    efficiency, 59
    legal systems, 60
    markets, 60, 61
    optimal outcomes, 59
    property rights, 60
complex systems and chaos
    theory, 59
contested facts, 9, 29, 30, 44, 52
contested values, 9
contingency fees, 42, 43
contingent valuation, 167
contract law
    freedom of contract, 12
    industry standards, 229
    infrastructure, 144
    preferences, 163
    surrogate motherhood, 44
    two-party exchange, 115

control
    corporations, 34
    decision-making, 66
    non-profit entities, 217
conventions
    decision-making, 66, 68
    infrastructure, 230
    interpretive conventions, 62
    interpretive hierarchies, 75
    legal forms, 66
    secondness, 80
coordination problems
    complexity, 118
    multi-party transactions, 118–22
    non-profit entities, 219
    public/private interest, 28, 125
copyright infringement, 39, 128
corporations
    agency, 33
    competing interests, 120, 216
    control, 34
    corporate culture, 66
    incorporation market, 34
    multi-party transactions, 120
    stakeholders, 32, 34, 35, 121,
        216
    stock *see* shares
cost and benefit analysis
    case law, 158
    constitutional violations, 43
    decision-making, 37, 38
    disabled persons, 159
    discount rate, 106
    discounted present value, 166
    environment, 167, 168
    general market frames, 106
    interpretation, 58
    interpretive hierarchies, 66
    legal standards, 159
    market theory, 94
    pesticides, 153
    representations, 157
    risk assessment, 169–74
    substitute goods, 153
    valuation, 166, 168
cost effectiveness, economics, 61
cost internalization
    externalities, 118

non-profit entities, 222
property development, 129
costs
    externalities, 117–18
    marginal costs, 27, 154, 156
    opportunities *see* opportunity
        cost
    out-of-pocket costs, 107
    rough proportionality, 128
    social costs, 27, 125
    spillover costs, 106, 117–18
    substitute goods, 152
    supply/cost curve, 154–5
    transactions *see* transaction
        costs
creative destruction, 6
creativity, 6, 76
credit risk, 171
criminal law
    drug offences, 117
    mens rea, 145
    property rights, 115, 116, 144
    risk aversion, 169
critical theorists, 6, 57, 79,
    88, 92
cross-over activities, 222–3
cultural-interpretive approach
    applied semiotics, 26
    clarification, 93–104
    conflict, 27
    critical theorists, 6
    economics, 56, 69
    law and market economy, 64
    law, markets and culture, 56
    values, 30
    variation, 20
cultural-interpretive connectors,
    self-interest, 65
cultural-interpretive hierarchy, 67
culture
    assumptions, 78
    cultural sphere, 62
    law and market economy, 56,
    62–9
    market process, 58
    meaning, 20
    public interest, 62
    secondness, 72

damages
    hedonic damages, 167
    lost opportunities, 176
dead capital
    developing countries, 108
    legal representations, 108
decision-making
    control, 66
    conventions, 66, 68
    cost and benefit analysis, 37, 38
    democracy
    discounted values, 66
    efficiency, 59
    experts, 184
    interpretive communities, 66
    interpretive hierarchies, 67
    legislation, 195
    normative foundation, 93
    participation, 39
    private sector, 216
    rational choice, 37
deeds, property rights, 10, 108
demand/benefit curves
    changes, 156
    economic model, 155–6
    quantity demanded, 155
Department of Transportation, 168
DeSoto, Hernando, 108, 109
developing countries
    dead capital, 108
    distributive justice, 18
    less developed countries, 108
diminishing marginal utility, 156
diminishing returns, 154
disabled persons, reasonable
    accommodation, 159, 205
discounted present value,
    valuation, 166
discrimination
    adverse selection, 134
    disabled persons, 159
    efficiency, 49
    exchange, 132–5
    hiring practices, 133
    irrational, 28, 133
    market power, 48
    misinformation
    profile, 134

discrimination (*cont.*)
  proxy, 133, 134
  race, 48
  rational, 133
distributive justice
  developing countries, 18
  lottery, 18, 19
  political/social organization, 16–17
Dolan v. *City of Tigard*, 11–13, 186–7
Dynamics Corp. of Am. v. *CTS*
  Corp., 33–5

Eco, Umberto, 5, 96
economic calculus
  flexibility, 47
  framing, 33
  market exchange process, 100
  normative judgments, 41, 103, 232
  optimal actions, 60
  social fabric, 29
economic profit
  efficient breach, 202
  opportunity cost, 149–50
  private sector, 216
  see also accounting profit
economic rent, 176
economics
  alternative choices, 26
  Arrow's Impossibility Theorem, 194
  Coase's Theorem, 177–85
  competition, 161–3, 216
  cost effectiveness, 61
  cultural-interpretive approach, 56,
    69
  efficiency, 189–94
  efficient breach, 199–203
  highest bidder rule, 18, 19
  information, 60
  Kaldor–Hicks *see* Kaldor–Hicks
    efficiency
  maps compared, 69
  market concepts, 68
  objectivity, xi
  opportunity cost, 45, 148–52
  Pareto efficiency, 189, 191
  production possibility curve
    (PPC), 151–2
  property rights, 17

rational ignorance, 146–8
rationality, 144–6
risk and return, 169–74
scarcity, 143–4
sign systems, 68
substitute goods, 152–3
transactional misbehavior, 174–5
understanding, 64
universal language, 4, 62
valuation, 165–9
wealth maximization *see* wealth
  maximization
efficiency
  ambiguity, 47, 59
  complex systems, 59
  decision-making, 59
  discrimination, 49
  economics, 189–94
  exchange relationships compared,
    70
  indicators, 50, 51
  Kaldor–Hicks *see* Kaldor–Hicks
    efficiency
  market judgments, 20
  Pareto *see* Pareto efficiency
  takeovers, 34
  traditional analysis, 47
  unemployment/welfare
    payments, 50, 51
  value, 189
efficient breach
  economics, 199–203
  paradigmatic market frame, 106
employment
  employment rate policy, 51
  wage rates, 9
endogenous preferences, 164
endowment effect, 107
environment
  airspace, 129
  commons problems, 124
  cost and benefit analysis, 167, 168
  urban growth, 126
  valuation, 166
  wetland habitat, 160
equilibrium
  competition, 162
  information, 94

market equilibrium, 156
  temporary, 94
equitable servitude, 118, 193
equivalence theory, 27
esthetics
  criteria, 100
  exchange, 64
  normative justification, 101, 103
ethics
  ends, 101, 103
  exchange, 64
Europe, social welfare, 51
evolution
  evolutionary change, 96
  objectivity, 231
  pragmatic evolutionary realism, 96
exchange
  cheating, 130
  cooperative exchange
    problems, 130–2
  differing experiences, 30
  discrimination, 132–5
  esthetics, 64
  ethics, 64
  firstness, 73
  forced, 190
  human actors, 20
  interpretation theory, 10
  limits of interpretation, 93–9
  mapping, 57, 61, 64, 68, 69–80, 84,
    85–93, 119, 142
  market concepts, 114–41
  methodological individualism, 20,
    227
  multiple parties see multi-party
    exchange
  networks/patterns, 58
  not-for-profit, 212–26
  public policy, 70
  representational signs, 83
  representations, 47
  scaling, 105
  social fabric, 29
  social meaning, 94
  strict liability, 159
  two parties see two-party exchange
  voluntary exchange, 15, 88, 90, 92,
    190

exclusion, property rights, 115
exogenous preferences, 164
experience
  differing experiences of
    exchange, 30
  firstness, 80
  interpretation, 58
  interpretive institutions, 64
  law, 76
  law and market economy, 1, 40, 64,
    227, 230
  preferences, 164
  scarcity, 144
  secondness, 72
experts
  decision-making, 184
  transaction costs, 184, 185
extensive externalities, 29
externalities
  absent, 27
  Coase's Theorem, 177, 184, 187,
    188–9, 193
  cost internalization, 118
  costs, 117–18
  extensive, 29
  meaning, 177
  multi-party transactions, 118
  negative, 118, 123, 177, 193
  positive see positive externalities
  public, 47
  resource allocation, 177
  rhetorical use, 118
  sources, 118
  spillover see spillover effects

facts, 9, 29, 30, 33, 44, 52
fair market value, 167
families
  adoption, 52
  market placement, 53
  parenting obligations, 53
  surrogate motherhood contracts, 44
Federal Aviation Administration
    (FAA), 168
Federal Trade Commission (FTC), 48
feminist theory, 3, 57, 72, 79, 88
fiduciary duty, 33, 34
first-in-time rule, 16, 18, 19

firstness
  experience, 80
  factual world, 97
  icon, 70, 73
  positional designation, 95
framing
  basic tool, 105–10
  case law, 41–50
  contemporary film, 30–3, 35
  cost and benefit analysis, 106
  cross-cultural context, 8
  general market frames, 105–6
  interpretive references, 8
  mining operations, 11
  paradigmatic market frames,
    106
  quasi-adjudicative processes,
    13
  real estate finance, 7
  references, 106–7
  referencing devices, 7, 107
  resource allocation, 19
  self-interest, 65
  value-enhancing opportunities, 6
Fred F. French Investing Co. v. City of
    New York, 128–30, 230
free rider problems, 122, 219, 221
Frigaliment Importing Co. v. B. N. S.
    Int'l Sales Corp., 8, n. 19

game theory, 3
general market frames, 105–6
global context, neoclassical
    economics, 62
grammar, 61, 62, 82
Grimshaw v. Ford Motor Co., 37, n. 19

habit, patterns of regularity, 94
Hall, Stuart, 20
Hand, Judge Learned, 158
Hausman, Carl R., 96, 97, 98–9, 103
Hayek, Friedrich, 6
hedonic damages, 167
hedonic valuation, 167
Hicks, John R., 190
hidden versus revealed preferences,
    164
highest bidder rule, 16, 18, 19

Honorable v. Easy Life Real Estate
    Sys., 48–9, 162
hypothetical efficiency, 191

icon, firstness, 70, 73
identity
  aboriginal, 17
  property rights, 17, 19
impact fees, 126, 127
In the Matter of Baby M, 44–7, 49
income flow, valuation, 166
index, secondness, 70, 73
indexical referents
  conclusions, 71
  interpretive hierarchies, 67
  resource allocation, 83
  secondness, 80, 97
indigent litigants, civil rights, 41
individual choice, 114–5
individual rights, 43
information
  assessment, 12
  asymmetrical, 169, 171, 219
  economics, 60
  equilibrium, 94
  lacking, 28
  market power, 49
  perfect competition, 27, 28
  rational ignorance, 146–8
intellectual property
  competition, 162
  copyright infringement, 39, 128
  property rights, 108
Int'l Union, United Auto., Aerospace and
    Agric. Implement Workers of
    America (UAW) v. Johnson
    Controls, Inc., 172–4
interpersonal utility comparisons, 164
interpretation theory
  alternative understandings, 52
  approaches, xiii
  cross-cultural context, 8
  exchange, 10
  market action, 26
interpretive hierarchies
  computer software, 67
  conventions, 75
  cost and benefit analysis, 66

decision-making, 67
dominance, 67
indexical referents, 67
influence, 66
interpretive institutions (language,
    communication, interpretation)
    experience, 64
    influence, 66
    mediation, 1
    new value, 84
    wealth formation, 1, 6, 59, 61
interpretive references
    framing, 8, 51
    risk allocation, 8
interpretive turn, 56
investment-backed expectations, 3,
    149, 150
investments
    accounting profit, 149
    risk and return, 169, 175
    uninsured, 169
investor risk
    ownership, 170
    returns, 169, 175
invisible hand, 27, 43, 152
irrational discrimination, 28, 133

Kaldor, Nicholas, 190
Kaldor–Hicks efficiency
    aggregate utility, 190
    compensation, 190
    efficient breach, 199, 200
    exchange, 46
    framing, 47
    hypothetical efficiency, 191
    liability rule, 191, 192
    public gains/private losses, 47
Kevelson, Roberta, xiii, 68, 228
Keystone Bituminous Coal Ass'n v.
    DeBenedictis, 11–12
Kirzner, Israel, 6

law
    experience, 76
    mediation, 62, 85
    rent seeking, 176
    resource allocation, 77
    substitute goods, 152

law and market economy
    additional concepts, 142–209
    basic tools, 104–10
    cultural-interpretive approach, 64
    cultural-interpretive
        environment, 67
    culture, 56, 62–9
    experience, 1, 40, 64, 227, 230
    framework, 56
    human agency, 64
    interdisciplinary approach
    introduction, 1–25
    multi-valued approach, 72
    new law and economics, 3
    primary concerns, 64
    sustainable wealth formation, 61
    understanding, 64, 84
    value formation, 64
legal arguments
    forms, 80–5
    precedent, 80, 81
    triadic approach, 76
legal forms, conventions, 66
legal reasoning
    market concepts, 93
    objectivity, 230
legal representations
    dead capital, 108
    stability, 108
    western world, 108
liability rule, 191, 192, 193
linguistics, 62, 77, 98
logic
    abductive logic, 93, 97, 231
    deliberative activity, 101
    interference, 12
    mapping, 103
lottery, 16, 18, 19
Lucas v. *South Carolina Coastal
    Council*, 150, 187

mapping
    exchange, 57, 61, 64, 68, 69–80, 84,
        85–93, 119, 142
    fair market value, 168
    logic, 103
    map is not the territory, 68, 110
    risk, 173

mapping (*cont.*)
  secondness, 73
  socio-legal action, 69
  triadic approach, 75
marginal costs
  market equilibrium, 156
  private/social, 27
  supply, 154
marginal utility
  diminishing, 156
  economics, 155
  market equilibrium, 156
  private/social benefits, 27
market action, 26, 28, 229
market arrangements, indicators,
  50
market choice
  complexity, 38
  market options, 26
  social situation, 30
market concepts
  economics, 68
  exchange, 114–41
  legal reasoning, 93
  single party/individual choice,
  114–5
market economy
  meanings, 77
  process analysis, 59
  property rights, 15
market focus, self-interest, 62
market opportunity, 79
market performance, contested
  measures, 50–2
market power
  cultural-interpretive hierarchy, 67
  dual strategy, 48
  exploitation, 48, 49
  information, 49
  market share, 48, 49
  neoclassical economics, 48
  racial discrimination, 48
market price, 165
market process theory, 6
market rates/returns, 175
market share
  market power, 48, 49
  strategy, 65

market theory, 63, 94, 97, 100
markets
  complex systems, 60, 61
  contested assumptions, 158
  contested meanings, 26–55, 58
  contested understandings, 67
  contested values, 9
  entry/exit, 27, 28
  equilibrium *see* equilibrium
  equivalence theory, 27
  exchange *see* exchange
  marketplace risk, 170
  meaning and value formation, 57
  segmentation, 49
Matter of Baby M. See In the Matter of
  Baby M
meaning and value formation
  competition, 39
  markets, 57
mediation
  interpretive institutions, 1
  law, 62, 85
Merritt v. *Faulkner*, 41–3, 49
metaphor
  human interaction, 103
  semiotic devices, 77, 81
  tools, 62
methodological individualism
  contested facts, 29
  exchange, 20, 227
  rationality, 21, 29
Microsoft Corporation, 67
Moore v. *Regents of the Univ. of*
  California, 11, 13–16
moral hazard, 115
multi-party exchange, framing, 47

narrative, 62, 77
natural rights
  first-in-time rule, 18, 19
  fruits of labor, 16
negative externalities, 118, 123, 177,
  193
negative servitude, 118, 193
neoclassical economics
  framework, 35
  global context, 62
  market power, 48

nexus
  impact fees, 127
  regulations, 13, 187, 188
  takings law, 186, 187
Nollan v. *Calif. Coastal Comm.*, 186–7
non-governmental organizations
    (NGOs), 212, 223–4
non-excludability
  commons, 123
  public goods, 122, 219
normative judgments, 41, 89, 219
normative sciences, 61, 93, 99–104, 231
not-for-profit organizations
  additional market
    considerations, 219–20
  agency problems, 220
  asymmetrical information, 219
  characteristics, 214
  constraints, 218
  control, 217
  coordination problems, 219
  cross-over activities, 222–3
  efficiency, 219, 221
  exchange, 212–26
  funding, 218, 220–1, 222
  mission, 218, 219, 221, 222, 223
  non-governmental organizations
    (NGOs), 212, 223–4
  non-profit sector, 217–9
  paradigmatic market frame, 106
  preferences, 220
  presence, 213–4
  private sector, 222
  public goods, 214, 217, 219, 220, 221
  public interest, 217
  religion, 217, 218, 220, 222
  special arrangements, 222
  taxation, 214, 221, 222

objectivity
  economics, xi
  legal reasoning, 230
opportunistic behavior, 175–7
opportunity cost
  accounting/economic profits,
    149–50
  economics, 45, 148–52
  income-producing opportunities, 45

meaning, 45
  production, 154
out-of-pocket costs, 107
ownership risk, 170

paradigmatic market frames, 106
Pareto efficiency
  breach of contract, 46
  economics, 189, 191
  meaning, 45
  two-party exchange, 47
Pareto optimality, 189
Pareto superiority, 189
path dependencies, 29
Peevyhouse v. *Garland Coal & Mining
    Co.*, 200
Peirce, Charles Sanders
  abductive logic, 93, 97
  American Pragmatism, 4
  applied semiotics, 26
  creativity, 6
  cultural-interpretive signs, 93
  dynamic process, 96
  economics, 76
  esthetics, 100
  ethics, 101
  exchange, 10
  framing, 6
  indexical referents, 71
  influence, xiii
  law and market economy, 72
  law and market theory, 5
  logic, 101
  normative sciences, 61, 93, 100,
    231
  pragmatic evolutionary realism, 96
  public policy, 75
  semiotics, 4, 70, 94
  speculative rhetoric, 93, 97
  triadic theory, 57, 70, 73, 80, 82, 83
  unlimited semiosis, 96
Penn Central Transp. Co. v. *City of New
    York*, 129, n. 9, 149–50
Pennsylvania Coal v. *Mahon*, 11
perfect competition
  assumptions, 27, 42, 49, 220
  hypothetical model, 28
  information, 27, 28

perfect competition (*cont.*)
  paradigm, 48, 220
  rationality, 27, 28
poison pills, 33
positive externalities, 43, 118
positive network externalities
  legal representations, 108
  value, 59
Posner, Richard A., 2, 42–3, 159–60
Prado, C. G., 97, 98
pragmatic evolutionary realism, 96
preferences
  economics, 163–5
  endogenous, 164
  exogenous, 164
  experience, 164
  hidden versus revealed
    preferences, 164
  non-profit entities, 220
  scarcity, 143
  shaping, 3
  social choices, 164
present value, 166
prior distribution, wealth/resources,
  28
prisoner's dilemma
  cheating, 130, 131, 132, 174, 203
  explanation, 130
  paradigmatic market frame, 106
private interest
  coordination, 28
  see also self-interest
private property *see* property rights
private sector, 216, 222
production possibility curve (PPC)
  economics, 151–2
  trade-offs, 151, 152
profile
  affirmative action, 134
  rational discrimination, 134
profit
  accounting profit, 149–50, 202
  economic *see* economic profit
  non-profits *see* not-for-profit
    organizations
profit margin
  market share compared, 65
  non-profit entities compared, 219
  normative values compared, 66

property rights
  commodification, 17, 129
  commons, 111
  complex systems, 60
  criminal law, 115, 116, 144
  deeds, 10, 108
  economics, 17
  exclusion, 115
  identity, 17, 19
  legal description, 68
  market economy, 15
  references, 12
  representations, 108
  restrictions, 186
  scarcity, 144
  semiotics, 82
  Soviet Union, 79
  torts, 115, 116, 144
  transfer risk, 171
  trespass, 192
  United States, 60, 79
  valuation, 229
  veil of ignorance, 16
property rule
  property rights, 193
  voluntary exchange, 190
proportionality
  assessments, 128
  regulations, 13, 188
  takings law, 186, 187
proxy
  adverse selection, 172
  rational discrimination, 133, 134
  social preferences, 164
public choice
  Arrow's Impossibility Theorem, 106,
    194
  paradigmatic market frame, 106
  rational ignorance, 146
public externalities, 47
public goods
  boundaries, 123
  characteristics, 122
  free rider problem, 122, 219,
    221
  mixed goods, 221
  non-excludability, 122, 219
  non-profit entities, 214, 217, 219,
    220, 221

paradigmatic market frames, 106
private/public mix, 122
public sector, 217
quasi *see* quasi-public good
self-interest, 29
transactions, 122–30
under-production, 122, 221
public interest
culture, 62
non-profit sector, 217–9
self-interest, 18, 20, 26, 27–30,
190
public policy
exchange, 70
qualities of life, 51
public sector
economy, 217
entities, 217, 219, 220
public services, 222
public values, invisible hand, 27

quasi-public good, health care, 120

radical anti-realists, 97
Raffles v. *Wichelhaus*, 8, n. 19
rate of return, 169
rational choice, decision-making, 37
rational discrimination, 133
rational economic person
reasonably prudent person, 145
substitute goods, 152
rational ignorance, economics, 146–8
rationality
economics, 144–6
perfect competition, 27, 28
reasonable accommodation, 159, 205
reasonable investment-backed
expectation, 3, 149
reasonably prudent person, 145
references
burden of proof, 13
conflicts, 9
cross-cultural context, 8
devices, 7, 107
framing, 106–7
interpretive *see* interpretive
references
property rights, 12
torts, 229

rent
economic rent, 176
rent seeking, 176
returns, 175
replacement cost, valuation, 166
representations
abstractions, 10
commodification, 108
cost and benefit analysis, 157
exchange, 47
framing, 108
genetic materials, 13–15
informal, 108
legal *see* legal representations
property rights, 108
referencing, 7
resource allocation
conventions, 66
equality, 43
externalities, 177
first-in-time rule, 16, 18, 19
framing, 19
highest bidder rule, 16, 18, 19
indexical referents, 83
law, 77
lottery, 16, 18, 19
medical treatment, 121
models, 16
multi-party transactions, 121
natural rights, 16, 18, 19
scarcity, 121
self-interest, 28, 65
restrictive covenants, 8
rhetoric, 3, 62, 77, 93, 97, 118, 231
Ricardo, David, 176
risk
adverse selection, 169, 171, 172, 175
asymmetrical information, 169, 171
case law, 172
credit, 171
disclosure, 172
entrepreneurial, 170
health and safety, 172
investor/ownership, 170
marketplace, 170
temporal, 169
transactional, 170
transfer, 171
warranties, 169, 172

risk allocation, interpretive references, 8
risk assessment, cost and benefit analysis, 169–74
risk aversion
    returns, 169
    self-interest, 17
risk and return
    economics, 169–74
    investments, 169, 175
rough proportionality, costs, 128

Samperi v. *Inland Wetlands Agency of West Haven*, 159–61
scaling, general market frames, 105
scarcity
    economics, 143–4
    experience, 144
    preferences, 143
    production possibility curve (PPC), 151
    property rights, 144
    resource allocation, 121
    time, 143
Schumpeter, Joseph, 6
secondness
    conventions, 80
    culture, 72
    experience, 72
    index, 70, 73
    indexical referents, 80, 97
    memory, 71
    positional designation, 95
self-interest
    cultural-interpretive connectors, 65
    distributive justice, 16
    economics, 17
    framing, 65
    greed, 31
    market focus, 62
    objectives, 67
    property rule, 190
    public interest, 18, 20, 26, 27–30, 190
    socio-legal discourse, 65
    transaction costs, 117
semiosis, process, 70, 74, 95

semiotic resistance, 97
semiotics
    abstractions, 10
    cultural-interpretive approach, 5
    devices, 81
    evolutionary change, 96
    property rights, 82
Sen, Amartya Kumar, 50–1
shares
    ownership interests, 121
    shareholder value, 31, 33
    undercapitalization, 109
signs
    cultural-interpretive signs, 93
    economics, 68
    independent reality, 96
    interpretation, 95
    meanings, 96
    rational discrimination, 133
    representational signs, 83
    scope, 4
    sign systems, 68
single party/individual choice, 114–5
Smith, Adam, 5, 27, 29
social construction, 93, 96, 102
socio-legal discourse, 65
Soviet Union, property rights, 79
speculative rhetoric/abductive logic, 93, 97, 231
spillover effects
    Coase's Theorem, 106, 184
    costs, 106, 117–8
    individual choice, 115
    see also externalities
stakeholders, 32, 34
stories
    law compared, 77
    semiotic devices, 81
substitute goods
    cost and benefit analysis, 153
    costs, 152
    economics, 152–3
    law, 152
    oil shock, 152
    remedies, 153
Suntrust Bank v. *Houghton Mifflin Co.*, 39–41

supply and demand
  basic model, 156–61
  economic model, 153–61
  market equilibrium, 156
supply/cost curve
  economic model, 154–5
  quantity supplied, 154
sustainable wealth formation, 61
symbols
  creditworthiness, 10
  thirdness, 70, 73

takings law, 12, 13, 186, 187
temporal risk, 169
thirdness
  argument, 80, 81
  doubt, 97
  positional designation, 95
  symbols, 70, 73
Throsby, David, 20
time-value of money, valuation, 165
torts
  contingency fees, 42
  conversion, 116
  property rights, 115, 116, 144
  references, 229
  risk aversion, 169
trade-offs
  interest rates, 169
  production possibility curve
    (PPC), 151, 152
trademarks, brands, 71
tragedy of the commons, 21, 106
transaction costs
  experts, 184, 185
  market action, 28
  negotiation, 177
  self-interest, 117
  zero assumption, 184
transactional misbehavior, 174–5
transactional risk, 170
transactions
  multi-party transactions, 118–22
  public goods, 122–30
  two-party exchange, 115–7
transfer risk, 171
transferable development rights
  (TDRs), 128, 129

transferable goods and services, 27, 28
triadic approach, 57, 69–80
two-party exchange
  coercion, 115
  contract law, 115
  framing, 47
  Pareto efficiency, 47
  public dimension, 114, 116
  transactions, 115–7

understanding
  alternative understandings, 52
  cognitive process, 70
  economics, 64
  law and market economy, 64, 84
  socio-legal problems, 66
unemployment
  Europe, 51
  welfare payments, 50, 51
Uniform Commercial Code (UCC), 58
United States
  employment rate policy, 51
  interpretive conventions, 62
  legal culture, 58
  not-for-profit organizations, 212, 213
  property rights, 60, 79
  taxation, 214, 221, 222
  three-sector economy, 215–21
U.S. v. Carroll Towing Co., 158–9
US Constitution
  Fifth Amendment, 11, 186
  free speech, 220
  individual rights, 43
  infants, 46
  legal representation, 41–4
  takings, 11, 186
  technical violations, 43

valuation
  benchmarks, 165
  commodification, 167
  comparable sales, 165
  contingent, 167
  cost and benefit analysis, 166, 168
  discounted present value, 166

valuation (*cont.*)
  economics, 165–9
  environment, 166
  fair market value, 167
  hedonic, 167
  human life, 168
  income flow, 166
  market price, 165
  property rights, 229
  references, 106
  replacement cost, 166
  time-value of money, 165
value
  discounted present value, 166
  efficiency, 189
  fair market value, 167
  positive network externalities, 59
  present value, 166
  shareholder value, 31, 33
  social understanding, 84
  value-enhancing opportunities, 6
values
  capitalism, 33
  contested values, 9
  cultural-interpretive approach, 30
  facts compared, 29, 30, 33, 44, 52
  meaning and value formation, 39, 57
  multi-valued approach, 72
  profit margin compared, 66
  public values, 27

Vande Zande v. *Wisconsin Dept. of
  Admin.*, 159–60
veil of ignorance, 16
veil of objectivity, xi
voluntary exchange, 15, 88, 90, 92, 190

warranties, 8, 78, 169, 172
Wealth formation
  coherence, 64
  interpretive institutions, 1, 6, 59, 61
  market process approach, 61
  networks of exchange, 58
  sustainability, 61
wealth indicators, well-being, 50
wealth maximization
  commodification, 39
  corporate culture, 66
  cost and benefit analysis, 38
  discrimination, 49
  market context, 62
  market judgments, 20
  market process approach
    compared, 61
  shareholder value, 31, 33
welfare payments
  intergenerational dependence, 84
  unemployment, 50, 51
willingness/ability to pay
  credit risk, 171
  revealed preferences, 164, 167